ON RELIGION AND MEMORY

On Religion
and Memory

Edited by

Babette Hellemans, Willemien Otten,

and Burcht Pranger

FORDHAM UNIVERSITY PRESS

New York 2013

Library of Congress Cataloging-in-Publication Data

On religion and memory / edited by Babette Hellemans,
Willemien Otten, and Burcht Pranger. — First edition.
    p. cm
    Includes bibliographical references.
    ISBN 978-0-8232-5162-9 (cloth : alk. paper) —
ISBN 978-0-8232-5163-6 (pbk. : alk. paper)
    1. Time—Religious aspects—Christianity.
2. Augustine, Saint, Bishop of Hippo.   I. Hellemans,
Babette editor of compilation.   II. Otten, Willemien,
editor of compilation.   III. Pranger, Burcht, 1945– editor
of compilation.
    BT78.066 2013
    231.7—dc23

                                      2012043900

Printed in the United States of America
15 14 13   5 4 3 2 1

CONTENTS

ABBREVIATIONS

CCCM   *Corpus christianorum continuatio mediaevalis.* Turnhout: Brepols, 1966–.

Conf.   James J. O'Donnell, *Augustine: Confessions*, Introduction, Text, and Commentary, 3 vols. Oxford: Clarendon Press, 1992.

SC   *Sources Chrétiennes.* Paris: Les Éditions du Cerf, 1942–.

PREFACE

On Religion and Memory was initially conceived at a colloquium held in December 2008 at the premises of the Dutch Royal Academy of Arts and Sciences (KNAW) in Amsterdam. The colloquium was designed as a preparatory exchange of ideas that was to materialize in a joint publication. Accordingly, all participants were invited to address a set of questions concerning religion and time from the perspective of their own discipline. "Discipline" was to be taken in a loose sense, however, since it was the organizers' explicit intention to approach religion, memory, and temporality from a variety of viewpoints, incorporating philosophy, literary criticism, musicology, history, and art history.

The editors would like to record their gratitude to the Netherlands Organization for Scientific Research (NWO) for funding the five-year research program *The Pastness of the Religious Past* that formed the background of this colloquium. This program, focusing on the status of the religious past, was a joint effort of the University of Amsterdam, Utrecht University, Johns Hopkins University, and the University of Chicago. A word of special thanks goes to Hent de Vries for his academic involvement and support throughout.

Finally, we would like to thank the anonymous readers for evaluating the manuscript and the staff of Fordham University Press, in particular Helen Tartar, Tom Lay, and Eric Newman, for their professional support in realizing the publication of the resulting book.

Babette Hellemans
Willemien Otten
Burcht Pranger

ON RELIGION AND MEMORY

Introduction:
On Religion and Pastness

Burcht Pranger

This volume brings together a number of studies dealing with the pastness of the religious, Christian past.[1] While it is generally accepted that
temporality and historicity are constitutive elements of the Christian religion to the extent that Christianity is sometimes credited with being their
founder, the actual status of time *in* religion is far from self-evident. First,
there is the issue of the proximity of eternity as it hovers over each and
every temporal manifestation of both Christian worship and reflective,
religious language. This incarnation of timelessness inside the Catholic
tradition was coined by Vincent of Lerinum in the crudest terms possible
as "that which is believed everywhere, always and by all." Yet it is not this
hyperbolic claim to timelessness within history that holds center stage in
this collection of essays. If anything, this study could be characterized
as aiming at the opposite of hyperbole: the fragility, scatteredness, and
multidimensionality of time beneath the surface of the literary Christian
tradition.

Resulting as this volume does from a research project that took its cue
from the Augustinian concept of temporality, it may make sense to sum up
the reasons why it is Augustine who provides us with the tools to do jus-

tice to the intricacies of time and eternity in the past, the present, and the future. Although less hyperbolical than Vincent of Lerinum, Augustine is first and foremost known for his grand design of history as outlined in his *City of God*. In that book we can observe Augustine tracing the vicissitudes of the heavenly city as it pilgrimates on earth under toilsome circumstances from a sinful beginning toward a blissful end. Although, inevitably, Augustine's interpreters throughout the ages, from Orosius to Ratzinger, have taken this grand design of time and history to be a narrative with a beginning and an ending, Augustine's skepticism with regard to the means at our disposal to delineate the events of history has gone mainly unnoticed. Yet skepticism is a key concept here, since time and again Augustine reminds his reader that the scope and presence of the celestial city—and, for that matter, of the earthly city as well—cannot be pinpointed. Neither can we distinctly separate the one from the other. And lofty though the presence of the Church may be and despicable the behavior of its opponents, there is no fixed point in time and history that guarantees the undisputed contours and recognizability of either.[2] In that respect Augustine maintains the skeptical view of time he had entertained in his *Confessions*. Not only does his famous quote hold true that we know what time is as long as no one asks us about it but that we are at a loss as soon as we have to answer that question.[3] Augustine also draws more drastic conclusions from the fact that time eludes us because its momentary status as present prevents us from holding on to that very moment. The implications of this view are that "time is and is not." It *is* to the extent that the present is always there comprising as it were the future and the past as "a present of the future and a present of the past."[4] It is *not* to the extent that time, whether future, present, or past, evaporates the moment we try to get hold of it, from expectation through the focus of the present to memory. Yet the fact that neither future nor past—and, by implication, neither expectation nor memory—can stand on its own but is always in the grip of the "present of the present," which, in its turn, cannot be pinpointed, leaves us with a skepticism that at the same time represents the force of destiny in the guise of eternity's pressure. For what else could this ineluctable present that governs the course of time be called but a reflection of eternity? That very pressure also blocks any attempt to characterize Augustinian temporality as subjective, since, in spite of expectation, attention, and memory being the vehicles of the soul that shape time, there is no moment at which they could act independently out of sight of the possessive presence of present time as eternity's emissary. In that respect the shaping of time through expectation and memory is nothing but a wake-up call to the soul preoccu-

pied with its inner stirrings—Augustine's famous "interiority"—to come
to the surface and seize the moment of voice: *"Tolle lege, tolle lege /* Take up
and read, take up and read."[5]

Now in using the Augustinian concept of temporality the emphasis is on
its usefulness rather than on its being "objectively" true or not. Time—not
least historical time—is too complex an issue for making claims of universal validity. Nor will this volume deal with the question, vexing though it
may be in itself, why the Augustinian concept of time has been passed over
in favor of a more simple, linear view of "ecclesiastical" time with the help
of which events, both sacred and secular, could be discerned and assessed
in a clear-cut way. The aim of this volume is not historical in that sense,
although, interestingly, such *historical* explorations would bring to light a
great number of medieval and early-modern sources—from Bernard of
Clairvaux and Dante to Pascal—which would be conspicuous for their
closeness to the Augustinian approach. As for heuristic usefulness, apply-
ing to a variety of sources an aporetic and nonlinear notion of time such as
Augustine's in which the extendedness of attention, memory, and expectation (the "stretching out of the soul,"—*distentio animi*—as Augustine calls
it) plays its role while all the time shrinking into the split moment of the
present, may produce interesting results. The aporetic aspect will enhance
the dynamic and suspenseful nature of our quest, whereas the nonlinear
dimension will demand a flexible and creative approach to sources that
hitherto may have seemed comfortably accessible, thanks to the support
of a clearly drawn narrative and temporal lines; a comfort that is somehow reminiscent of the support of linear emplotment versus the versatile
and "contingent" composition of the modernist novel. Renouncing such
comfort asks for an asceticism of sorts on the part of the interpreter. With
regard to asceticism, less is more.

With these preliminary thoughts and questions in mind, the contributors to this volume were asked to address the following questions

> Given the temporal concept as described above, what exactly does it
> mean to talk about the history of Christianity? In other words, what
> is left of the prospective aspects of Christianity, its futurology, what
> exactly is its pastness?
> Following this general question, what is left of notions such as de-
> scriptivity, depiction, and narrativity in the light of a nonlinear
> conception of history? If, for example, in an Augustinian concept
> of temporality, distinctions between past, present, and future are by
> definition problematic, how can a reduction to the present as the

reflection of eternity and immovability be avoided? And, can this
question be put in a positive way so as to open up new avenues of
research into the "course" of time? Is it possible to reassess notions
of temporality that depart from a present yet open up a past and a
future, and keep an eye on notions such as movement and repetition (for instance, rhythm and ritual)?

In a more general way, if past and future are no longer merely seen
as points on a historical line but instead as "living" constitutive
elements of the present, how does the interpretation of texts and
objects, as elements of the past, embedded as they are in context,
negotiate this tension between contextualization and constitutive
singularity?

How should one respond to Augustinian "skepticism" as part of the
question exactly where—if anywhere—in the process of knowing
and desiring, the human subject is to be located?

It goes without saying that the questions as formulated above are not necessarily restricted to the realm of religion. What is more, one of the major
issues the volume deals with is the problematic status of religion as such.
Here Hent de Vries's work on the secular appearance of the tropes and
figures of religion in modern discourse, in particular his *Philosophy and the
Turn to Religion* (1999),[6] is of importance. It is the stated purpose of the volume not to focus on "positive" religion but rather on the dynamics and the
stasis of temporality as such. That such dynamics and stasis are, traditionally, first and foremost to be found in religion as it hovers between time
and eternity provides an eminent opportunity to use religion as point of
departure for musings on temporality. More specifically, Augustine's vertical concept of time as "present" under the aegis of eternity radicalizes the
temporal status of each and every human phenomenon, including religion.
Rather than reaffirming a fixed status of human existence, this view of religious temporality introduces unrest and skepticism from which religion
is not exempted. This less than reassuring nature of (Augustinian) time is a
leitmotiv in the various contributions to this volume. Or to put it the other
way around, the wish on the part of the contributors to explore aspects of
uncertainty and scatteredness inside religious temporality accounts for the
prominent presence of Augustine, as it does for the prominent presence of
a modern thinker such as Stanley Cavell, whose dealings with skepticism
and the uncertainties of "arrogating voice" only reinforce the tenor of the
various essays.

The volume is divided into five parts, all dealing with the clash between time and eternity—past, future, present, and eternity—resulting in yet another confrontation between the immovability of temporal dimensions as, for instance, in rhetorical figures and tropes and ritual on the one hand and the underlying skepticism with regard to the knowledgeability of time on the other.

In Part I, "Time and Eternity: Between and Betwixt," Burcht Pranger and James Wetzel address Augustinian temporality head-on. Pranger examines the status of the (seemingly) supratemporal moment in the famous vision at Ostia in book 9 of *Confessions*, during which Augustine and his mother touch upon *esse solum*, pure and undivided being. Countless interpretations have emphasized the Neoplatonic origins and connotations of this vision, which, among other things, manifests itself in the strong language of desire. With the help of a fragment by Kafka called "The Desire to Become a Red Indian," Pranger argues that the reading of this vision as driven by a desire that moves from longing to fulfillment should be turned around. In view of Augustine's emphasis on time as governed by the present of the present, any move of the human mind in any direction whatsoever has to be accounted for in terms of perseverance and the gift of grace. As a result, Augustine's notion of time as a distention of the soul, *distentio animi*, should be reassessed. The width of distention is not as far reaching as it seems. Like the density of Kafka's desire, Augustine's dynamic language of longing is absorbed in a present that turns the extension of future and past into a frightening presence of sorts.

While in the vision at Ostia we find Augustine and his mother at the point where language is on the verge of exhaustion, Wetzel, in his "Memory and the Sublime: Wittgenstein on Augustine's Trouble with Time," tackles, with the help of Wittgenstein, the problem of time and eternity from the viewpoint of language and its origins. Here memory and oblivion come in. Augustine's meditation on time in *Confessions* 11 follows his (aborted) attempt in *Confessions* 10 to locate God in his memory (God was everywhere and nowhere at once). A remembered God implies the sanctification of time, and it is not at all clear that Augustine's usual experience of time has been of something holy. Perhaps the best he can hope for in *Confessions* 11 is to remember his forgetfulness of time—the oblivion that has sundered his life from his knowledge. Wittgenstein's gloss on Augustine suggests that such a recognition on his part would be neither a logical insight (a misplaced sublimity) nor a scientific discovery (a misplaced mundanity). In *Confessions* 11, Augustine calls time an *affectio animi*; basically he says, as strange as it may sound, that time is an emotion. It is movement out of a living source of movement and perhaps away from it. Augustine's time begins with his birth, his exit from Monica's womb; his lifetime is his soul's movement from birth to death—and this indeed proves to be his basic conception of time, as movement towards nonexistence. Wetzel's essay considers Augustine's sense of the beginning of that movement, his retrospective portrait (couched as a memory) of his desperate infancy. He affects to give words to his once infant desire for words, and the curious preemption of language by language speaks worlds about his tendency to forget—to want to forget—his life's tie to time. "Augustine describes the learning of human language as if the child came into a strange country and did not understand the language of the country; that is, as if it had already had a language, only not this one" (Wittgenstein, *Philosophical Investigations* §32).

After the discussion of Augustinian time and eternity proper, the authors of the next section, "Moving Progressively Backward," zoom in on the status of pastness and futurity. Along the road they hit upon stumbling blocks that are in the way of assessing the past as mere pastness, ranging from the fixity and atemporality of logic, grammar, and rhetoric—tools, in other words, required to "make" history at all (*faire de l'histoire*)—to the almost immovable presence of nature.

In her article on Abelard, "The Man without Memory: Peter Abelard and Trust in History," Babette Hellemans takes up Wetzel's discussion of memory as "oblivion that has sundered life from knowledge." "Lucky the man who can say 'when,' 'before' and 'after,'" she quotes Robert Musil's *The Man without Qualities*. In Abelard we have someone whose multitalented brilliance has produced an utterly deceptive image of both himself and his work. First, there is the gifted logician whose passion for argument is often supposed to have foreshadowed the timeless framework of Scholasticism. Next there is the autobiographer who, in his famous *History of My Misfortunes*, does seem to prove to have had a historical (and emotional) sensibility of a kind. And, finally, there is the moralist who, with his concept of moral intention (*intentio*), is often thought to have paved the way for a *temporal* assessment of human behavior. Hellemans takes none of those premises for granted. Instead, she demonstrates how Abelard's dealings with the rules of logic and grammar, rather than being timeless in themselves, are a product of memory in the process of producing meaning. This process is, in turn, part of a relentless quest for insight: *vis intellectus*. Efforts to get hold of the past are as much part of that quest as, for instance, the philosophical inquiry into the status of universals. "Status" is the right expression in this context, since it contains stasis and movement, time and fixity. Just as for Abelard the game of logic is tied up with the flexibility of brilliance (*ingenium* as he calls it), reconstruction of past events and intentions, rather than being part of the endless chain of mnemonic reconstruction for the sake of events and intentions themselves, has to operate without a *point fixe*, narrative or otherwise; a skeptical stance if ever there was one, which is somehow reminiscent of Stanley Cavell's views discussed in Asja Szafraniec's article in this volume. Whereas from a (post-) Romantic perspective we tend to qualify brilliance (*ingenium*) in terms of expansion and scope (bent as the Romantic subject is on the infinite), for Abelard it means the narrowing down of the polyphonous voices of thought, action, and emotion to a life-form that, by creating, assessing, and honoring rules (of logic, and life as in the monastic rule), carves out room for insight. That insight (*vis intellectus*) overcomes the flux of temporality by artificially structuring reality (including the past) while tentatively and lightly—as "a leaf in the wind"—establishing a "when," "before," and "after."

With Willemien Otten's article on nature in Johannes Scottus Eriugena and Emerson, "Creation and Epiphanic Incarnation: Reflections on the Future of Natural Theology from an Eriugenian-Emersonian Perspective," we move closer to the suggestion of atemporality, albeit it as a trompe l'oeil. For dealing with the topos of the "book of nature" it is precisely the temporal aspects, the "when," "before" and "after," Otten wants to distill from the slowly moving flow of the universe as depicted by both authors manifesting itself through both the incisions of epiphany and a comprehensive contraction *and* expansion of that universe through Christ's incarnation (Eriugena) as well as in Emerson's futurology foreseeing a bookless "new Teacher that shall follow so far those shining laws [of Hebrew and Greek Scriptures] that he shall see them come full circle." As for the "book of Nature," in recent years ample attention has been paid to its meanings, with the book model serving as a trope to indicate how nature can be a revelatory repository of resources, comparable to Scripture, and even rooted in it. It would seem that the tradition of natural theology could be read productively through the use of this trope, insofar as natural theology regards creation as a direct manifestation of the divine and its attributes. And yet there is a sense in which nature, once endowed with revelatory power, exhibits an inherent tendency to break out of its creaturely bounds and dismiss its divinely assigned tasks thus shaping temporality in a very special guise indeed. Such is the case in various medieval allegories of nature in the twelfth century, whose overall intellectual climate invites us to consider nature not just as book but as a mirror of the human self, and even earlier in Johannes Scottus Eriugena's *On the Division of Nature*. After a medieval preface the article focuses on the nineteenth-century American author Ralph Waldo Emerson as a modern author sensitive to nature's rich potential as a voice of divine proclamation. From a temporal perspective, the article analyzes Emerson's concept of nature as channeling "epiphanic" incarnation rather than serving as the static locus of creation.

In many respects, Charles Hallisey, in his "The Care of the Past: The Place of Pastness in Transgenerational Projects," stays close to the "transgenerational," Scotian and Emersonian problems discussed by Otten. Hallisey purposes to use a Theravada Buddhist example of a transgenerational project, the Sasana, sometimes translated as the Buddha's dispensation, to trace one aspect of the place of time in religions, an aspect that might be called the onwardness that is part of pastness in religions (like Otten, Hallisey uses here Cavellian and Emersonian and Thoreauvian notions). In the case of Theravada Buddhist visions of the Sasana, there is an onwardness (another concept coined by Stanley Cavell) in human care as it is received in time, recognized as having been given in the past, and then subsequently given again, precisely because of the care received. This onward motion of human care is revealed when acts of care for the Sasana that were done in the past are perceived in the temporal framework of a transgenerational project, allowing the perceiver of these past acts to see herself, in the framework of nextness, as having already benefited from them and also providing the conditions for new acts of care for the Sasana.

After the pulse of Eriugena's, Emerson's, and Buddhist universes, Mette Bruun, in her article "Trembling in Time: Silence and Meaning between Barthes, Chateaubriand, and Rancé," returns to the problems addressed by Hellemans with regard to Abelard's "grammatical" handling of the status of past events and intentions. How to account, in Barthesian terms, for the proportions and ambiguous relation between historical fixation and superhistorical connections? As for Roland Barthes, on the one hand, the literary function is historical, and literature is thus a sign of history; on the other hand, it cannot be reduced to its historical situatedness and thereby offers resistance to that history. Cohesion is created through a register of literary intentionalities, the similarities of which connect authors across centuries while their dissimilarities separate contemporaries. Form constitutes a repository for such intentionalities. In its gravity, form is a value that transcends history in the same way as the ritual language of preachers. With those Barthesian ideas in mind, Bruun presents a case in the negative; a religious concern with the moment whose emptiness is nothing but renunciation but which is invested with a literary surplus by others.

It explores the Trappist reformer Armand-Jean de Rancé's (1626–1700) conflict with the Maurist propagator of textual criticism, Jean Mabillon. The conflict revolves around the position of the monk between the past of the monastic tradition and the future of eternity. The struggle, and particularly Rancé's stance in it, is viewed through the prism of Roland Barthes's introduction to Chateaubriand's *La vie de Rancé* (1844) and his basic question: "What is it to which *La vie de Rancé* could convert us, who have read Marx, Nietzsche, Freud, Sartre, Genet, or Blanchot?" Barthes suggests that Chateaubriand's development of topoi, the function of which is to "*faire entendre, en même temps, autre chose* / to create the opportunity to hear something else at the same time," makes his work survive the anachronistic distortion between author and reader and comes across as a masterpiece. The article approaches Rancé in this vein. It is the underlying presupposition that, in this age of Louis XIV, profoundly concerned with the presentness of the past and the future of the present, Rancé saved the generically correct consistence of his own Trappist Reform with tradition through a seamless and historically disinterested appropriation of the monastic topoi of penitence, solitude, and silence; but that his development of these features lacks, intentionally perhaps, the rhetorical moment that can take them beyond this immediate situation. That the figure of Rancé was to have something like a future outside Trappist circles owes mainly to Chateaubriand's literary skills in filling out the aesthetic and spiritual void of the abbot's rather dry texts, doubling, like other biographers before him, the abbot's somewhat unimaginative penitence with his, apparently, ardent premonastic life in the salons, and mediated in turn by Barthes's critical sophistication. Aesthetical parsimony may suit a penitential reformer bent on silence, less so generations who are eager to "*entendre, en même temps, autre chose.*"

The third section, "Time and the Ordinary," resumes problems, discussed in the previous sections, of the status of language and, as a sequel to Monica's motherly presence to Augustine, of the Thoreauvian transition from the mother tongue to the father tongue. In his "The Literary Comfort of Eternity: Calvin and Thoreau," Ernst van den Hemel examines the fixed position of the believer whose trust in and presence inside divine eternity entitles him to address himself to God as his Father, "Abba Father," versus the doubts with regard to confidence and assurance within the practice and process of faith starting at the stage of "the mother tongue." To bring to the fore the relevance of Calvinist particularity, Van den Hemel discusses two voices in the debate on Calvin's theology that make a claim on how Calvin's notion of faith can offer assurance for the believer. After clearly locating the two sides of the debate, a suggestion is put forward about how the relation between eternity and reassurance in Calvin's theology can be thought of as not only doctrinal content but as a linguistic *charge* to theological language as well. For an example of such a "charge" that is important in interpreting a text, the author takes a look at Henry David Thoreau's *Walden*. By reading *Walden* as a project that attempts to communicate the charge of eternity that can be read in a text, we can perhaps see how the notion of the literary voice can help in reading theological texts that grapple with the double danger of dogmatism and self-referentiality that lies in emphasizing under the slogan *sola fide*, faith, and faith alone.

As I have briefly stated above, the influence of Stanley Cavell in this volume is prominent indeed. The reason I elaborate on this fact here and not at the beginning of this introduction is because it is the stated ambition of the contributors to this volume not to approach their subject matter on the basis of one theoretical, modern philosophy or theory. To take Augustine's notion of temporality as point of departure is part and parcel of the *experimental* nature of this volume, bent on creatively exploiting and opening up a dense notion of temporality such as Augustine's comprising the budding potential, like a Proustian madeleine, of bursting into a variety of perspectives. Taking that approach, the closure often implied in the use of theoretical models is hopefully avoided. That said, the presence of Stanley Cavell—another "open thinker"—is all pervasive as has become clear from the use of notions like "voice," "skepticism," and the prominent place of Emerson and Thoreau.

In her "The Past and History in Ordinary Language Philosophy" Asja Szafraniec deals explicitly with Cavell's philosophical musings on pastness and skepticism. In *Must We Mean What We Say?* Stanley Cavell addresses simultaneously a historian and a philosopher when he writes: "This is what a historian has to face in knowing the past: The epistemology of other minds is the same as the metaphysics of other times and places." Envisioning ourselves as spectators of our past is in other words just as misguided as an attempt to penetrate the privacy of another mind. That human beings nevertheless try to do both is due to our "all but inescapable temptation to think (. . .) in terms of theater"; i.e., to our temptation of either being spectators or having spectators. When in *The World Viewed* Cavell writes that "like religion, art had to learn to defeat theater," this necessity can also be projected on historiography. In *The Melodrama of an Unknown Woman*, when taking up his relation to Derrida's work, it is again an attitude to history (or lack of it) that Cavell indicates as a defining characteristic of American philosophy (and his own): "No American philosopher plays off history [of philosophy]." Instead, he says "[history of] philosophy approaches me, like a conversion." This suggests that the correct attitude to the past is not an (active) attitude at all, that the past only makes its claim upon us in the guise of an experience akin to the phenomenon of Proustian involuntary memory, set into motion by our engaging in, and attending to, present and shared forms of human interaction. Here we are back at Augustine, Abelard, Eriugena, Emerson, Rancé, Calvin, and Thoreau—in short, all authors discussed so far. The past is only real to the extent that it reveals itself in our present, and the only proper way to attend to the historical past is to absorb it in an orphic mode, with our back turned, without looking. The sustained attention to the present is the best and the only archaeology of the past: "The time is always now." Absorption of the past in the present is here opposed to the attitude of spectatorship with respect to the past. But is absorption without loss possible? Already in 1980, in his *Absorption and Theatricality*, Michael Fried had to concede that "there can be no such thing as an absolutely antitheatrical work of art."[7] This remark can be taken to apply to historiography, too. Is an absolutely antitheatrical approach to the past possible (i.e., one in which the past would be absorbed without loss, but also without facing it directly)? To what extent should the proposed absorption of the past in the ordinary language philosophy be seen as an evacuation?

Let us once more turn to Augustine: "[O]n that day when we had this conversation . . . as we talked on (*inter verba*) . . . my mother said . . ."[8] In a volume in which the notion of voice is so prominent the presence of two contributions on sonority seems only appropriate.

In Part IV, "Time and Lateness," Rokus de Groot and Sander van Maas deal with closure in music and late style respectively. In his "From Past to Present and from Listening to Hearing: Final Indefinable Moments in Bach's and Stravinsky's Music," de Groot—musicologist and composer— discusses the mysterious theme of sound dying out as well as the emergence of (eternal) silence. Unsurprisingly, musical pieces on death, Bach's *Trauerode* and Stravinsky's *Requiem Canticles* take pride of place. In this context de Groot speaks of "final indefinable moments, so similar to dying, when the musical ordening of time is fading away, while no new order is presenting itself, and when we are invited to enter a non-order, a moment which has been likened in the literature to the ending of time, infinity, eternity." As for Stravinsky, several of his compositions end with the presentation of mechanical time measurement in sound (repetition of the same sound events using identical time intervals) and, simultaneously, with the presentation of sound patterns that are at odds with this mechanicity. The tension between these two is conducive to a heightened sense attention to sound and silence, while, paradoxically, the course of time stops being perceived as a course. Here the role of the listener becomes important. For the listener the ending of sound may take on the shape of an initiation as a shift from listening to hearing. While listening is bound up with intentionality, hearing involves a nonrestricted openness of attention. Significantly, the biblical dictum is not "Who hath ears to listen, let him listen" but "Who has ears to hear, let him hear."

The notion of late style discussed by Sander van Maas in his "Late Style Messiaen" reminds one of Augustine's famous phrase in *Confessions:* "Late have I loved you, beauty so old and so new, late have I loved you."[9] "Late style" is often used to refer to a period of consummation in an artist's output in which he or she looks back on previous work in harmony and resolution. However, just as in Augustine, so with other authors and artists, "lateness" may also express more fundamental dimensions of temporality, which are not necessarily dependent on a "before" and "after." Since Theodor Adorno's and Edward Said's writings on the topic, the notion also evokes the intransigence, difficulty, and unresolved contradiction occasionally found in such works. Rather than evincing the breakthrough of biological reality in the creative biography, these authors contend, late style is what happens if art does not abdicate its rights in favor of reality. Late style suggests a mode of being apart from one's life while continuing to claim its full rights, a mode of being in time without completely belonging to it, and without belonging to history, or to the Elysian Fields, either. In van Maas's article this mode of artistic production is tested against French composer Olivier Messiaen's "late" musical works, many of which appear to thematize, in a monumental manner, the same eschatological themes found in his earlier work. Is there a late style Messiaen? Would such a thing be possible in the first place?

If the last section of the volume centers around the theme of oblivion, it is not because that notion had been absent from the previous sections. The density of the Augustinian concept of time, present throughout the book, takes care of the simultaneous presence of all aspects involved, just as, for instance, "lateness" comprehends the possibility of fading away while maintaining or even reinforcing a remembrance of sorts. This paradoxical simultaneity of time as the interaction between memory and oblivion under the aegis of the present is so characteristic of Augustinian temporality *and* of the ambition of this volume to present the past and present in their most vulnerable guise.

Before waging the ultimate experiment as undertaken in Peter Cramer's exercise in giving (discursive) shape to both the epiphanic present of the present and the shakiness and scatteredness of time, Brian Cummings, in his "Of Shakespeare and Pastness," discusses the "timelessness" of Shakespeare. All the more intriguing becomes the question of Shakespeare's past. The subject of Shakespeare's past and of his future has been opened up in novel ways in the last few years by the previously unspoken question of Shakespeare's religion. "What was Shakespeare's religion?"— once a matter of indifference—has now become something of an obsessive quest. Some of this quest for Shakespeare's religious identity ("Was Shakespeare a Catholic?") can be seen to have been fruitless—attempting to find documentary evidence for personal truths that are now irretrievable. We cannot finally know what Shakespeare himself believed. Much of the evidence produced has in any case been about Shakespeare's father and not about Shakespeare himself. Yet the quest, and even its failure, can also be reformulated in more productive ways. We are confronted here by the impossibility of Shakespeare's own past. We are also confronted by Shakespeare's sense of the past and its recoverability. For his religion can only be constructed (it seems) by reference to a constant regression: The religion of Shakespeare is bound up with the religion of his father, and more generally, with the religion of England's past. Shakespeare's religion is therefore to be imagined as the recuperation of a lost religious identity—the pre-Reformation religion of his fathers and forebears. The irreducible fact of religion in Shakespeare's time is that it is constantly on the point of oblivion. As one confessional identity replaces another it buries a host of former practices, which had previously been taken for granted. Shakespeare's religion is thus residual and memorial: It is a religion of the past. Investigating these questions opens a new set of possibilities for thinking about how Shakespeare imagined the past, about how we imagine Shakespeare's past, and how we reconstruct the past through religion.

By way of conclusion, Peter Cramer's "The Anger of Angels: From Rubens to Virginia Woolf" brings together the various aspects of temporality raising the issues discussed so far to a superior level of subtlety bordering on the limits of what can be expressed in discursive—or should we say "academic"?—language. Starting out with the exuberant, drunken pen of Rubens in drawing his *Landscape with Mill Buildings*, Cramer focuses on the issue of historical temporality and objectness up to the level at which Rubens breaks through the object as firmly fixed between the eye and what it looks on "back to the rudimentary force with which once the seen object struck at the eye and was struck by it: the suppression of difference." This being so, once more questions of distinctness in time and form come to the fore as in the problem of absorption, earlier discussed by Szafraniec. And, once more, we face the abysses of skepticism when theatrical spectatorship is replaced by absorption as coined by Michael Fried: "withdrawing paintings from the beholder and depicting action turned in on itself without the bridge to the beholding consciousness provided by a 'theatrical' figure who looks out from the scene of action and invites the gaze into its story-line." In a daring yet logical move Cramer turns from Rubens to Virginia Woolf and her portrayal of scatteredness and fragments. "Instead of being the *occasion* of reflection [theatrical in Fried's sense] (as Auerbach [in his famous *Mimesis* dealing with the historicity and temporality of western realism] began by thinking), the fragments that drift in the memory, in a state of mind close to dream, are the very stuff of reflection."

This discussion of Woolf's dealings with the fragility and fragmentedness of time in people and objects sums up the dimensions of Augustinian temporality by which this volume is permeated. Less is more. So much is clear that the concept of time at which the contributors have been trying their hand is—razorlike—bent on reduction both by acknowledging the relentless, eternity-wise present of the present and its abysmal absence and, by implication, honoring reality as the *esse solum*, the singular and unsupported being it is.

PART I

Time and Eternity: Between and Betwixt

CHAPTER I

The Vision at Ostia:
Augustine's Desire to Become a Red Indian

Burcht Pranger

The concept of time that is central to this volume derives from Augustine's aporetic notion of temporality as it has been handsomely summarized by Garry Wills—Wills, in turn, evoking Nabokov to support his own reading:

> Vladimir Nabokov had obviously been reading Augustine when he made Humbert Humbert describe his own self-awareness as "a continuous spanning [*distentio*] of two points, the storable future and the stored past" (*Lolita*, Section 26). Time is a shuttling of the future into the past, moving through an immeasurable point. "If we could suppose some particle of time which could not be divided into a smaller particle, that alone deserves to be called the present, yet it is snatched from the future and flits into the past without any slightest time of its own—if it lasted, it could be divided into part-future and part-past. So there is no 'present' as such." (T, 11.20) And yet, paradoxically, we know the past only as a present memory and the future only as a present anticipation. There is, then, no real *present* and nothing *but* a real present. The mind brokers this odd interplay of times in a no-time.[1]

Wills's emphasis on time as "no-time" is to the point and rescues Augustinian temporality from countless efforts to lend it robustness and extension where it seems to be badly in need of some filling up. What is even more important is the stringency and urgency of the corollary "nothing but real present." While the empty notion of time may still suggest room for mystical interpretation, the overwhelming present of the present, whether in the shape of grace, perseverance, continence, or integrity, overturns the sequential order of human language and desire. Last but not least it does not seem to leave much room for what Wills coins as the function of the mind (in the so-called *distentio animi*) to stretch out and mediate between the various phases of temporality. If Augustine's concept of time holds, mind (*animus*) is part and parcel of the gift of grace, of that which is "nothing but real present." Consequently, "brokering the odd interplay of times" comes down to moving within parameters and distinctions that are less than realistically clear. Any attempt to postulate a stance in the guise of an *anima* or a human subject beyond temporality's fray would be cut off by the razor of the special Augustinian present of the present.

One of the reasons why the aporetic nature of all this has not always been felt to be of the utmost urgency is that the nature and the development of Augustine's work have allowed for a considerable degree of breaking up into isolated segments. The resulting compartments (time, grace, philosophy, theology, Platonism, existentialist tenor of unrest, etc.) were subsequently sheltered in the save havens of categorization. The experiment I want to wage is to act for once *as if* the density of Augustinian temporality as it survives in his concept of grace and perseverance should be accounted for in the strictest terms possible. For reasons of space and time I proceed as follows. Focusing on the *Confessions*, I confront images of human decision making, desire, and hesitancy with the notion of the present as "nothing but present," acting on the assumption that the latter (the present) is of no less performative a nature than the former (desire, etc.). To that purpose I will discuss a counterintuitive example by highlighting a scene that seems to move beyond the parameters of temporality, the famous vision at Ostia. Hopefully, this will bring out a problem that is too often taken for granted: How to square the will's utter dependence on grace as dramatized in the *Confessions* ("*da quod iubes, iube quod vis*/ give what you command, command what you will") and theorized in later works, with the process of decision making in conversion, continence, or for that matter, in failure and sin? By that I do not, of course, mean the issue of free will versus the force of grace as it has been discussed ad nauseam throughout the ages. I am, rather, interested in the *image* presenting the drama of decision making and desire that pervades even grace itself. That I will call on Kafka for a little help in tackling the present of the present may come as no surprise if one realizes how badly a steady hand is needed to discern the contours of a reality that has absorbed its potential future and past before coming into being or moving out of it.

Generally speaking, Augustine's language seems not to be lacking in desire. "What man can enable the human mind to understand this? Which angel can interpret it to an angel? What angel can help a human being to grasp it? Only you can be asked, only you can be begged, only on your door can we knock. Yes indeed, that is how it is received, how it is found, how the door is opened."[2] Clearly, this "knocking on the door" does not one-dimensionally represent the patient quest of the God seeker. It is, in fact, being given throughout the search process itself. That is what the thrice-repeated outcry in *Confessions* "give what you command . . ." is about. Before being able to assess this supratemporal gift as perseverance in time, we have to confront Augustine's moments of delay and hesitancy as well as the lengthy and languid trajectory of desire in the *Confessions* with the epiphanic brevity of conversion and the "the heart's beat" (*ictus cordis*)[3] of "mystical" vision. Confronted with this almost timeless moment, what is the nature of "the intermittences of temporality" as they become manifest in the variety of ways and moments the divine call to conversion and a life of integrity can be heeded? What, for instance, about the criminal from the Gospel—one of them—on the cross, mentioned more than once by Augustine as the perfect example of instant conversion?[4] Like Augustine he has taken his time to live his sinful and criminal life. Unlike Augustine, it did not take him long to say the word. Hanging on the cross, his was apparently not the leisure of struggling with divided wills. This is more than a matter of rhetorical variation, although that device is important enough in itself. In a sense, our criminal reminds us of the quick deciders in *Confessions* such as the soldiers in Milan whose stroll—leisure here indeed—in the imperial gardens resulted in the immediate conversion of one of them.

> In their wanderings they happened on a certain house where there lived some of your servants, poor in spirit: "of such is the kingdom of heaven" (Matt. 5:3). They found a book in which was written the Life of Antony. One of them began to read it. He was amazed and set on fire, and during the reading began to think of taking up this way of life and of leaving his secular post in the civil service to be your servant . . . Suddenly he was filled with holy love and sobering shame.[5]

Thus the soldiers' function in the conversion narrative in book 8 of *Confessions* is unambiguously clear: to counterpoint Augustine's own hesitancy and to heighten suspense. But underneath the notion of suddenness and immediate decision making something mysterious lies hidden, and that is the operational intensity of abbreviation that brings any conversion and any decision, including the protracted conversion of Augustine himself, within the reach of gift. As such it erases any middle term (which I would like to coin as *medium quiddam*) between longing, decision, and gift. Consequently, we face an ironic question rising from the intermittences of temporality as created by Augustine: The endless *distentio* of time into delay and hesitancy does not have any subsistence of its own. In the end—but exactly what does "end" mean?—any decision, regardless of the slothful time it takes, is made *sub specie praesentis*, under the aegis of suddenness. As a consequence, the criminal's abbreviated performance on his cross is no different from Augustine's procrastination. Conversely, the opposite holds true: The criminal's quick decision emerges from the realm of hesitancy and desire. How do we account for all that?

If we now turn to the vision at Ostia proper, the major challenge presenting itself is how to characterize, and to hold on to, the moment at which mother and son touch upon the immovable and eternal *esse solum* while the confessional conversation moves on uninterruptedly. In that dynamic capacity, Augustine's confession seems to succeed in representing the so-called *distentio animi*, the stretching out of the soul in the region of dissimilitude. It seems to fail, however, in capturing the fixity of time and remembrance, the moment at which the unquiet soul is at rest. As such this feeling of melancholy fits in with a more general sense of abandonment, which we also know from other mystical texts:

> If only it could last, and other visions of a vastly inferior kind could
> be withdrawn! Then this alone could ravish and absorb and enfold in
> inward joys the person granted the vision. Is not this the meaning of
> "Enter into the joy of your Lord"? And when is that to be? Surely it is
> when "we all rise again, but are not all changed."[6]

Yet the parameters of *Confessions* do stay in place, which means that they do not allow the moment of touching the *esse solum* to move out of the text and turn into a mystical or psychological experience pure and simple. Honoring those parameters is a precondition for assessing the vision at Ostia in terms of time and eternity. That means, among other things, that, while taking in that mystical vision, we have at the same time to account for the place and status of the *da quod iubes, iube quod vis*, the presence of grace, conversion and perseverance as well as hesitancy and delay inside the flow of uninterrupted prayer by which that vision is framed. What it emphatically does not mean is adding an extra religious layer to the text of the vision at Ostia, thus turning a passage replete with Plotinian terminology into a theology of sorts. In that respect, a kind of semantic impoverishment is needed that prevents the reader from prematurely moving out of the literary parameters of *Confessions* and indulge in the sweetness and timelessness of religious and mystical experience. What this semantic impoverishment brings to light is a bare structure converging with a nuclear power: time and *distentio animi* governing the discourse, backward and forward, as the point of reference through which the confessor gets in touch with his invisible and unfathomable Confessee. If there is indeed any *structure* to *Confessions*, it is the establishing in time of this point of reference. Accordingly, the reader is not at liberty to abandon that temporal structure once the discourse verges on the eternal. With this impoverishment a new semantic urgency makes itself felt: How, as a matter of survival vis-à-vis this unlivable verticality, to draw from and to this point of reference dividing and connecting lines that do justice to the "story" of *Confessions*. How to identify the texture of the text?

Here Samuel Beckett may be of some help. About Beckett's play *Endgame* Hugh Kenner once wrote perceptively that "the play contains whatever ideas we discern inside it: no idea contains the play."[7] Kenner's remark points to precision, to the diamondlike hardness of the text, whether written or performed, which reduces efforts to embrace and contain the play with an "idea" to secondary nonsense. Suppose, for instance, one tries to read the play as telling us something about the grimness of human communication such a liberty would be freely granted; yet to claim that the play is *about* human communication would be wide of the mark. Such a move would be ridiculed, be broken off, fragmented and absorbed by other, more powerful and denser mechanisms at play "contained" by the untouchable wit with which (non-) communicative language is charged.

As for Augustine's text, here, too, all protecting walls have to be broken down. Thus the conversion scene just cannot bear to be covered with a frame of religious devotion to the same extent that *Endgame* is not about existential problems. Analogously, although much less recognized, the vision at Ostia is neither about mysticism nor is it framed by (Neoplatonist) philosophy and offered as such to a privileged class of interpreters. It is our notion of semantic impoverishment that prevents the anger and contempt of philosophers with regard to vaguely mystical and religious readings of that vision from being justified, since precisely what they fear—a false semantic enrichment in terms of Christian devotional or existentialist mysticism—is cut off *ab ovo* by the economy of impoverishment. A different view presents itself: the flow of confessional language being inserted with, and governed—"contained"—by, vertical points of reference such as Augustine's conversion in book 8 and the vision at Ostia in book 9. As for texture, it is up to the reader to discern the connecting and dividing lines between those points of reference that do indeed lend power and melancholic urgency to the text: "*modo, modo . . . si continuetur!*/Let it be now, let it be now . . . O, that it could last!" Thus it is not as nonsensical as it seems to link seemingly contradictory notions (vertical versus horizontal) as, for instance, protracted perseverance to the brevity of ecstasy. Semantically different and irreducible though they are, they also represent two sides of the same coin: *esse solum*, divine mercy, grace, both briefly bordering on the eternal and all pervasive in time. Semantic impoverishment means that there is not a third corpus of language at hand that could forge them into an artificial unity imposing its own frame, whether theological, philosophical, or psycho-biographical. But neither is there a third corpus at hand to separate them. The arrogance of power putting in place a set frame of what ancient philosophy including Augustine should look like is as poor an "idea to contain the play" as the claims of religion, devotion, and theology. "No idea contains the play."

After this preliminary round of cleansing activities the question arises as to the nature of the reading practice within parameters that honor the presence of frameless grace and perseverance. What about Augustinian desire in the guise of the knocking (*pulsare*) on the door with the gift of life hovering over, in, and preceding it? Surely this cannot mean that the door is opened already. But neither is it closed in a normal way (that is, closed so as to be opened as a result of the knocking). What about the *medium quiddam* between closure and opening, the fathomless, "nonexisting" space in between the word spoken by the criminal and his being launched into paradise, which, as we have seen, is essentially no different from Augustine's own protracted language of desire and delay?

Let us have a more detailed look at the spiraling language of desire in the vision at Ostia and quote the passage in full:

> Alone with each other, we talked very intimately (*conloquebamur ergo soli valde dulciter*). "Forgetting the past and reaching forward to that lies ahead" (Phillip. 3:13), we were searching together in the presence of the truth which is you yourself. We asked what quality of life the eternal life of the saints will have, a life which "neither eye has seen or

ear heard, nor has it entered into the heart of man" (1 Cor. 2:9). But with the mouth of the heart wide open, we drank in the waters flowing from your spring on high, "the spring of life" (Ps. 35:10) which is with you. Sprinkled with this dew to the limit of our capacity, our minds attempted in some degree to reflect on so great a reality.

The conversation led us towards the conclusion that the pleasure of the bodily senses, however delightful in the radiant light of this physical worlds, is seen by comparison with the life of eternity to be not even worth considering. Our minds were lifted up by an ardent affection towards eternal being itself. Step by step we climbed beyond all corporeal objects and the heaven itself, where sun, moon, and the stars shed light on the earth. We ascended even further by internal reflection and dialogue and wonder at your works, and we entered into our own minds. We moved up beyond them so as to attain to the region of inexhaustible abundance where you feed Israel eternally with truth for food. There life is the wisdom by which all creatures come into being, both things which were and which well be. But wisdom itself is not brought into being but is as it was and always will be. Furthermore, in this wisdom there is no past and future, but only being, since it is eternal. For to exist in the past or in the future is no property of the eternal. And while we talked and panted after it, we touched it in some small degree by a moment of total concentration of the heart (*modice toto ictu cordis*). And we sighed and left behind us "the firstfruits of the Spirit" (Rom. 8:23) bound to that higher world, as we returned to the noise of our human speech where a sentence has both a beginning and an ending. But what is to be compared with your word, Lord of our lives? It dwells in you without growing old and gives renewal to all things.

Therefore we said: If to anyone the tumult of the flesh has fallen silent, if the images of earth, water, and air are quiescent, if the heavens themselves are shut out and the very soul itself is making no sound and is surpassing itself by no longer thinking about itself, if all dreams and visions in the imagination are excluded, if all language and every sign and everything transitory is silent—for if anyone could hear them, this is what all of them would be saying, "We did not make ourselves, we were made by him who abides for eternity" (Ps. 79:3, 5)—if after this declaration they were to keep silence, having directed our ears to him that made them, then he alone would speak his word, not through the tongue of the flesh, nor through the voice of an angel, nor through the sound of the thunder, nor through the obscurity of a symbolic utterance. Him who in these things we love we would hear in person without their mediation. That is how it was when at that moment we extended our reach and in a flash of mental energy attained the eternal wisdom which abides beyond all things. If only it could last, and other visions of a vastly inferior kind could be withdrawn! Then this alone could ravish and absorb and enfold in inward joys the person granted the vision. So too eternal life is of the quality of that moment of understanding after which we sighed. Is not this the meaning of "Enter into the joy of your Lord" (Matt. 25:21)? And when is that to be? Surely it is when "we all rise again but are not all changed" (1 Cor. 15:51).

   I said something like this, even if not in just this way and with exactly these words (*Dicebam talia, etsi non isto modo et his verbis*). Yet, Lord, you know that on that day when we had this conversation, and this world with all its delights became worthless to us as we talked on, my mother said "My son, as for myself, I now find no pleasure in this life. What I have still to do here and why I am here, I do not know. My hope in this world is already fulfilled. The one reason why I wanted to stay longer in this life was my desire to see you a Catholic Christian before I die. My God has granted this in a way more than I had hoped. For I see you despising this world's successes to become his servant. What have I to do here? (*quid hic facio?*)."[8]

How else can such a passage be read but as a "coherent" act of reaching out and stretching forward toward the brief moment of vision? Yet, in my view, another dimension should be taken into account which, as said, does not diminish desire but, in a sense, reverses and, as a result, intensifies it. This is not so "unnatural" as it seems. Take the following fragment of Kafka's, which seems to defy the laws of "narrative" nature:

> *Wenn man doch ein Indianer wäre, gleich bereit, und auf dem rennenden Pferde, schief in der Luft, immer wieder kurz erzitterte über dem zitternden Boden, bis man die Sporen ließ, denn es gab keine Sporen, bis man die Zügel wegwarf, denn es gab keine Zügel, und kaum das Land vor sich als glatt gemähte Heide sah, schon ohne Pferdehals und Pferdekopf.*[9]

> If only one were a Red Indian, always prepared, launched into the air on one's galloping horse, a brief tenor over the trembling ground, till one let go one's spurs, for there were no spurs, and threw away one's reins, for there were no reins, and could barely make out the land in front of one opening out as smoothly mown heathland, with horse's head and horse's neck already nowhere to be seen.[10]

A succinct and striking analysis of this passage has been given by Heinrich Detering. Since it brings to the surface all the major elements that are in play in our reading of Augustine's spiraling sentences of desire, I quote it in full:

> This is the first line from Kafka's first book entitled *Desire to Become an Indian*, and at the same time his first prose text. In it he conceives of an adventurous film scene moving at a fast pace: a glance of desire into the world of the lonely hero, the boy scout and pioneer, "*gleich bereit* / ready to act." So much is for sure, it is hard to think of a way in which a wish could be crushed more restlessly. It does not suffice that "one" (for the desire does not even get as far as the "I") is not an Indian on a horse—since there is no horse at all, no harness and hardly any broad countryside. For this film runs backward. The "desire to become an Indian" (not simply "to be" one) begins with its imaginary fulfillment. Next it turns itself back as far as the disappointing absence from which the desire has sprung. The first words point to an exclamation mark; the sentence itself ends almost inaudibly with a laconic full stop. First the optative mood, then the indicative: the one thing that is for sure in this world is that which is denied. No spurs, no reins, no horse—only the desire that governs the sentence right from the first word and lives on, unfulfilled, after it is suddenly finished.
>
> Kafka's sentence transfers the economy of desire into the linguistic material. "Until," he writes, as if the issue here were just a merely temporal sequence and not a phased revocation of the presuppositions. A "then" figures twice where a "but" would have been more plausible as if "one" had given up the spurs and thrown away the reins, because they were not there, as if the deception that dreams prove to be ghosts would be compensated by the idea that this at least would be the result of one's own acting. Thus does Kafka's short story insert the dream of boys and films into the calculatedly confusing logic of an oblique grammar. This, then, is the first sentence of his first book. The storytelling begins where the air is being let out of desire.[11]

Detering's analysis is all the more admirable given the sense of finality Kafka's *verbum abbreviatum* imposes on the reader, including the latter's subsequent reluctance to add anything to it. In Kafka's "poetical" prose it does not matter whether one takes an isolated sentence or an entire text: It is all charged with nuclear power. All is said and done. Paradoxically, out of this very finality spaciousness rises to the surface spreading out, filmwise, albeit disconcertingly so, into the width of the countryside, which is on the brink of receding into nothingness and taking with it the contours of the horse's neck and head. Coincidentally, in view of the semantics of "west-

erns," this scene seems close to the opening shot of the Coen brothers' film
No Country for Old Men.[12] Zooming in, slow motion, on a barren American
western landscape and, farther, much farther, on a group of burned-out
trucks and shot-down dogs, a scene of deserted violence, the filmmakers
not so much set the melancholic, slothlike tone for more violent things to
come as, rather, close in, slowly and violently, on any possible event to follow. Enclosure as end and beginning. Any "future" event will be set within
this frame. As a result, dividing lines between events—and, by implication,
between ideas—are hard to draw, having become accountable to—and
absorbed by—the "mood" of the opening scene. Yet, drawn they should
be, to the utmost degree of precision.

Both Kafka's *Desire* and the film are "stories" melancholically emptied
out right at the beginning. At the same time the desire to become an Indian, before evaporating into its flattened disguise as "one," remains the
expression of a boy's dream, a *vox pueri.* The problem we face here—that
is, in trying to get to the bottom of Kafka's picture by taking in, in one and
the same breath, youthful desire and adult resignation—lies in the fact
that "melancholic"—or, more precisely, "slothlike"—appears not to be
the right expression. It would be, to make a preliminary correction, more
to the point to speak about the "*suggestion* of melancholy and sloth." In
between the slippery and sticky space of "melancholy" and the "suggestion
of melancholy" a violent turnabout is executed, and it changes the entire
landscape. In the Coen-brothers approach this turnabout is spun out in the
slow pace of the film full of retarded action just to culminate, in correspondence with the zooming in of the opening scene, into the same receding
contours of the scenery as in Kafka's version. As for Kafka, the execution
takes place right at the beginning, causing the suggestion of speed and
adventure (the optative mood of desire) to be overtaken by reality (indica-
tive). The reason why, the absence of melancholic slowness notwithstanding, I insist on reintroducing the notion of sloth even in Kafka is twofold.
First, the suggestion of receding horizons of imagined opportunities supported by a willingness to act and go (*gleich bereit*) is exceedingly strong,
and, second, it is a priori being overtaken by reality (not being an Indian,
no spurs, no horse, no reins), in being objectified into a factuality (*es gab
keine Sporen*), does not for one moment excuse or remove the acting subject (*gleich bereit*) even though all images seem to vanish into the thin air of
a dream losing its grip on, and articulation of, reality. Detering's comment
is particularly insightful here. The economy of desire (*Wunschökonomie*)
has its unbalancing effect on language. Once more we have a suggestion
on our hands: The narrative sequence *seems* to keep the markers of tempo-

rality alive ("until," "then," *bis, denn*), *suggesting* a trace of the *gleich bereit*, as if *one* (*man*) had been in the position to let go the spurs and throw away the reins. Yet this is not a luxury the narrator/protagonist—meanwhile shaped, not as "I" but as "one" (*man*)—can afford. Before one can even try, the markers of temporality are gone, leaving "one" cut off, overtaken by reality, *esse solum*.

To all the suggestions made in the text I want, as said, to add another one: the presence of sloth. In my view the *gleich bereit* mirrors itself in the *decision* not to move and not to persevere, whose characteristic it is to be indistinguishable from the barren fact. The absence of any *medium quiddam* to prove or even establish this link is as much part of the enigma of Kafka's factuality and the unseen nonperseverance of his protagonist as it is of Augustine's *esse solum* and the unseen perseverance of Jacob as well as the nonperseverance of Esau.[13] Admittedly, this is more than Kafka's text allows for and, rather, part of the dreams it *seems* to contain, or trigger, yet as much worth a try as the desire to become an Indian.

It is hard if not impossible to make a next step after Kafka—and in my search for eternity's ennui I deliberately move in a direction where next steps get stuck in the finality of being (for what it is worth): the gift of perseverance / *donum perseverantiae*. On the other hand, inside the volcano of Kafka's text things do move. Thus we can approve of Detering's reading of desire so thoroughly emptied out yet continuing to make itself heard: "No spurs, no reins, no horse—only the desire that governs the sentence right from the first word and lives on, unfulfilled, after it is suddenly finished." At the same time we see how difficult it is to say anything meaningful after the "fact," since "unfulfilled" may be too much said already overruled as it is by the "suddenly finished." What we have here is the implosion of fulfillment, so to speak.[14]

If we now return to the Augustinian voice in the vision at Ostia, we can hardly argue that reading the long sentences spiraling up to the moment of touch have the same effect on the reader as Kafka's *Desire to Become an Indian*. We are not at one stroke drawn into the emptiness of unfulfillment, nor is our desire overtaken by reality. Rather, it seems to be allowed ample time to develop width and perspective until it touches upon the *esse solum*. Consequently, we do not watch a film running backward here. But is this really true? If persistent knocking on understanding's door was ever required, it is now in the face of Augustine's language of desire.

I would not have made this Kafkaesque detour if I did not believe that somehow, somewhere, and at some time the vision at Ostia is turned around and cut across with the same power or, rather, violence, as *Desire to Become an Indian.* For that to be the case, however, the impression should be as immediate and gripping as Kafka's, which it clearly is not. Yet, appearances notwithstanding, I believe the opposite holds true.

Wo der Wunsch ins Leere geht, fängt das Erzählen an. Detering's fine concluding remark in a sense captures the problem we face. Not only does it recycle his brief analysis (a digression, still) to a starting point of a kind thus subtly mirroring the dynamics of the text under discussion. It also, more drastically, reveals the utter impossibility of talking about beginnings and closures, since meanwhile any attempt at a beginning is drawn into, and absorbed by, the volcano of text itself: no wide countryside, no horse, no reins. No beginning, no story. In other words, that desire is being emptied out is not extrinsic to the story, since there is no *medium quiddam* between that failed desire, the beginning of the narration, and the narration itself. *In medias res.* Long since (reminiscent of Proust's *longtemps*) the storytelling was begun: The longueurs of brevity are in the air. And so we are back at Kenner's Beckett: "[T]he play contains whatever ideas we discern inside it: no idea contains the play."

This said, it may be rewarding to have a look at Augustine's "narrative," which, on the surface, would seem to run squarely counter to Kenner's maxim. If ever a mystical experience was embedded in a narrative frame, it is the vision at Ostia. To "begin" with, the theme of book 9 does not leave much room for doubt: It is about Monica's death as a "natural" consequence of her son finally having said the word "continence" at the end of book 8. Temporal markers abound as a clear indication of some finality in the air, oscillating between speeding up and slowing down: "I made a decision "in your sight" not to break off teaching, but quietly to retire from my post as a salesman of words in the markets of rhetoric . . ." (9.2.2), ". . . full of joy I tolerated the interval of time until it [the teaching job] was over" (9.3.4), "When can time suffice for me to recall all your great benefits toward us at that time, especially when I have to hurry on to other more important matters?" (9.4.7), "The prophet cries: 'How long?' and cries 'Know'" (9.4.9), "When the time came for me to give in my name for baptism, we left the country [Cassiciacum] and returned to Milan" (9.6.14), "While we were at Ostia by the mouths of the Tiber, my mother died. I pass over many events because I write in great haste" (9.8.17), "The day was imminent when she was to depart this life (the day which you knew and we did not). It came about, as I believe by your providence through your hidden ways, that she and I were standing leaning out of the window overlooking a garden. It was at the house where we were staying at Ostia on the Tiber, where, far removed from the crowds, after the exhaustion of a long journey, we were recovering our strength for the voyage. Alone with each other, we talked very intimately, Forgetting the past . . . " (9.10.23). Then follows the actual vision just to spiral straight down into Monica's death and Augustine's mourning.

Multa praetereo, quia multum festino. Here we might have an inkling of the desire speedily to become an Indian. But before getting to that, we have to assess more accurately the precise status of this temporal and narrative framework. Exactly what is this frame supposed to support? A straight answer to this question could be given if we were to follow the path of Platonic-Plotinian interpreters of this passage and take all this "small" talk about conversion in book 8 and the miseries of our earthly existence as preparing deficient temporality for perfect eternity.[15] In that view the vision would be a remarkable piece of "philosophy" rising out of and beyond Augustine's gloomy view of life as it is. Beginning at the other side of the story, the moment of touching the eternal, I want to stress that I do not wish to lessen its status and have it embroiled in the vicissitudes of temporality; it is and remains *esse solum*—and what is more, without any *distentio animi* in it. This said, the only option open for the Augustine's and Monica's "story" is indeed to function in a supportive role as shaping and blending their desire into their spiraling sentences. Yet the resulting language of desire is far from being a one-way route. Both in *Ad Simplicianum* and *Confessions*, we are left with the primacy of grace, the robber's seamless reception and acceptance of grace as symbolized by his sudden elevation into paradiseor, for that matter, Augustine's conversion as mercy bestowed "on him who is not running (*non currentis sed miserentis*)."[16] The same principle applies to the markers of temporality. Each and every such marker is governed by the *praesens praesentis*, and that is how the *multa pratereo, quia multum festino* is electrified and in turn electrifies the "narrative" discourse. As a result, the narrative framing of the vision by the story of Monica's life and death as humbly reflecting, so to speak, the *esse solum*, loses much of its supportive flavor, to say the least. The frame is still there, but it has to be cleansed, as it were, of its supportive elements and linked to the *esse solum*, not as a kind of prelude (or reflection) but as being overtaken by it. Desire being a gift—whether accepted or refused—there is no way back to its narrative independence and its functioning as a one-way forward-reaching drive or its plotlike status, just as Monica's death and Augustine's mourning cannot be seen as a mere after-play—a *"post-ipsum."* All this is quite confusing considering that, as a matter of course, no reader can avoid reading Augustine's account precisely on the level of narrative sequence and well-ordered desire. But neither can Kafka's *Desire to Become an Indian* avoid initially to be read as a "real" story expressing a genuine wish although *his* reader's illusive expectations are short lived indeed.

One little question remains: *Wie zu lesen sei*? As a first effect of a "cleansed" reading effort, a reversal of supporting and leading roles should be noted. Precisely because the *attingere*/touching of the eternal—*esse solum*—is not contaminated with any *distentio animi*, its retroactive range is so far-reaching and powerful. As such it takes the storytelling under its wings, depriving it of its supportive nature, since any support has been overtaken by reality right from the beginning. What is left? Nothing. How, then, to articulate "that which is—not—left"? In my analysis of Augustine's mourning the death of his mother, I have shown how his probing into his mother's affection for him and his own response, both failed and successful, to that affection, in the end were ordered into the position of the solitary weeper *coram deo*.[17] "Solitary," that is the inevitable state of the confessor addressing himself to the unfathomable Confessee, since he is only capable of really sharing his full confession with someone else if it moves on the same level of unfathomability. Paradoxically, it is precisely this fundamentally vertical fact that, symbolized here by Monica's state of equality during the vision at Ostia, underlies the *Confessions'* ambition as indeed Augustine's linguistic ambitions at large, socially to start and take up communicating with others on the level of human speech. Ultimately, it is all about arrogating voice. But before being able to "speak," the combined forces of the unfathomable Confessee and the *attingere* of the *esse solum*, while not containing any distension in or between themselves, create a unique picture of those being overtaken and touched. Miraculously, its full enforcement is to be found in—and within the parameters of—human language. *Wo der Wunsch ins Leere geht, fängt das Erzählen an.* It should be noticed, then, that throughout the "narration" of the vision at Ostia the conversation between mother and son at no time looses or transcends its status of speech and "narrative."[18] And, even at the *moment suprême* the talking goes on: "While we talked and panted after it (*dum loquimur et inhiamus illi*), we touched it [eternal wisdom] in some small degree by a moment of total concentration of the heart (*toto ictu cordis*)."[19] Now an obsessively mystical reading of this text emphasizing the latter's Neoplatonist infrastructure, would inevitably and justifiably highlight the unique moment of supratemporality, including the standard display of disappointment with regard to the lack of durability: "If only it could last/*Si continuetur . . .*" However, on closer inspection the *dum loquimur et inhiamus illi* appears to play a more prominent part than the force of oblivion resulting from the ecstatic moment of mystical union—if that is the right expression, which, of course, it is not—would seem to suggest. Not only does Augustine fail to express the moment brought about by the *ictus cordis* in terms of vision, of seeing the invisible. He also makes it abundantly clear that, vanished though the moment of eternity's touch down may have into thin air, the entire process, both the rhetorical buildup and the unique moment of *ictus cordis*, is and remains embedded in speech: *dum loquimur*. If Augustine subsequently concludes this episode with some reservation as to the verbatim rendering of the linguistic exchange between his mother and himself, he nonetheless keeps it all firmly within conversational bounds. "I said something like this, even if not just in this way and with exactly these words. Yet, Lord, you know that on that day when we had this conversation, and this world with all its delights became worthless to us as we talked on (*inter verba*) . . . my mother said: '*Quid hic facio?* / What am I (still) doing here?'"[20]

What we have here, is a considerable degree of slippage in the very heart of the language of desire ("I said something like this . . ."), which tends to go unnoticed as long as one does not feel the duty to account for the speech, the voice, hovering between sustainability and unsustainability, in which the vision of *esse solum* is and keeps embedded. Again, that does not mean that the moment of the *ictus cordis* is brought down. We are rather faced here with the subtle picture of the *distentio animi* both on the brink of being dissolved into the intimacy of communicative speech and hence into the *esse solum* and, and at the same time, caught in the act of processing the *esse solum*, so to speak, into the very unsustainability of voice. Appearances notwithstanding, this is far more dramatic than merely recognizing the inevitable deficiencies of human language. "*Wo der Wunsch ins Leere geht* / Where desire is emptied out . . ." In the absence of a *medium quiddam* that could help us to distinguish between the *esse solum* on the one hand *and* the conversation between mother and son on the other, all we can say is that Augustine, accounting for the monumentality of being while blending his own "solitary" voice with his mother's, moves between the slippery and the sticky. It is the split second during which that voice is on the brink of being both sustained and not sustained that triggers a shot from the hip on the part of the *esse solum*. It clinches the invisible bond between ecstasy and perseverance. That is where the storytelling begins.

CHAPTER 2

Memory and the Sublime: Wittgenstein on Augustine's Trouble with Time

James Wetzel

Augustine writes his *Confessions* under the assumption that God's experience of time must be radically different from his own. This assumption of his proves to be problematic, not for the unsurprising reason that Augustine is not God and so has little acquaintance with divine time-consciousness, but because Augustine, from his own time-bound point of view, finds that he cannot say what time is. He is clearly surprised by his loss for words. Time, he readily concedes, is a frequent topic of human conversation. Everyone talks about time. We are all, in various ways, obsessed with the subject—time being a good that we crave, an intangible we seek to measure, a limit that we lament. Is it possible to talk about time, to dress it up in clocks and calendars, to feel it in our bones, and not really know what time is? "If no one asks me," Augustine writes, "I know, but if I want to give an account to someone asking, then I don't."[1] Wittgenstein, who greatly admired Augustine for his philosophical honesty, had this to say about Augustine's sentiment: "Something that we know when no one asks us, but no longer know when we are supposed to give an account of it, is something that we need to *remind* ourselves of." This is not a simple matter of recall, but "something of which for some reason," Wittgenstein tells us, "we have trouble reminding ourselves."[2] It is worth noting that Wittgenstein's invocation of Augustine on time concludes a section of the *Philosophical Investigations* that begins with the question, "In what sense is logic something sublime?"[3]

In both of his major works, the tightly wrought *Tractatus Logico-Philosophicus* and the more loosely constructed *Philosophical Investigations*, Wittgenstein is concerned to battle the disposition, not least of all his own, to mistake where the sublime lies in human experience, to look for sublimity where none can be had or even intelligibly wanted. He takes aim against the subliming of logic in the *Tractatus*, where in seven propositions, six annotated, he reminds us that the general form of a proposition, the form that makes any proposition make sense, is impossible to abstract from ordinary discourse and render into an object of knowledge.[4] There can be no science of logic, no metalanguage of language, nothing that could be exulted as a paradigmatic form of intelligibility, in comparison to which more mundane ways of speaking would seem defective. In retrospect, Wittgenstein will come to notice an unintended subliming of logic in his *Tractarian* farewell to philosophy. True, he resolutely avoids the temptation to think that there is some special form of the logos that is the philosopher's job to perfect and serve, but then there is his idea, determinative for the *Tractatus*, that all of human language has to admit to a completely determinate, fully general form of analysis—albeit one that no one is able to express directly in words. An ideal of intelligibility, omnipresent but strangely unspeakable, still hovers over spoken language like some despotic doppelganger. In the *Investigations*, Wittgenstein seeks to exorcise that ghost and strip it of its pretensions of spirit.

Along the way he invokes the time-perplexed Augustine, haunted by an apparent loss of words and on the verge of giving into the temptation that Wittgenstein knows so well. "We feel," writes Wittgenstein, "as if we had to *penetrate* phenomena."[5] The better course, he suggests, would be to stop looking for the meaning behind the appearances and let our ways of speaking remind us of unnoticed, if familiar, possibilities of sense. He credits Augustine with having at least an inkling of this better course, the turn from metaphysics to grammar: "Thus does Augustine recall to mind," he notes approvingly (same passage), "the different statements that are made about the duration, past, present, or future, of events."

Wittgenstein does not quote any of these statements; he simply identifies them as not being philosophical in nature. I think he must have in mind Augustine's normal disposition, evident when he is not being asked about time, to speak of the past as no longer, the future as yet to come, and the present as now. But this leaves me with two basic puzzlements about Wittgenstein's treatment of Augustine on time.

One has to do with the selectiveness of his reading of book 11 of the *Confessions*. Augustine does affirm, grudgingly, all the customary ways that people talk about past, present, and future, but he also deems this usage inexact and even misleading. Over the course of his analysis of time, he has been quite struck by the apparent impossibility of an objectless name. If there is no object for a name to name, then the name is meaningless, a piece of nonsense, and not simply empty. On the assumption that the past and the future name something, what would be that thing, given that the past is no longer and the future not yet? Augustine moves quickly from his sense of the essential unreality of the past and future to an idealized reformulation of time-language: "It is not rightly said," he suggests, "that time's trio is past, present, and future; it would perhaps be better to speak of a present of things past, a present of things present, and a present of things future."[6] But this is not a serious suggestion for revising time-talk. Let the customary usage stand, says Augustine, as long as we remember what we *really* mean when invoke the past or future: that the past, as we are given to speak of it, is always present, and likewise the future.

Whatever one thinks about the utility of this reminder, it is abundantly clear that Augustine is far from willing to restrict himself to the intramural complexity of ordinary time-talk in *Confessions* 11; he is, on the contrary, looking to find the one uncomplicated thing that would tell him, if he could just bring it to words, what time means. Augustine's hunch seems to be that time's tendency to lapse into nonbeing, its stretch into the no longer and the not yet, must be underwritten by some kind of eternal presence, available to the concentrated mind; we'll have to see whether he is ever able to muster much affection for the concentration required.

But for now let's envision an Augustine who resists the temptation to penetrate the phenomena and affects to arrive at the supposed ground of time's intelligibility—that to which time-talk must always ultimately refer. Our Wittgensteinian Augustine rejects the very idea of a final analysis of time; he humbly embraces the rootless phenomenology of ordinary time-talk and comes to participate ever more fully in the form of life that this phenomenology, in its rootless way, delimits. This brings me to my other puzzlement about Wittgenstein's treatment of Augustine on time, a puzzlement having to do with the supposed boon of being freed from a false sublimity. I don't immediately see why it should be especially cathartic for Augustine to plunk down for ordinary, unsystematic time-talk once he has tried and failed to resolve his fundamental question about time by way of some compellingly determinative analysis. Why not think of his return to the manifold sphere of the mundane as yet another human failure to attain a godlike perspective? We may well be stuck as human beings with limits to our knowing that we can see but never transgress, but why do we have to accept such a self-chastening recognition as if it were some kind of a gift?

My questions, I admit, still presuppose the intelligibility of a sublime point of view on time—enough intelligibility for me to say, with some sense, that this is what I don't have. In fact I am more inclined to think, in keeping with Wittgenstein but not so much with Augustine, that God is in no better position than I am to answer the question, What is time? The perspective I would otherwise be attributing to God—the one that reduces time to a timeless essence—would be self-defeating. Or to make the point with a little less cheek (though not much less), God answers the question of time not by engaging in supernatural science but by creating beings with a sense of time and sharing a form of life with them. My Augustine side encourages me to think that this is a better answer to the question of time than I could give, not so much because of God's superior leverage, but because God is so much better at sharing. But, again, it is not clear to me that my attention to the ordinary time-talk that I exchange with others can be anything like sharing in the sublime sense. And so I am still wondering whether losing an idyll of sublimity, an Eden of intelligibility, is ever anything but deflating.

I should say that my puzzlements over Wittgenstein's take on Augustine are not meant to be criticisms, politely renamed. It has, after all, never been the business of the *Philosophical Investigations* to be Augustine exegesis. When Augustine enters into the text, he is there only to lend his authority, his spiritual and intellectual gravitas, to the temptation to sublime logic. It would be wholly contrary to the spirit of Wittgenstein's philosophical practice to assume that the disposition to sublime logic is solely an intellectual failing, such as a failure to see when a question has been posed and analyzed apart from any context of possible application. If this is all that philosophical catharsis amounts to, a sobering return of a metaphysical logic to logistics, then it is enough for us when doing philosophy to remind one another that we fail to assign a sense to the terms we often consider the most sublime, or more to the point, that when we sublime a term, like "time" or "truth," we evacuate it of sense.

Imagine Augustine trying to play this game. He has one term, "God" (*deus*), that he cannot help but sublime, for it refers essentially to the being whose very being enforces the distinction between absolute and relative existence. Augustine feels deeply moved to love God absolutely and not be bound by the genealogical history that would surely qualify his love as temporary, particular, and limited. Obviously he cannot evade this history without having to undo his own birth and miraculously return to the nihil of uncreatedness—a metaphysical fantasy if there ever was one. But it is only in the wake of finding his ascent out of time godless that Augustine is able to return to his own natural history with something more than disillusionment to inform his intellect. If disillusionment were the only offering of a frustrated transcendence, then he would hardly be able to resist the temptation to absolutize the relative and mistake the created order for something authoritatively ordinary. There is no name for God in the ordinary language philosophy of a dispirited world. Augustine's name for God—Jesus of Nazareth—suggests why he cannot so easily abandon his question What is time? to an investigation of the grammar of time-statements; those statements have no authority for him while he remains unsettled between an impossible memory of eternity and an anticipation of lost love.

Wittgenstein had a profound, sometimes melancholy, sense of how difficult it would be for most of his readers to detect the confluence of spiritual and intellectual struggle in his writings. He felt that he lived in clever but not especially honest times, where there was little appreciation for how deep the demand for clarity in philosophy went and little sense for the damage that cleverness could do when taken for wisdom. "One *cannot* speak the truth," he once wrote, "if one has not yet overcome oneself. One *cannot* speak it—but not because one is not yet clever enough."[7] "The truth," he goes on to explain, "can be spoken only by someone who is already *at home* in it; not by someone who still lives within untruthfulness and does no more than reach out towards truth from there." While I believe that Wittgenstein would have indulged honest doubts about his or anyone else's comfort with truthfulness, I think that he was probably right not to underestimate the disposition that most of his readers would have to read the confessional elements out of his philosophy altogether and take him to be a clever, if not always wholly successful, debunker of metaphysical pretension. "When philosophers use a word—'knowledge,' 'being,' 'object,' 'I,' 'proposition,' 'name'—and try to grasp the *essence* of the thing, one must always ask oneself: is the word ever actually used in this way in the language which is its original home?—What *we* do," Wittgenstein invitingly summarizes, "is to bring words back from their metaphysical to their everyday use."[8]

I have to admit that apart from scattered references in the *Philosophical Investigations* to Augustine, I would have had little inclination myself to hear much of spiritual moment in Wittgenstein's desire to reacquaint philosophers with the ordinary usage of their sublimed terms. And in truth I still don't hear much, despite my inclination. Perhaps I overestimate my inclination to read Augustine, the more overtly confessional writer of the two, with something like a confessional intent or resolve of my own, or perhaps I just underestimate the importance of this kind of resolve for truthfulness. In either case I owe mostly to Wittgenstein my sense that I do not read Augustine especially well, and not because I am not clever enough.

To give you some sense of the difficulty I have in mind, the difficulty to which I am in effect confessing, I turn now to the passage in *Confessions* 11 that many of Augustine's readers, the self-described philosophers especially, have taken to be his resolution to the problem of time.[9] Prior to this supposed high point in his analysis, Augustine has come fairly definitively to associate time's mysterious stretch across past, present, and future with his mind's distention (*distentio animi*)—the mental stretch of his perceptiveness into a memory or an expectation.[10] Association apparently slips into identification in the climatic passage. I quote it in full:

> In you, my mind, I measure stretches of time. Don't clamor against me,
> or more to the point, don't clamor against yourself with your crowds
> of unruly affection. In you, I repeat, I measure stretches of time. The
> affection which passing realities make in you and which remains after
> they have passed, that is what is present for me to measure, not the
> things which have passed to make it. When I measure time, it is this
> very affection that I am measuring. It follows either that this affection
> is what stretches of time are, or that I don't measure stretches of time.[11]

In my attempts to interpret Augustine's conclusion, that time for him is some kind of mental reflex, I have tended to ignore the force of the framing imperative. It is only when he is able, if he is able, to cut through the confusion of his affections and focus on a single affection—his affection for time—that Augustine is in a position to resolve his disjunction and claim with some confidence that he has sufficient self-awareness to become aware of time. If I am to meet him on the other side of his self-directive and judge there whether he really has captured what time is, then I must have the ability to quiet the unruly crowd of my own affections and focus my mind on time; only in this way am I able to isolate my affection for time—my unambivalent disposition, that is, to know what time is. Whenever I assume that I have the requisite focus, I start to see clearly what so many of his other readers have professed to see: that Augustine has left out of his conception of time the irretrievable pastness of the past and the ever elusive futurity of the future. All that remains to him is a poor man's eternity, a present that, for lack of a viable alternative, refuses to budge.

But note. The unadventurous claim that neither the past nor the future is ever really present hardly counts as a revelation. I haven't discovered anything about time when I insist on the past being the past, the future the future. I simply impose a condition—an impossible one, as it turns out—on what I can know, the condition being that I absolutely differentiate what I can know from my means of knowing it. To know the past as past, I have to disown my memory in my very act of relying on it. I think here of a memory of forgetfulness, my vague sense that my present awareness has slimmed down, but without my being able to say how.[12] Matters aren't any better when it comes to knowing the future: My mind's expectation does double duty as what the future both may and cannot be. In pushing my knowledge of time toward a putative objectivity, I will have resolved Augustine's disjunction—that time is either his affection for time or he doesn't know what time is—toward unknowing. He and I can be reasonably sure of only one thing: that whatever time's stretch happens to be in itself, it is nothing that we can measure.

When I find myself imposing a condition on my knowing that is guaranteed to keep me in the dark, I begin to wonder whether I really want to know what I profess to want to know. Augustine does not specify which affections among the crowd in his mind were doing the most to wreck his focus on time. But in imagining that I have achieved a focus sharper than his, I have identified in my own mind one of the principal culprits. It is my affection for not being able to know what time is, for having to take time for granted, for living my life within my own self-imposed horizons. I call this my affection for not dying. And if there is that part of me that really doesn't want to bite into the fruit of knowledge and come to know what time is, then how nice to have the philosophical reassurance that any answer to the question What is time? would be a waste of time, a venture into the ether of a sublimed logic.

Here it is worth pausing to remember that it is not the time-perplexed Augustine that Wittgenstein holds up as a saintly sublimer of logic, but the Augustine who affects to assign a language to his infancy—some kind of wordless mentalese, it would seem, but not so hopelessly mind-embedded that that it fails to translate, however roughly, into words. The first entry of the *Philosophical Investigations* starts off with quotation from *Confessions* 1.8.13, the part where Augustine is recalling his emergence out of infancy and into a life of communicable desires. It reads as follows:

When adults were calling something by name and doing so by moving their bodies in accord with an utterance, I would notice this and commit to mind the sound they were making when they wanted to point this thing out. That they wanted to do this was further apparent from their body language, the language that is, as it were, the natural speech of humankind: a change of countenance, a look, a gesticulation of limbs, a tone of voice that indicates an intent to seek and possess something, or reject and avoid it. Over time I made the right associations between words in sentences and sounds frequently used to point out objects, and once I had wrung the requisite sounds from my mouth, I used them from then on to announce my desires.

When Wittgenstein ventures to comment on Augustine's recollection, he passes over the odd spectacle of an infant's soliloquy and confines his attention to what the infant, by some lie or miracle of Augustine's memory, is saying to us: "It seems to me," Wittgenstein writes, "that these words give us a particular picture of the essence of human language. It is this: the individual words in language name objects—sentences are combinations of such names."[13] So far this description of the so-called essence of human language is as innocent as the infant who articulates it. What can be more natural, more basic to language than the correspondence of words to things? Wittgenstein digs a bit deeper. "In this picture of language," he continues, "we find the roots of the following idea: every word has a meaning. This meaning is correlated with the word. It is the object for which the word stands."

It is one thing to claim that a name in a language corresponds to an object; it is another, less innocent thing to claim that the object is what the name means. To get at the difference, let's enter into Augustine's infant mind-set for a moment, taking his recollected infancy, as Wittgenstein has done, more or less at face value. The infant wants to be a speaker of words and no longer an infant because he hopes through words to announce his desires more effectively to the adults who surround him and who, he presumes, have some interest in meeting his needs. Although the infant Augustine is precociously self-conscious, I will assume that he has fairly ordinary objects of infant desire: breast, blanket, binky, bed. Imagine that tiny Augustine wants his mother, who is usually the one to furnish him with all those alliterative desirables; she is absent from his sight. He calls out "Monica!" perhaps for the first time in his life, and she returns: happy day. The name "Monica" surely corresponds to the person who is his mother, or there would be no sense in which Augustine calls out her name. But is she also the object that is the meaning of her name? We have two avenues of response here. We can assume that her name has meaning only in the presence of the object that gives it its meaning, or we can resist this assumption.

Let's start by not resisting. What is the object, the presence that supplies the name "Monica" with its meaning? Why not say that this object is Monica herself? The rub here is that tiny Augustine is moved to call out for Monica when she is absent from him and not when he is basking in her presence. If he still in some sense calls for her in her absence, he is nevertheless, in keeping with our current theory of meaning, using a name that refers essentially to a presence, something that is always available, that is, to a properly focused mind. We may be tempted to surmise, along the lines of Augustine's talk of a present of things past, that this something is a memory. The physical Monica may come and go, but tiny Augustine's memory of her endures and furnishes her name with meaning. A moment's reflection, however, should reveal what a disastrous move this would prove to be. To the infant Augustine, and I daresay to the adult version as well, there is a world of difference between remembering Monica in her absence and being aware of her while she is present in the flesh. If the meaning of her name is to be a mental presence, fully in place whether she is there or not, then Augustine has no meaningful way to express a son's ordinary, time-conditioned love for his mother. The memory that is furnishing him with the meaning of her name is never the memory of an absence. Of course Augustine can utter the words, "I miss my mother," or words to that effect, but in whatever way he invokes her he uses a name whose meaning ends in a timeless object—something whose passage into nonbeing would be nonsensical, not sad.

The implication I draw from this oddly analytic route to immortality is not that we will find ourselves speaking of eternal things, and only them, once the fog of time and desire has been lifted from our minds, but that Augustine's memory of the sublime, in all of its apparent innocence, threatens to put him out of touch with everyone he truly loves. It is as if he were imagining himself essentially orphaned in this life of the flesh and not just occasionally bereft. "Augustine describes the learning of human language," Wittgenstein observes, "as if the child came into a strange country and did not understand the language of the country; that is, as if it already had a language, only not this one."[14] And yet the boy surely loves his mother and thinks of her as home.

Obviously I think that we should somehow resist the temptation to expect meaning only from eternal things. The logos is for loss and longing, too, though meeting language there does seem to keep us constantly emerging out of infancy, as we struggle to find our feet and our words with others. At the extremity of Augustine's desire to break his tie to woman and quiet the desires of his unruly flesh, he hears the voice of a child at play, one whose body he never locates. It tells him to pick up and read—*tolle, lege*—and he does.[15] He picks up the Apostle's book and, on the authority of a child's voice, divinely assumed, he applies the words of Romans 13:13–14 to himself: "No more wild parties and drunken fits, bedroom antics and indecencies, rivalries and wrangling; just clothe yourself in Jesus Christ, your master, and don't look to lusts to care for your flesh."[16] Augustine remembers being immediately reassured by these words; they flood his heart with a securing light and whatever doubts he was having disappear—like shadows in daylight. I have long found this reassurance of his unsettling. Why should it be particularly reassuring for a man whose habits of desire have been resisting reform to be told that he must stop all the sexual nonsense, stop trying to be the flesh beloved of all women, of woman herself, and just, once and for all, put on Jesus? One possibility is that Augustine is reassured to learn that God, from all eternity, has already given him the power to secure his own integrity and walk like Jesus, confident of his father's love. All Augustine needs to do is to remember that. But this of course means that he will have to travel the route of a sublimed logic and expect meaning only from eternal things. Maybe putting on Jesus means something else entirely.

Since I have no charitable reason to doubt the authenticity of Augustine's conversion, I'll assume that he does put on Jesus and that he ceases in some profound way to nurse himself on lusts. Augustine comes to know that in the eyes of his heavenly father he is as Christ Jesus is—a beloved son, now and for all eternity. And yet, despite all this or perhaps because of it, he fails to find himself perfected in time. Here is a bit of his confession, a passage that both follows and haunts his supposed resolution to the problem of time:

> Now I spend my years sighing, while you, Lord, my solace, my father, are eternal. Still I am being scattered into times whose order I know not, and my deepest thoughts, my soul's viscera, are by happenstance and tumult being torn apart—until into you I flow, purified and made molten by the fire of your love.[17]

The question I am most moved to ask here is this: Is Augustine in a position to assume that matters were much different for Jesus? Perhaps he is in only this one respect. Augustine notices that the passage of time is keeping him from himself and putting him into God's keeping. He imagines a life that stands inherently in need of consolation. Jesus, who had a better sense of his father's love than Augustine's had—he was, in fact, at one with it—acknowledged faith in the place of selfhood and went to his cross an honest man.

Our language tends to perpetuate a grammatical fiction. It suggests to us a subject that is never identical to the thing that changes. I change over time, presumably become more or less myself. How can I be both the subject and the object of that change? "Philosophy," says Wittgenstein, "is a battle against the bewitchment of our intelligence by means of our language."[18] Augustine tries to say what time is, resolves his options into a disjunction, and confesses that his life is a *distentio*—a stretch beyond his mind's ability to stretch. He cannot resolve his disjunction because both sides are true. Time is his mind's affection for time, and time is not what he measures. Like any one of us, he cannot help but give into the fiction that he has a hold on time, but the fiction, and the self that it constitutes, never ceases to pass. "You cannot face it steadily," T. S. Eliot reminds us, while he ponders Krishna's words to Arjuna on the field of battle, "but this thing is sure, that time is no healer: the patient is no longer here."[19]

Every moment of a human life calls for a surrender of self, a sacrifice, a dispossession. But in dispossession there is also receptiveness, a prior grace. The failure to know what time is, when consecrated in the attention, becomes the disillusionment that Augustine calls love.

PART II

Moving Progressively Backward

CHAPTER 3

The Man without Memory:
Peter Abelard and Trust in History

Babette Hellemans

> What puts our mind at rest is the simple sequence, the
> overwhelming variegation of life now represented in, as
> a mathematician would say, a unidimensional order:
>
> the stringing upon one thread of all that has happened in
> space and time, in short, that notorious "narrative thread"
> of which it turns out the thread of life itself consists.
>
> Lucky the man who can say "when," "before" and "after"!
>
> —ROBERT MUSIL, *The Man without Qualities*, VOL. 2, 435–36

In the first section of this volume (on Augustine and Wittgenstein) it has been pointed out how the structure of language becomes scattered in the realm of history, especially when language uttered by the "confessional self" is at issue. This article will turn toward a more theoretical approach of this problem. It seeks to explore how one of the most famous confessional accounts in Western history, *The History of My Misfortunes*, dismantles the historical status of language up to the point of facing an abyss of oblivion. Peter Abelard (1079–1142) represents the central figure of this document. Multitalented, Abelard wrote a set of highly diverse texts, which makes it difficult to categorize his philosophy. It will suffice to resume the variety of his work as concerned with the ethical use of language "under the realm of time" (*infra abitum temporis*). Before zooming in on the details of Abelard's idiosyncrasy, we can generally state that the ethical implications of running against the boundaries of human language preoccupied twelfth-century intellectuals. Their culture, rooted in the ancient tradition of withdrawal and asceticism, abounds with a persistent drive to understand the human and the divine status of language. Because language belonged to the world created by God, it was by definition part of the human condition. This also implied that language was considered intrinsically *temporal*. The uttering confessional self, then, as an act of historicism that determines why the turn to God as an event that is present here and how, causes some serious philosophical problems. Abelard was particularly aware of such a breakdown of history, caused by the status of language. As we will see, one of his main concerns was to return to the nucleus of what we might call "the event." In order to come closer to Peter Abelard's reading of "the pastness of the event" we will gradually peel off the following question: Can one be truthful toward remembering factuality in events while at the same time transfiguring these events through language into a "dramatization" of serendipity?

Giving Up Authority

In describing theories concerning the past, medieval scholars drew on a long tradition of authoritative texts (*auctoritates*) often written by ancient philosophers. The debate of intellectuals was often directed toward the question of whether the past was "present and universal" or "past and particular." In this academic tradition, memory seemed to incorporate something very different from an intellectual cognition of the past. The reason for this separation between cognition of the past and memory was based partly on the historically recurring idea that the human soul was not compelled to use sense-dependent images but can independently construct likeness (of the past in the present). While on the one hand, the growing corpus of authoritative texts reflected knowledge of the past in an excessively optimistic way, the status of an individual past through memory as a specifically intrinsic operation was rather opaque. In the twelfth century, however, some intellectuals started to question the confidence in the status of these authorities, as well as the ontological status of the mental operations of the inner soul. For Peter Abelard in particular, famous for questioning the confidence in the authorities (*Sic et Non*), as well as the ontological status of the soul capable of transforming itself into all things, meant shaking up the structure of language and narrative. It is my hypothesis that Abelard's *skepsis* toward knowledge of past events relates much more to a positive act of investigation of history than mere doubt, which would represent in the Christian medieval context a contempt of God (the word "*skepsis*" used here in the sense of the Greek metaphor of vision). With these notions in mind, I will argue that the process of structuring language into a new system of thought parallels an extratemporal conception of "events" in history. In addition to what I will be calling "trust or distrust in the past," this parallel will help to explain the possible interactions between time, performance, and language in an eschatological world. Such a dynamic interpretation will also prove to be important for the understanding of memory as emotion and cognitive knowledge of the past. This article thus provides another, perhaps more nihilistic, perspective on current academic theories of cultural memory, historiography, ritual, and commemoration.

Memory as a Principle of Structure

Few movements were further removed from a sense of historicity than the movement of scholasticism when it occurred at the dawn of the rise of nonmonastic schools in the early twelfth century. After the reintroduction of Aristotelian philosophy in the twelfth and thirteenth centuries, the epistemology of the mind was meant to be forever different: Henceforth the mind was capable of abstracting and grasping integrated conceptions of matter. As a result, scholastic teaching was based on a more naturalistic interpretation of the cosmos than practiced in the world of monastic learning, implying a widening spectrum of knowledge and commemoration of Scripture, from a rhetorical framework of interpretation to theoretical principles of knowledge. This shift would exert pressure on an authoritative weight of the past. What these medieval scholars who were trained in new logic first and foremost needed to figure out, was how to handle the flux of time within a world which was definitively physical.[1] While trust in the senses could not claim access to knowledge (*scientia*), their general truthfulness guaranteed by coherence prohibited a rejection of the truthfulness of senses into general doubt. Not that legitimacy of a new kind of human existence was being acknowledged by the senses, so that knowledge of the sincere truth (*veritas sincera*) would be merely shaped by knowledge of the external world, but that it was *worth* acknowledging its presence without transgressing the Christian contours of eschatology. That it was possible to achieve knowledge within the frame of divine laws of nature, signs, and language.[2]

The way in which these twelfth-century "missionaries of reason" imparted codes of moral values and ethics ran counter to some established practices of learning and expressing the ancestral heritage: monastic training. In these circles the influence of Augustine can hardly be exaggerated. He took Aristotle's doctrine of signs (transmitted through Cicero) as a basis on which he elaborated his theory of language in which words were necessary to connect the signs—as objects of knowledge—to the interpreter.

Within this interaction between object of knowledge and the subject, Augustine introduces time not as something measurable by reason but only mentally; that is, as the "stretching out" of the mind itself.[3] In addition, he developed a theory of knowledge of the past, which he connected to the threefold, intertwined presence of the Trinity. According to Augustine in his *De Trinitate*, remembering implies a simultaneous set of "trinities" of representations in the mind: *memoria, intellectus,* and *voluntas*.[4] Western intellectualism as it flourished in the monastic schools would be immensely influenced by this Augustinian theory of three interconnected elements in the mind. The third element of the will (to remember, to understand) refers to the imminent end of the world, the essence of eschatology. Indeed, the core business of monastic life was (and is) to wipe out any sense of an earthly reference of temporality. In practice, this was realized by means of the ever-returning rhythm of the divine offices, seven times per twenty-four hours, every day and every season. *Saecula saecolorum*, for ever and ever, thus mimicking a human understanding of eternity. Augustine's notion of a three-partite chain of knowledge of time, hovering between an extra-mental reality and the inner human soul, would leave an imprint on almost any articulation of medieval intellectual thought. This "imprint" was intrinsically ambivalent. For although Augustine holds the view that knowledge has to pass all the elements of this chain—via the shape of things, images, similitudes, or species through memory trace—the cognitive process ultimately comes full circle by an act of the will.[5] How, then, could it be possible to achieve a universal knowledge of the past?[6]

According to Janet Coleman, medieval scholars adopted two epistemological attitudes toward the past that are incompatible with each other:

> Medieval theories of memory are, in part, theories of reconstruction. This is because learning to read and write depended for many centuries on late classical grammar and logic texts which effectively argued that things in the world, to which language referred and thinking referred, could not be "touched" except through the mediation of linguistic or mental signs. Hence, the examination of a text which was a surviving fragment of the past in the present, could only be an examination of coherent ways of grammatically and logically speaking about experiences, rather than an examination of the events themselves. The nature of reliable evidence is at issue in medieval historiography and epistemology, intimately bound up with the nature of language and men's confidence in its conventionally established means to refer to and report nontextual evidence accurately. Physics and mathematics were taken to have their

own ways of dealing with the world. Historical knowledge and understanding is of the world but only through language.[7]

Roughly, Coleman distinguishes here a theory of the past and memory that
deals with the *language of texts* as dealt with in the *arts du langage* (grammar, rhetoric, logic) and one of nonlinguistic *experience* as in physics and
mathematics. The relationship between those two aspects is far from clear.
All we know is that, while the Augustinian-Platonic influence persisted,
scholastic thinkers, all of them, somehow took the problem of sense experience as a basic element of human knowledge seriously. As a result of this
amalgam of old and new philosophical and theological elements, we cannot expect a clear-cut synthesis. Yet precisely that which retrospectively
looks fragmented and incoherent to us may have to be seen as a manifestation of profound thinking (as in the case of Abelard), precisely because
it lacks the overarching synthesis of the later, scholastic period. History
being part and parcel of this amalgam, medieval scholars conceived the
past rather differently and in a less clear-cut manner than we do: This is
the reason why, for instance, medieval conceptions of the past often seem
anachronistic or heuristically wrong for modern scholars.

Coleman considers the thinker of our interest as a turning point in the
understanding of history: "And we are now in a position to discuss one
of the most sophisticated theories of knowing and remembering to have
emerged from the medieval concern to describe how man uses language
to understand both present and past: that of Peter Abelard."[8] Let us have
a closer look at her discussion. In order to understand what Coleman is
saying in her chapter on Abelard, which is about halfway in her book, we
should keep in mind that she positions him as partly responding to the still
powerful old ideas on logic, language, and literary structure embedded in
Aristotelianism, as well as on the previously sketched influence of Augustine. This implies that the use of language (*usus*) is a crucial instrument in
order to understand the past. Instead of using the monastic techniques of
memory within the frame of the apostolic *disciplina claustralis*, Coleman
explains how Abelard constituted a theory of "historical understanding" of
texts. But what did this understanding look like? When the new logicians
of the twelfth century developed their theories on knowledge of the world
(including its past), they replaced one set of metaphors for structures of
memory with another. I do not mean this as a criticism, as if it would be
possible to describe the medieval concept of the Creation in a nonmeta-
phorical sense. Instead I want to point out the knotty character of intellect

and matter—couched in Christian language—as both aspects manifested themselves as an undivided whole.[9]

Peter Abelard was very aware of this intersection between reality and mental operations. According to Coleman, his theory provides us with a study of language in which a logical and linguistic development of Augustine's belief in the uniqueness of experience is developed. Since he "substituted texts for events [. . .] texts are primarily significations of events," "Abelard believe[d] that language reflects the stability of the nature of things over time."[10] We realize how important Aristotle was to Abelard's thought, since from an Aristotelian perspective historical time cannot be of crucial importance in the physical world.[11] Remembering can only take place after having experienced, sensed, and learned from things around us. When we remember according to Aristotle "the present content of our mind is an image which is a copy of a past thing, the image being similar to and derived from our past act of perceiving something."[12] This was obviously not the case for Plato, for whom the object of knowing was something eternal and stable. Learning and remembering in Plato's view meant recollecting knowledge that is already present in the mind. In order to understand the nature of "pastness," then, ancient and medieval intellectuals who interpreted Plato and Aristotle (almost always indirectly) would argue that the nature of the past was metaphysical rather than historical, meaning by "metaphysical" the science that studies things that do not change. The question was pivoting around the status of reality in experiences that happened out of the realm of *praesens*. Are "past" and "pastness" to be considered as things (that don't change)? And what about movement, experience, or passage in time? From the beginning, interactions between the mental and the physical were interconnected with time and space. It seems as if "pastness" is to be found where these poles cross. All this preoccupied Abelard immensely. He held a theory of his own in which abstract concepts—including events, times other than the present, relations or wholes—would be a matter of *language*, not something of the world. The power of an individual intellect (*vis intellectus*) would be decisive in the nature of knowledge. This is important. Meaning for Abelard is not naming. Put in competition with statements of logic and grammar, a moral statement—"I ought not to kill this man," for instance—will presumably lose.[13] Meaning is interpretation. Abelard thus emphasized not merely the relevance of context but its enabling power. The nature of a thing or its properties was related to the *structure of language*. Ultimately, it made him conclude that in the case of the Trinity we can speak of something distinctive (the Father, the Son, and the Holy Ghost) without speaking of separate forms *in* God.[14] For this, Abelard would be condemned.

We have seen how for Abelard the plurality of interpretations and intellections was crucial. It led him to adopt a singular position in the polarizing and widespread discussion on the universals. Against the common opinion of twelfth-century intellectuals, Abelard considered the notion of context (he used the words *status*, *dicta*, or *statement*) essential in order to understand the abstract nature of these universals. For Abelard a universal, "being a man" for instance, is not simply "seen" by others like a bent stick in the water but a performance, an act of understanding that is manifested by the thinking individual him- or herself. Intellection is *validated* by language. If "being a man" was a thing, for Abelard it would refer to Plato's eternal realities. But there is action and performance. But "because we are not God, we do not have correct or complete conceptions of natures that our ideas are of; indeed, intellection is limited."[15] The thrust in an intellection (*vis intellectus*) allows the understanding of universal "things"; it does not tear apart the process of understanding the sincere truth. On the contrary, it is the *vis intellectus* that shapes veracity according to the thrust and counterthrust in the intellect itself.

This theory of knowledge also influenced Abelard's understanding of actions performed in the past. Indeed, past actions are to be considered as universals, even though they are not things *in the present*. In Coleman's words Abelard's concern is "to deny that talking about 'being a man' or 'past actions' (both of which cause universals) or, indeed, any such nature or *status* that may be signified, forces us to accept that there is some universal to which we are referring over and above the concrete individuals that share such a name."[16] In other words, past actions cannot be separated as "things." Rather, they are differentiated events. Abelard's neo-Aristotelianism led him to picture the understanding of things as structuring reality that our language presupposes, as logic that was not concerned with ontology.[17] For Abelard, then, language is established by rules. But it is caused and experienced by the world in the fact of "being language." Indeed, the logic of language has no temporality in it. Coleman concludes "Abelard's concern for literal textual exegesis along dialectical or logical lines, therefore, affirms that it was possible to come to an understanding of a past author's intention in the present. The truth of the conception of a past intention, expressed through its logical coherence, may be discovered by a present activity of mind analyzing fixed grammatical and logical conventions."[18] Therefore, understanding the world as it *was* depends on how we understand the world as it *is*.[19] But how can language account for the veracity of one's own history?

Parallel Worlds

Until now we have discussed "pastness" and memory as features of knowledge; that is, knowledge of past actions and their ethical *meaning*. In this section I will try to examine a possible connection between a rational knowledge of past actions and the status of a "personal" history. Different dimensions of "pastness" will fuse together, from the life narratives of an individual to historiography and the ethics of history. We will see how ill defined the concept of memory is; with good reason, since we all experience daily the fragility of our memory. What is important, therefore, is a possible interpretation of memory not as something fixed that is holding the past together in its most trustworthy sense but as something that constructs meaning.[20] Not merely by considering a testimony as a narrative or composure but as a synthesis of remembering and oblivion, knowledge and religion, akin to a twelfth-century anthropology of reason. I now propose to test Abelard's consistency in the application of his own rules of logic and grammar as he recalls the morality of his own past actions. Does he recall these actions as "memories" in our sense of the word? Or is he connecting those past actions with the present status of his intellect? And what about the notion of factuality with respect to emotion in those past events?

The most obvious text to have a look at is the famous *History of My Misfortunes* (*Historia Calamitatum*). The nature of this "history" is highly ambiguous. The text is written in the guise of a letter, as *memoirs* of sorts, and it especially gives attention to a "personal" intellectual development, intertwined with all kinds of events in the world, including sex, power, and politics. The *History's intentio operis*—as expressed by the author, genre, and content—has been the subject of strong debate among historians, mainly pivoting on the question of whether an emergence of individuality could be traced back to this "auto-document."[21] One of the major historiographical difficulties is to estimate the degree of authenticity and veracity in this text, molded by commonplaces of stylistic and rhetorical conventions. This difficulty especially concerns the use of typology; that is, to see the history of Abelard's life not as exceptional (as we modern individuals tend to do) but as an example for others. What is most "typological" about Abelard's account in the *Historia* is its firm representation of rules, authorities and principles to be sought out, developed, and followed—or rejected. The author's protagonist, Abelard himself as it seems, imitates writers of the past and further elaborates ancient and medieval literary topoi. With great ability and knowledge the protagonist seizes hold of many great authorities: the Bible, the Church Fathers (especially Augustine), as well as the commonly known figures of classical antiquity in the period such as Cicero, Boethius, Lucan, or Aristotle. In style as in genre, the key figure Abelard consistently shows a desire to use all aspects of language. He also demonstrates a specific attitude toward authorities. This can be read in passages in which Abelard is struggling with his masters, such as Anselm of Laon, one of the leading figures in Paris at the time. Abelard demonstrates great disdain toward Anselm's lack of improvised intellect (*ingenium*):

> One day it happened that after a session of Sentences [summaries of authoritative arguments, BH] we students were joking amongst ourselves, when someone rounded on me and asked what I thought of the reading of the Holy Scriptures, when I had hitherto studied philosophy. I replied that concentration on such reading was most beneficial for the salvation of the soul, but that I found it most surprising that for educated men the writing or glosses of the Fathers themselves were not sufficient for interpreting their commentaries without further instruction. There was general laughter, and I was asked by many of those present if I could or would venture to tackle this myself. I said I was ready to try if they wished. Still laughing, they shouted "Right, that's settled! Take some commentary on a little-known text and we'll test what you say." Then they all agreed on a highly obscure prophecy of Ezekiel. I took the commentary and promptly invited them all to hear my interpretation the very next day. Then they pressed unwanted advice on me, telling me not to hurry over something so important but to remember my inexperience and give longer thought to working out and confirming my exposition. I replied indignantly that it was not my custom to benefit by practice, but I relied on my own intelligence, and either they must come to my lecture at the time of my choosing or I should abandon it altogether.[22]

It goes without saying that the text recalls how brilliantly the protagonist Abelard succeeded in his demonstration of *ingenium*. Admittedly, it is hardly surprising that the Abelard of the *History* was attacked by critics who felt that this kind of improvised intellect was not intellect at all but rather an unrelated series of moments of intelligence that served merely to impede narrative progression. Abelard's rather "spectral" reflection on the past influences our way of interpreting the events in the *History* as well. Historians and literary historians certainly have generated valuable insights into the way in which Abelard described his life events as a narrative, but it might be worthwhile as part of our experiment to draw on concepts deriving from Abelard's own debate within linguistics, for the *historical status* of this narrative may be seen in at least two ways. Analyzing the historical context, it represents an account of past events. Grasping deeper linguistic structures and meanings that organize this text we might add another perspective to Abelard's view on history. The first interpretation of *The History of My Misfortunes* is based on a cyclic narrative, in which an individual story of rise and decline is "told" to a friend. The second, however, draws its structure from a more dramatic view of eternally contending binary oppositions. In other words, if we are to take this *History* merely as a testimony, we do not have sufficient evidence to interpret this text as a frozen series of events. In terms of Abelardian linguistics, language understood as a *status* in which statements and propositions are made, is intrinsically atemporal, and I would add, intrinsically dramatic. Is this "letter of consolation," then, demonstrating another *meaning* of *history*? Let us read some other examples of past events in the narrative.

The events Abelard encountered as a teacher in Paris are of world fame. Invited by the chancellor of the Notre Dame, he became a scholar in residence at the cathedral. Here he would meet the chancellor's niece, Heloise, a student at the Cathedral school who "in her looks she did not rank lowest, while in the extent of her learning she stood supreme."[23] They had a dramatic love affair. During this period of his life, Abelard would have only inspiration to write love songs and "not the secrets of philosophy."[24] The scandalous incident—as a cleric Abelard was not supposed to have sexual intercourse—ultimately resulted in the birth of a son and the decision to adopt the vow of the Benedictine order and to live a life as a monk and nun in separated cloisters. Both would pursue their new vocation as leader of monasteries. Although separated, the couple would stay in touch during their lifetime. This is all written in *The History of My Misfortunes*. Ever since, the story of Abelard and Heloise has been seen as ideal when it comes to faith in love. After their lives, they were buried next to each other, a token of eternal love. Do we have here a happy ending, *after all*? The symbolic burial is not described in the *History*. Actually, the story does not reveal any specific sense of emphatic emotion or judgment about the loss of love towards the beloved. Some of the letters placed after *The History of My Misfortunes* reveal tensions and remorse, albeit reluctantly as far as Abelard is concerned. Anecdotes, such as the one just read, humor, and irony in the *History* also serve the performance that is inherent in any epistolary-historical encounter. We should not forget the shape of the text:

The goals of the performer—Abelard—will only be met if both audience and narrator share a mutual understanding. The key feature of genre is the sharing of rules of interpretation—genre is never explicable by shape alone. So if we take into account the specific incidents described in the *History* as well as the way in which they are embedded in the structure of language, we have a problem of trust in the past. The acknowledgment of such a *skepsis* with regard to the veracity of history issues a challenge: Can one know the truth of history?[25] Let me first point out that the understanding of Abelard's inquiring can be seen as a radical form of *skepsis;* that is, to see beyond the metaphysics of history. By that I mean that the simultaneous layers in the narrative function, as it where, like polyphony in the field of music.[26] If, for instance, the first "polyphonic chord" opens with an emphasis on the topos of consolation, a different "layer" of historicity can be added, such as the history of Abelard's difficulties in schooling. A more complex construction is thus added to the shape of the *Historia.* The architecture of this text becomes more complicated when the affair with Heloise is added. Exchanges between the topos of a letter of consolation, the monoseries of the intellectual *Werdegang* in which Abelard performs and transforms, and the rhythms of developments such as the encounter with Heloise are casting their shadow forward. Together they represent the complexity of series of narrative transformation. I want before all to try to get rid of the idea of a monolithic history meant for testing the "veracity" of past events alone. If we honor the complexity in which all "narrative sequences" can be organized, whatever their nature or historical status (in the logical sense I pointed out above), it becomes hard to isolate the "monostructure" of the love story that has had such a strong imprint on this *History*. It is this specific rhythm that results from the way in which narrative sequence arguments and emotion are woven together into one polyphonic "history." The singular structure of a work, then, consists of the way in which the rhythm sequence is constructed through the protagonist's performances in different series happening at the same time. If we are able to honor the serial narrative and to multiply the series by itself, between the *a* and *b* of an initial polyphony, not as parallels but as serial structures proper, we realize that the structure of the text is composed with interchangeable structures, counterpoints and structures of counterpoints interwoven into emotional and rational transformations. To get a hold on past events, then, may be hardly more than prejudice here: a happy ending. If we recall the problem evoked by Janet Coleman on Abelard's theories of the past, what might these similitudes of events (of a different nature) represent?

My juxtaposition of different kinds of "pastness" is meant to suggest that it is not possible to know the answer to the question of quality (of opinions or past events) without thinking about the moment insight occurs. It may become clear that all my attention in this article is given to the widening of the scope of series of past events in order to make it homogeneous: *History*. What we are to read in the narrative of events is the intelligence that a text has already brought to its making; and hence we have to think about what improvisation of intelligence is. History indeed is assigned another meaning; technically speaking it becomes allegorical. I think that "history" for Abelard does indeed contain a metaphysical vision of the world. If Plato thinks that being and Being are in different places, particular beings and Being are not located in the same realm. This is what I mean to say with "parallel worlds." But, as we have seen, for Abelard the Aristotelian sense of existence as a way of knowing the past is equally important. Here we feel as if the awareness of being belongs to a *real experience* of a presence of the present (*praesens praesentis*—see the introduction to this volume). Pastness itself cannot be objectified. For when our *vis intellectus* in relation to things or universals (and their context or *status*) are reduced in temporal significance, and crushed by the reminiscences of post factum morality, the possibility of an improvised and self-performing intellect (*ingenium*) will be left vacant. The ambiguous status of the past events will have the effect of undermining our efforts to come to a conclusion about the *status* of the narrative. According to Abelard, here language comes to the rescue. But what exactly does it save? The emphasis on the author, presented as *the* actor, diverts our attention from a qualitative judgment, unnoticeable in its obviousness. In a way, Abelard casts himself in his *History of My Misfortunes* as an individual who is seeking a rational way of living with an analytical eye toward the use of language in the world. With a rather superior disdain toward the world itself, Abelard the actor puts his trust in another worldly kind of language. While rudimental in its topological use but fundamental in its placing, such an attitude is illustrated by the concluding lines of the text. Here, the author of the letter and the actor of the events conclude: Those who follow their own will rather than God's "rebel against their secret hearts [that is] against the meaning of the words 'Thy will be done.'"[27] The historical meaning of words is to be found in the domain of secret hearts. Such a conclusion, after the turmoil of events, is indeed puzzling. For it implies not only that Augustine's tripartite chain of knowledge is broken, precisely at the intersection between memory and the act of will (*voluntas*), but also that the line drawn between history as a memory trace and the will as a cognitive act is blank. No connection, no past, no memory, no happy ending—nothing. Is the effort of describing the past events to his friend *a waste of time*? Or is a "polyphony" of events the meaning of "consolation"? In the *History of My Misfortunes*, Abelard casts himself as light material, delivered to the wind. The scene is of loss followed by a sigh of divine redemption, after having experienced earthly love, ambition, and the quest for truth in a degenerated world. It is somehow rather similar to the celebrated poem of the contemporary *Carmina Burana* written by his "confrere" the Archipoet († after 1165):

> Foaming from within with the most violent anger
> I speak to my mind in bitterness
> I have been made from material of nimble elements:
> similar to a leaf about which the winds tease
>
> [*Aestuans intrinsecus ira vehementi*
> *in amaritudine loquor meae menti:*
> *factus de materia levis elementi*
> *folio sum similis de quo ludunt venti*].[28]

With a satirical position in relation to hegemonic values, the poet enumerates a series of specific incidents, ultimately leading to longing and a feeling of trust in time: "I will get whatever you order with a willing soul."

I do not intend to suggest that the events described in the *History* did not "really happen." They may have taken place and they may have changed people's opinions. But I also wish to ask whether one can accept a description of past events in such a work—fleeing into the divine redemption—as dictating the events of the protagonists of the story; to wit, Abelard flirting with Heloise, his teaching and directing her, her achievement of humility in accepting the monastic veil—reluctantly. In anticipation of what I want to say at the end of this article, let me just comment that Abelard's memory (including the notion of will and *vis intellectus*) is focused toward the very limits of language and meaning. At the center of the performance language, metaphors, meanings of culture are brought together by improvisation, as it were, but before that moment all these elements are free floating. They collapse into a "composure" in which past, present, and future (anticipation) are reconciled.[29]

We should, in short, ask ourselves whether the status of Abelard in his *History* is a matter of trust in the past, in which events occurred during a couple of troublesome years a long time ago, or if the narrative demonstrates the misleading power of individual memory, tongue in cheek. As well as the description of events Abelard analyzes himself in the most sarcastic way, to start with the fact of writing a "history of my misfortunes" in the guise of a "letter of consolation."[30] In the text the author casts himself as the protagonist, someone who practiced various forms of self-deception, especially in matters of his love affair with Heloise. But he also made of this personage a persecuted intellect, an epic figure who has difficulties in identifying himself, since he is surrounded by people who have become victims of some scholarly obsession (the universals, for instance) or theological slogans (such as the possibility of understanding the Trinity) and have thereby achieved a false sense of significance. All the participants of the story have given a kind of narrative plot, a *point fixe*, to their lives. Instead, Abelard, the protagonist of his own "history," stands aloof. Uncommitted to any intellectual institution (hovering in between monastic and nonmonastic schools), Abelard pitilessly observes various representations of twelfth-century monastic culture that advocate pseudo-solutions to questions of knowledge and human condition. These solutions suggest meaning to life as if a totality of complexity were possible. And this is a key notion I think, to an understanding of Abelard, namely his conviction that comprehensive totality of knowledge is a chimera. Abelard's disdain toward the external world is based on two objections: His "colleagues" lack any semblance of the improvised intelligence (*ingenium*) and they live their life by reacting to events, reconnected through narrative. While Abelard's cognitive language experiments are directed toward a solution in which rationality leads to redemption, the people who surround him—perhaps Heloise should be excluded for her self-imposed "silence" after the love affair simulates oblivion—tend to advocate a return to the past in the sense that the events in their lives and the fact that they only *react* to them express a reaction against the *vis intellectus*.[31] So indeed, the simultaneous existence of parallel worlds represents the complexity of events in the past and the present and how we judge them. What is important with respect to the notion of parallelism, however, is that I do not intend to say that Abelard considers a "past world" paralleled to a "present world." This would be a rather simple solution that would distort the complexity of moral possibilities. With parallel worlds I intend to evoke a sense of complexity that is not fixed, indeed, which is the nucleus of dynamics framed by the extremes of dialectical statements.

We now have two different statements with regard to the notion of narrative, historical events and the structure of language. As we have seen in the previous section, the one type of statement is designed to understand the rationality of language and its structure. It is characterized by reason, knowledge, and logic. The second statement, however, is characterized by love, irrational impulses, and the mystical. This statement is framed within a sphere of intellectual developments, rationalistic attitude, and experiments of language. Under the surface of historical factuality lies the powerful process of thinking (*vis intellectus*), the will to know. The stone-like and massive reality is a metaphor; it is built with words, signs, and agreements under which "things" (universals) are bursting to get out and acquire *meaning* through the one who interprets them. As such, the reality of events has no meaning when they are not considered within their "crystalline" status. What is more, morality of the present is built on past authorities rather than proper judgment. People are only good and sincere through habit (*usus*), not through their proper intellect. Abelard's attitude toward reality (of the past) in the present is complex. He seems to realize that reality cannot be conceived by examining its dialectical opposite, either.[32] The reality of (past) events is interwoven with different phenomena in the world into a status of contemplation, "the meaning of the words 'Thy will be done.'" In *contemplatio*, there is no desire, nothing of cause, no *differentiae* or accidents. There are no distinctions of opposite worlds, such as reality versus the imaginary, or ration versus passion. In "Thy will be done" the outward reality represents oblivion, a lack of memory.

I should add a final remark about the notion of dialectics in the "parallel worlds." Any competition between these two "worlds" is imaginary, since *a priori* judgments that presumably stand for the understanding of events in parallel worlds in fact distort a possible proliferation with "polyphonic" developments. The essence of Abelard's schoolbook *Sic et Non*, to give an example, in which he questioned the context in which statements of authorities were put, was not intended to create new rules about absolute truth. Put as general statements, the propositions would seem either too obvious or patently false. But if power in intellection (*vis intellectus*) is stimulated by an active judgment of existents via words, images, and intellections in the present, what of Abelard's attitude toward knowledge of the past world? What of his contemplation of what existed already? Why does Abelard set the sights of knowledge that high? In other words, why does he turn an everyday problem (the use of ordinary language) into an epistemological impossibility?

Apologies and Wasting Time

It is the eminently chiastic sequence truly characteristic of Abelard's mind that bears the burden of his reality: the respect—in a moment of insight—for truth and time. Hovering between scholarly knowledge and ascetic contemplation means precisely *not* to be a master of life itself. Deep down lies the eternal "wedding of the opposites." At a trial, for instance, an event also mentioned in the *History of My Misfortunes*, Abelard defends his own writings against the Church, who considered him a heretic. Abelard acts like an illusionist. Gestures and words evaporate into thin air and come out as something entirely different—remember the power of irony—and their meaning is turned upside down. We can feel something of its magic power while reading the prologue of Abelard's *Apologia* against his opponent, Bernard of Clairvaux:

> In keeping with that dictum of Boethius, "Time should not be wasted in prologues that accomplish nothing," it is indeed needful to come to the matter at hand, so that the truth of the facts rather than a superfluity of words may establish my blamelessness. First, the charges are to be recorded which seem to have been brought forth from my writings against me; then responses will be apprehended on the basis of which the logic of truth may refute the ill will of falsehood.[33]

We read how the shade of words, the originally fixed nature of their truth, move elsewhere, to different realms outside the "reality" of this world: Truthfulness of facts is established by a specific *structure in language*. Argumentation is set against narrative. But also, this first phrase of the *Apology* has already presented Abelard as the master of performance who assembles and reassembles words to warn against the tricks of time. It is a prologue and it is not—it is an apology and it is not. His theatricality is partly a matter of the performer's surroundings: By the twelfth century, masters in "theology-to-be" were trained in the *trivium* (the language section of the liberal arts) and virtually lived in their monastic habit. It is hard to know whether these wandering scholars had a "home," a place where they could lock the door and be safe after something like a trial, whether this is the kind of drama of a pre-urban northern France as we might have seen it in our imagination, too, or a theatricality that has been later on established in its passage from the scholar's brain to hand. Put another way, did Abelard ever write an *epistola* that did not tell a history?

The *Apology* continues, and nineteen accusations promulgated by Bernard of Clairvaux against Abelard are summed up. The accusations are anything but reassuring: "Thus you say that I wrote concerning God [. . .] that God can do only the things that he does, or renounce the things he renounces, either only in that way or at that time and not another [accusation 6]," or "[. . .] that neither action nor will nor desire nor the delight that occasions desire is a sin, and that we ought not to want it to be extinguished [accusation 19]."[34] These are accusations that free-float somewhere between orthodoxy and heresy, and the rhetorical phrasing of Abelard— "Thus you say that I wrote concerning God . . ."—makes the content of the accusations a nightmare in which the position of the dreamer is variable. The shiver of heresy is followed by Abelard's denial of being the author of these claims (which we just read as belonging to *him*).[35]

Letters can represent panoramic personal insights, such as for instance love letters with lovers declaring to each other their "genuine" feelings, but they also tell terrible stories of corruption, violence, or calamity, and they give us the measure of our own lives with pitiless precision. The lack of distance evoked by the medium of letter writing is the reason why the "trap" of historicity is that subtle. The reader—is he the friend, the addressee, or the adversary?—can never be entirely sure about the status of historical truth in the described events. The point of history is to resist classifying letters as autobiographical while, ironically, their author supplies compelling reasons to conclude that the author *is* the protagonist of the letter. For one of the most striking features about Abelard and his contemporaries is the extent to which they still inhabited a world pervaded by the omnipresence of intellectual authorities (*auctoritates*) in their thinking. Despite Abelard's famous efforts to use his improvised intellect and to critically study authorities in his *Sic et Non*, in the prologue of the Apology—*in keeping with that dictum of Boethius*—we feel the strong presence of this peculiar kind of "pastness" in his thought. Intellectual inheritance was not smashed into the abyss of forgetfulness, and authorities did not vanish away, not at all. This is not intellectual iconoclasm. The reassuring presence of the Church Fathers, for instance, was as endlessly flexible as was the verbal playing with their thoughts and words, and "playing with words" is how, in essence, intellectual authority began: authority about God, Passion, Trinity, saints, and gifted minds with an all-prevailing immortality. Abelard is one of the kindred souls when it comes to the traditional status of authorities and the "plays on words." In section four of the very same *Apology*, Abelard provides us with some authoritative background while shifting to the primacy of the argument, since

the devil is held to blame who, interpreting the Scriptures wrongly, said to the Savior "that he has given his angels charges over you" [Matt. 4:6 quoting Ps. 90:11] and so forth. Yet the devil, even if he interprets the Scriptures wrongly, does still cite the words of the Scriptures, to whatever meaning he may twist them back. But you, diverging from my words as well as my meaning, endeavor to make arguments on the

basis of your fancies rather than my statements, and you boast that you
condemned my writings together with their author, you promulgate
a sentence against yourself and your own writings instead. As charges
you also bring against me some [of my words] as if heretical, which can
be refuted by neither reason nor authority.[36]

Even if we accepted all of Abelard's efforts to relate the meaning of
authority to the owner of the *vis intellectus* and even if we accepted his
pointing to the human limitation as far as the understanding of sin and
redemption is concerned—in fact he accuses Bernard of misplaced pride,
superbia, the greatest and most serious of monastic vices—it is anachronistic psychologizing to say that Abelard's personality was intellectually
self-contained.[37] Without exception, scholars had no autonomous intellectual power in the twelfth century as we think we have "It" today. As
such, the modern ideal of Abelard representing the unrecognized genius
living and working in solitude like a Don Quixote fighting the windmills
is largely a myth. We have seen the epistemological limits of his "history."
If we consider Abelard's "letters" as the only real clue to the concerns that
might have been going on in his mind, and when these texts are at best ambiguous, it seems a simplification to consider his more conventional works,
based indeed on authorities, as mere "linguistic virtuosity." The world of
grammar and logic separated from the world of letters and history, indeed
differ. But neither are they dialectically opposed. If we read the underlying linguistic structures and sequences of Abelard's letters—to a friend,
to Bernard—we learn more about the truth of complexity. With this I
intend to say that rewriting or remembering past events might represent
for Abelard a kind of *artificial structuring* of reality. History represents a
process of simplification that does not refer to the complexity of context
in the present (and knowledge of the past in the present). But, as we have
seen, intellect also requires similitude. Is it possible for the mind with its
singular *vis intellectus* to account for the reality of complexity in which the
flux of time is only one of the different possibilities of structuring? How
are intellect and knowledge of the world related to love and redemption?
While a dialectical vision is certainly present in all of Abelard's work, it is
not easy to find a terminal point in which all his generated ideas come to
a halt. Since there is no process of objectification (*Verdinglichung*) in his
thought, Abelard's ideas endlessly circle around the possibility of achieving
a true understanding of complexity in the world and its language.[38] Abelard
will remain, like the writer of the *History of My Misfortunes*, the wandering
scholar who, in the furthest regions of the intellectual and emotional realm,

hovered between example and doctrine, between rationality and love, between the old monastic world and the university to come. Abelard ends his *History* long before he would die, and we can safely conclude that there is no happy ending (in the Hollywood sense). At the end of his life Abelard was drawn toward the abbey of Cluny, with abbot Peter the Venerable's blessing, by the monastic life of the Benedictine order in its most glorious form. In this huge edifice of Western Christianity, individual withdrawal had to take place amid the large number of monks present. With its satellite building structure, dispersed over acres of land, counties and countries, Cluny encouraged yet another kind of ascetic life and abandonment of the self to God's will. Abelard would die, severely ill, in one of those "satellite" buildings.

CHAPTER 4

Creation and Epiphanic Incarnation: Reflections on the Future of Natural Theology from an Eriugenian-Emersonian Perspective

Willemien Otten

Nature's Voice: From Creatio ex Nihilo to Epiphanic Incarnation

Why should there be an essay about nature in a volume about temporality? In terms of Christian theology one may be inclined to say that time is all about linearity and horizontal progression, while nature is about God's vertical intervention in the world, styled in the final analysis as his single-handed invention of it. The latter position is what has become reified over time in the locus of *creatio ex nihilo*, which continues to be the dominant way in which Christian theology thinks and speaks about nature. All this seems to point to a chasm rather than a connection between nature and time.

But is this really the best way to approach nature, or does the environmental crisis inaugurate a kerygmatic paradigm shift, forcing us to reconsider the traditional role of nature in Christianity? After all, it seems that the hardened defense of *creatio ex nihilo* has bared Christian thought about nature as increasingly vulnerable. This is in part the result of scientific development, in response to which Christianity depicted creation as increasingly objectified. But it is also the result of various developments internal to theology, which since Schleiermacher has become more and more focused on Christianity's vertical dependence on God and his teleological redemption of humanity. Most of all, however, I see the reification of *creatio ex nihilo* as the result of obliviousness to the voice of nature, ringing ever more distant over time even as it tried to make itself heard. For there is a case to be made that nature, while engaged in conversation with the divine and the human, also has a distinct voice of its own, through which it projects its own sense of justice. Upon such a conception of nature, it has much in common with Augustinian temporality, as it projects a sense of presence as fleeting presentness, of syncopation rather than duration, of epiphanic incarnation rather than solidified creation.

In this essay and in conformity with this volume's plan as a whole I will try to retrieve the voice of nature as one more amenable to the integration of God, humanity, and the cosmos than traditional *creatio ex nihilo*. To do so I will engage in a kind of thinking progressively backward: Starting with a diagnosis of the contemporary situation, I will weave a series of historical and constructive arguments spread out over two interconnected parts, followed by a conclusion. Pursuing a historical line of argument, I hold that the voice of nature has been available throughout the tradition but was suppressed as a side effect of both the scholastic and the scientific processes of objectifying nature. Continuing in a more constructive vein I argue that retrieving an Eriugenian-Emersonian view of nature, which allows space for the reflexive self as a precondition for thinking conversationally about nature, may remedy some of the ills of traditional natural theology. It thereby offers viable new prospects for thinking about nature in our current age.

Contemporary Ecological Criticism, the Hold of the Sciences, and the Building of Cosmos

In recent years nature appears to have had a comeback in the world of the humanities.[1] This has much to do with the ecological crisis faced by Western civilization, which is the result of the application of ever intensifying and more advanced technological industries and strategies, distributed on a global scale and turning the natural environment into a wasteland. It is tempting to explain this comeback in part as related to the relevance of the humanities themselves, eager as they are to add to the widespread social and political protest against the global ecological crisis. Even if in the short run their contribution will not lead to any practical "scientific solution," it may lend new meaning and credibility to the field. Because the humanities have so little to offer by way of concrete ecological solution, however, it is tempting to disregard their contribution as a mere elegiac lament over the loss of the once-favored *locus amoenus* of pastoral, classical literature. This rings particularly true if one connects the long tradition of nostalgic representation and romantic advocacy of nature's decorative place with a deep longing for a fixed, ordered, and harmonious universe, characterized by what can be termed not so much nature's ecological as, more broadly, its environmental role.[2]

The fact, however, that literary scholars like Lawrence Buell have recently embraced the term 'environmental criticism' to describe their new branch of eco-aware literary criticism, thereby replacing the earlier ecological criticism or ecocriticism,[3] counsels against dismissing their input too quickly. In addition to indicating a deep awareness that the role of nature in literature transcends its function as the Aristotelian "setting" for human activity, it gestures toward a more programmatic intent to reach beyond the stalemate of a "natural" versus a "built" environment.[4] It is relevant in this context—and will become central to the unfolding of my argument further on in this article—to borrow terms from the twelfth-century cosmologist William of Conches (Normandy) here by stating that what Buell and others want to avoid is the hardened opposition between what William called the *opus naturae* ("the work of nature") versus the *opus artificis* ("the work of the craftsman"). In his glosses on Plato's *Timaeus*, William of Conches depicts *opus naturae* as the intermediate cosmological level on which we find nature operating, procreating, and germinating more or less by itself, in a semi-personified guise. That is, nature broadly obeys the divine will but does not take its direct orders. By contrast, William speaks about *opus artificis* with specific reference to human deeds instigated by indigence or need, such as the building of a house against the rain or the cold. While the human craftsman may find himself imitating nature, William intimates that there is something contrived about the craftsman's work, as militating against the exigencies imposed by nature forces him to violate nature's integrity. Adding further nuance, he stipulates that the work of the creator endures permanently whereas that of the human craftsman is transitory. The work of *natura operans*, positioned as it is on the intermediate level, will come to an end, but nature will continue to be active through its seeds.[5]

The above distinctions from William's Platonic glosses resonate well with the way in which the contemporary humanities, having long taken the dichotomous approach of nature versus culture/nurture for granted, now see critics like Buell drop this divide upon reflecting on the current environmental crisis. From the perspective of the nature-culture dichotomy within the social sciences William's distinction seems to resonate strikingly well also with the criticism launched recently by Bruno Latour against the entire nature tradition of the West. A scientifically trained philosopher who divides the nature tradition of the West into a political and a scientific sphere, Latour aims at bringing us around from what he calls a "bicameral" view to the building of a new multiform and collective *cosmos*. Latour's agenda of "political ecology" is driven by his radical thesis that nature is not where we find the victim, and hence the possibility of a solution, but that our very idea of nature is part of the problem. In Latour's view "political ecology has nothing to do at all with 'nature'—that blend of Greek politics, French Cartesianism, and American parks."[6] His proposed solution for a true political ecology, whose work has only just begun, is to foster scientific production, to abandon nature, and to redefine the political. By striving for "the abandonment of nature" Latour advocates a comprehensive and embedded approach to the *cosmos* that abstains from privileging either politics or Science—an overarching term for the individual sciences which he capitalizes because of the near-religious, monolithic respect in which they are held. For Latour the facile antagonism between politics and Science has led society to become entrenched in their separation, based on the exaggerated claims of each to absolute authority, and thus yielded a stalemate that perpetuates nature's underlying hybridization.[7]

Although Latour talks little about the humanities, and hardly ever mentions religion, his pungent criticism of Science but also of the political mobilization against it echoes Charles Taylor's argument in *A Secular Age*,[8] even as in other ways Latour subverts Taylor. What both authors have in common is a desire to move beyond postmodernism and create a livable future for the collective of nature and society. While Latour's discourse does so by combining the register of science and democracy, Taylor criticizes the suffocating effect on our age of the so-called immanent frame,[9] under which he subsumes the post-Enlightenment mindset defined by the (strangle)hold of the sciences (what Latour calls "Science"), which he sees as a suffocating paradigm that no longer tolerates but forcibly excludes any discussion of transcendence and conversion.

What I take away from Latour's and Taylor's critical approaches, which I see as reinforcing each other on the above points, while resonating also with Buell's insight, is a growing awareness of how much contemporary thought is deeply "bicameral" and locked into the stalemate of nature/ Science versus culture/society, even as individual explanations and proposed solutions differ substantially. Thus there is a strong sense in Taylor that our present secular mindset has somehow become anesthetized by the sciences, a fact that, in Latour's view, has provoked a surreal ecological battle between sciences and politics about an ever more elusive sense of nature. While this spectral sense of nature has solidified enough to become the direct object of Latour's criticism, for Taylor the stated dominance of the sciences, summed up in his notion of the "immanent frame"—to which he adds the idea of "buffered identity"[10]—has spearheaded into the threat of exclusive humanism,[11] whose inherent drive is to marginalize, if not force out religion. Still, when Taylor identifies secularization with "excarnation,"[12] he echoes to some extent what Latour means when criticizing our mindless servitude to Science.

What remains as yet unclear to me, and cannot be resolved in this article, is how far Latour's and Taylor's analyses can be stretched to address the contemporary predicament of nature with one voice. To put it differently, is there a point where Latour's relentless intellectual rigor, enabling him to demythologize Science, to end "Naturpolitik,"[13] and undertake the work of political ecology all in one sweep, inevitably folds into the "immanent frame," rejected by Taylor due to its formal secularity? Or does Latour's analysis generate its own openness to transcendence in a constructive attempt at building *cosmos*—expressed in nonreligious but nevertheless expansive terms—that coalesces with and may even strengthen Taylor's goal of having society come together by fostering porous rather than buffered identities?

Leaving the last point for another time, in this article I want to take up the future-oriented approach that characterizes the outlook of both analyses by trying to design a view of nature that avoids the kind of romantic literary tropes of a pastoral paradise, which Buell sees rightly pushed out as naive, while taking up both Latour's and Taylor's valid criticism of the dominant, largely abstracted concept of nature, emptied of any value besides its instrumental use for a technocratic society. Reading progressively backward will be helpful not just in allowing us to bring in historical materials alongside contemporary ones but especially in turning the scripted and prescriptive text of *creatio ex nihilo* into a fuller and livelier conversation about the place of nature in the Christian tradition. While I reluctantly label my own project of attuning us to the echoes of nature's muffled voice a natural theology insofar as it emphatically includes the divine, I leave unanswered the question whether that makes the instrumental view of nature the unavoidable product of secularization. The latter seems to me the starting point rather than the upshot of Taylor's analysis.[14] I also do not want to commit as yet to the idea that any constructive position forward, including my own natural theology, must stand by definition in opposition to secularism.

Given that my explicit aim is to preserve the autonomous role of the literary and especially the religious imagination, the view of nature to which I aspire has its starting point neither in Science nor in the sciences. Yet it should stop short of scientific antinomianism, which I see as self-defeating by leading to a fragmentation of knowledge that defies the purpose of the humanities. Instead, my view of nature should allow it to break through the immanent frame, to borrow Taylor's expression, for which I shall draw on religion. I see religion as a constructive force and a source of inspiration rather than an inherited feature or, worse, a cause of Latour's bicameral stalemate. It goes without saying that only when the above conditions are met do I see a new tradition of natural theology that has a chance at succeeding.

Nature as a Source for Right Religion

To develop a new project on natural theology it is important to inculcate a keener sense of nature as a source and possible criterion for right religion. With that purpose in mind I want to go back now to the "French" (contemporary and medieval) scientific analytical thinkers Bruno Latour and William of Conches.[15] As indicated, Latour puts much of the blame for the hybridization of the sciences and politics on the Platonic tradition. Whereas William of Conches felt himself eminently at home in that tradition, Latour sees it as the chief culprit of the "metaphysics of nature" that forced the West to organize public life around the two elliptical poles of "nature" and "culture." Imposing on the world a bifurcation of human subjects and predominantly nonhuman objects, Platonism is for Latour an attempt to keep us doomed forever to life in the Cave.[16]

While William of Conches clearly saw himself as a Platonist, the open medieval way in which he molded this tradition, alluded to above, rather contradicts Latour's accusation of Platonic philosophy as tending by definition toward dichotomous models. In fact, William carved out a place for *natura operans* precisely to avoid this, intent as he was on overcoming any disjointed view of divine creation. Given William's identity as a premodern Christian author, moreover, the crucial subject—object dichotomy for him would not be that between humanity and nature, as Latour diagnoses our problem, but rather the chasm between God and nature, including both human and nonhuman nature.[17] Operating on a Christian-Platonic cosmological paradigm, William held that God *could* in principle do everything, as he did not doubt divine omnipotence. According to his much-celebrated example God could even make a calf out of a tree trunk, should he choose to do so.[18] But why should he? Hence the more important question for William becomes whether there was *need* for God to make everything, and if not, why not? For William, who increasingly endowed his twelfth-century Platonic worldview with the endemic aestheticism of *ornatus mundi* ("arrangement of the world"), answering this question led him to develop a more intricate and synthetic alternative to creation whereby we see his focus shift from divine activity to a divinizing creativity inherent in nature itself.

A further comment on William's twelfth-century milieu may be in order. It appears that William is best seen as part of the movement of twelfth-century humanism—a designation that I use as an offshoot of the associative term "medieval humanism" coined by Richard Southern.[19] Among other things Southern used the term "medieval humanism" to foreground the intelligible structure of nature, allowing humanity to make full use of its divinely bestowed but created, and hence limited, powers of rational insight. As I have argued elsewhere,[20] in twelfth-century humanism the understanding of nature fulfills the express task of furthering the unity of humanity with the divine, thereby closing the gap between creator and creation. Thierry of Chartres with his physiological commentary on Genesis and Bernard Silvestris and Alan of Lille with their influential personified Nature poetry can all be connected to this same movement. Using their shared background for better insight, we can rephrase the central problem occupying and energizing their thought as follows. If an emphasis on divine intervention did not further the intended celebration of nature, how else could the presence of the divine be channeled to the natural sphere in such a way that God's role to call the world into being was preserved but his surplus of power to crush it was reined in?[21]

It is relevant to observe here that for William and his twelfth-century peers the threat of Gnosticism, against which the orthodox warrant of *creatio ex nihilo*—however perceived as true—was once directed, had long subsided. Far more urgent and exciting to them was the challenge to keep up with nature's fast gaining prominence in a more active, celebratory, and integrative role due to the remarkable rise of interest in Plato's *Timaeus* and to connect this with biblical exegesis. The resulting concept of *natura operans*, which is unique to the age, is best understood as the combined result of a scientific or physiological interest in Plato's *Timaeus* (as well as in other sources of cosmological knowledge coming through the Arabic world) and a simultaneous attempt to forge a more sophisticated hermeneutics, including an expanded exegetical vocabulary, by which to integrate the *Timaeus* with Genesis.[22]

As a consequence of the rapidly expanding and diversifying role of nature, God's creatorship is not so much marginalized—as if adumbrating seventeenth-century deism—as much as it becomes suffused throughout the entire cosmos by *natura operans*, as nature in quasi-independent form takes on certain divine traits. As a consequence, William sees God's tasks as heavily concentrated ones, as he situates the divine at the edges of existence, there where being meets the void of nothingness. Thus he considers God exclusively responsible for the creation of the elements and the human souls out of nothing, for Christ's birth from a virgin, and for the resurrection of the dead.[23] What all these divine actions have in common is that they operate in the liminal sphere of life and death, and for that reason they transcend human insight even if they are not thereby irrational.

What my brief sketch of William's medieval Platonic worldview has attempted to make clear is that, if the twelfth-century idea of nature suffers from conceptual heterogeneity, contrary to Latour's analysis this does not reflect a gap between man and nature or between "nature" and "culture." As pointed out, the major disconnect is rather between God on the one hand and the collective of humanity and the natural universe on the other. This is the major disconnect that William and his age strove to overcome by stressing the work of nature (*opus naturae*). To put it in hermeneutical terms, what William tried to do by locating his own philosophical arguments as much as possible on the level of *natura operans* was to think "inside nature" rather than about nature.

Just as William is not a protodeist, it is likewise wrong to misconstrue his attempt to wean nature from the hold of the divine as a kind of scientific emancipation *avant la lettre*. To counter this misguided impression it is important to keep in mind that the apologetic dimension is never far from William's mind. He is very keen to exonerate the divine from having supposedly wreaked havoc by causing chaos at the elements' first creation. To this end he vehemently refutes the idea of a random "lying around" of the elements (*inordinata iactatio*), on which God violently needed to impose order to demonstrate his power.[24] His famous example of the calf and the tree trunk has its rightful place in the same context, as it brings home to us how there are endless options available to God to manifest his power. For William, however, God moves in far subtler ways. And since in the tradition of medieval humanism these are seen as underscoring rather than defying reason, even when transcending direct human insight, they pose an exciting challenge as humanity is invited to scrutinize them. Rather than randomly throwing elements into the world, William argues that God created them together "rude and mixed" in a big body of sorts in which, based on their weight and other innate qualities, they began to gravitate to their natural place, as *natura operans* teased out their inherent arrangement. For William and his colleagues then, investigating the twists and turns of *natura operans* yields the most comprehensive and representational insight into the origins of the world by extending God's creative activity to merge with nature's inherent divinizing creativity. What William's cosmology with his attention to *ornatus mundi* reveals at the same time is that God's originary creative act is ultimately more about attuning the world to love and beauty than about activating power and intervention.

To portray William as a Platonist, if we stay with Latour's terms without adopting his accusatory and dismissive stance, is accurate insofar as William employs the *Timaeus* as his privileged source of nature-speculation. But building on William's idea of *natura operans* as unfolding a dynamic world of cosmic love and aesthetic arrangement, I submit that calling him a Platonist may be truer in a moral sense. Such a perspective may help us to refute Latour's position that the central Platonic dichotomy, which both he and I want to overcome, is by definition that of idealism versus realism, of epistemology versus ontology. It is helpful to know that, since the *Timaeus* followed on Plato's *Republic*, which dealt with positive justice, William saw the reading of the former as inevitably bound up with natural justice.[25] The idea of nature as a moral force, even if closely related to its aesthetic quality of *ornatus mundi*, informs William's notion of *natura operans* in a way that is distinct yet has mostly gone unobserved.[26] Coloring and affecting the twelfth-century cosmological outlook as deeply integrated, it is typical for twelfth-century humanism also in a broader sense, as it helps to explain why interpreters like William were able to draw freely upon the *Timaeus* and on Genesis without feeling any rivalry or chasm between Christian creation and other views of nature. Seen as God's mouthpiece and filtered through the delicate hermeneutics of *natura operans*, the natural world constituted for William its own alternate text. Rather than a faint reflection of divine action, nature harbored its very seat, expressing it in a creative way that reflected, communicated, and also added to God's luster.

Compared to William, whom I have used as my launching board to develop a new and fuller natural theology, what I see as the problem with its classical guise found in William Paley is that the same atmosphere of interpretive openness is no longer maintained.[27] Coming out of the tradition of Protestant literalism, whose iconoclastic unseating of (religious and classical) authorities according to Peter Harrison accelerated the emerging science of nature, Paley and others read nature in much the same detailed and meticulous way as scripture.[28] But the price for this progress is that the supple and elaborate hermeneutics of old, linking nature and scripture, virtually disappears, thereby illustrating how much Latour's problem is a modern rather than a Platonic one. Consequently, Paley's attempt to reconcile the new hold of the sciences with the religious hegemony of Protestantism imposes an invasive hermeneutics of closure and constraint, as views of creation not set up in explicit contrast to nonbiblical concepts of nature seem no longer tenable. As Harrison has argued, as a result of seventeenth-century debates between science and religion not only did science validate itself by usurping the role of arbiter, but we also see Christianity in the process morph into the new status of a modern, propositional religion.[29]

Although I do not reject Harrison's conclusion that "with the passage of time the power relation between these two enterprises [science and religion] has been almost completely reversed,"[30] we should not take it to mean that religion henceforth eschewed the notion of creation by adopting a scientific worldview. Instead, what the Enlightenment project of natural theology by Paley and others most clearly expresses is how creation emerged as a viable category in science, thus reinforcing rather than loosening Christianity's monopoly of nature compared to the medieval outlook. While the divine power of *creatio ex nihilo* seemed to become severed from the natural world as a result of scientific development, it actually became lodged in creation's sanctified but fixed object status. Thus we see a tilting toward the bicameral view of Latour, even if for Paley humanity is included in the system of nature as its highest form.[31] Furthermore, since science cast the connection between the divine and creation in a predominantly causal mode, the study of nature became heavily teleological. In consequence, any language of nature that was free-flowing, or seemingly strayed beyond the trodden path became inevitably (mis)construed—and rejected—as idolatrous or pantheist.

In the vision of *longue durée* that I want to adopt for my own project, however, the rise of pantheistic nature speculation is more than a Romantic reaction to the advancement of the sciences; it must also be seen as the long-term consequence of the structural reining in of nature's innate powers, both theological and scientific, ever since the end of twelfth-century humanism. After all, it was the imaginative combination of both science and theology (or philosophy for that matter), avoiding any bicameral position, which endowed that earlier culture with such powerful inspiration.

Desiring a more integrative model, in what follows I will give two counterexamples to the way in which modernity, which both provides the setting for this development and is its driving force,[32] has led the early-modern ethos of religious reform, so powerfully thematized by Taylor,[33] to become teamed up with the scientific revolution, yielding in the end to a delimiting conceptualization of both the category of nature (in science) and creation (in theology). Prompted by an interest in cosmological conversation which I see as overriding problems of historical context, I will draw on the thought of Johannes Scottus Eriugena and Ralph Waldo Emerson, whose roles will be further explained below, to pick up echoes of what above I called nature's muffled voice. What is particularly interesting about these two chosen authors is how each in his own way tries to preserve humanity's integration with nature, allowing them to develop a sense of natural justice that is true to nature as both moral compass and criterion for right religion.

From Book to Experience: Nature as Source of Religious Inspiration in Eriugena and Emerson

JOHANNES SCOTTUS ERIUGENA (810–877 CE)

The Book of Nature

A familiar way to conceptualize creation as accessible to human understanding is by seeing nature as a book rather than a stage, with Calvin's famous description of creation as the "theater of his glory" providing the model for the latter.[34] In recent years ample attention has been paid to the trope of nature as book, a revelatory repository of resources that invites comparison with the inexhaustible well of scripture.[35] Invoking Romans 1:20, we can even see the revelatory potential of nature sanctioned by scripture.[36] It seems fair to conjecture, therefore, that reading nature through the book trope may be of help in trying to revitalize the tradition of natural theology. By enabling different reading techniques, moreover, ranging from the literal to the allegorical, a natural theology based on this trope would allow us to regard creation as a manifestation of the divine and its attributes in the widest sense, thereby transcending the teleology of causality.

Because of his subtle use of this trope, a review of the case of Johannes Scottus Eriugena proves particularly interesting and fecund, even if he does not employ it very frequently. One may find a first insight in his creative use of it by looking at his *Homily on the Prologue to St. John's Gospel* (14:5–7). Following Maximus Confessor, he establishes there a subtle connection between the four senses of scripture and the four elements of nature, whereby the earth represents history, the waters surrounding the earth represent moral exegesis, the air represents natural science, and, finally, the ether is the highest contemplation of divine nature.[37] Of particular interest in the context of this article is the original way in which Eriugena molds this trope to accommodate his insightful but alternative physiology, programmatically laid out in his *Periphyseon* or *On Natures*, in which the centrality of nature develops in tandem with scriptural relevance.[38]

I want to further unpack Eriugena's deployment of this trope by connecting it to recent scholarship. In contradistinction to the way in which philosophers like Stephen Gersh and Dermot Moran have typecast Eriugena as belonging to the idealist tradition—the legitimacy of which claim I do not want to dispute, although it oddly accords with one of the Platonic dichotomies rejected in Latour's political ecology; namely, that of idealism *versus* realism—approaching Eriugena through the metaphor of the book of nature makes me in the final analysis critical of their position.[39] For if Eriugena's molding of the book trope makes anything clear, it is that the *Periphyseon* wants to reshape Christian-Platonic cosmology in such a way that it structurally attends to incarnation. The deep incision and impact of incarnation as a prime theological theme punctures in my view the broad climate of intellectual immaterialism, seen as central by Moran.[40] To assess better the impact of incarnation, as well as evaluate my difference from Moran's position, I will explore Eriugena's exegetical craftsmanship as he navigates not just the exegesis of scripture but also, simultaneously, must ward off the perceived idealist *stasis* of *natura*. This latter theme may not be immediately evident but is nonetheless important precisely because Eriugena's nature, famously divided into four species, seems if not idealist, then at least monolithic and pantheist. And yet, underneath its meandering exterior, Eriugena's *natura* reveals in my view an urgently forward motion, however subtle, which is lodged deep inside the recesses of creation itself. It is precisely through Eriugena's attention to incarnation that we can begin to draw this out.

Taking my cue from Eriugena's modification of the book trope, I see two specific points on which I want to comment below, as they may help to nuance my difference from Moran's assessment of Eriugena. My points regard on the one hand the structural influence of Maximus Confessor on Eriugena's parallelism of nature and scripture, which causes a fundamental change in his application of the book trope to nature, and on the other his adoption and modification of the Maximian notion of incarnation as *incrassatio*, or "thickening," through which Eriugena is able to ground the book trope ultimately in *natura*. What I find most important is that as the combined result of these points Eriugena's *natura*, which like in William acts in dynamic, semi-independent form even if it is never personified, manifests itself as engaging rather than resisting temporality, insofar as in the final analysis it is more about affirming eschatological potential than about sustaining idealism.

Transfiguration and Incrassation

Although Eriugena can make use of the book trope as in the example from the *Homily*, in the end he clearly prefers another analogy, namely that of nature and scripture as Christ's two vestments at his Transfiguration. We find him commenting *in extenso* on the Transfiguration scene in *Periphyseon* III. In the context of what unfolds there primarily as an exegetical discussion, as usual Eriugena wants to probe deeper, in the course of which he comes to make the following statement:

> And if Christ at the time of his Transfiguration wore two vestures white as snow, namely the letter of the Divine Oracles and the sensible appearance of visible things, why we should be encouraged diligently to touch the one in order to be worthy to find Him whose vesture it is, and forbidden to inquire about the other, namely the visible creature, how and by what reasons it is woven, I do not clearly see. For even Abraham knew God not through the letters of Scripture, which had not yet been composed, but by the revolutions of the stars as other animals do, without being able to understand their reasons? I should not have the temerity to say this of the great and wise theologian.[41]

The quotation makes helpfully clear that Eriugena's attachment to the book trope for the study of nature must inevitably be tangential, outshone as it is by the more attractive idea of nature as vestment. But this does not alter the fact that in the final analysis both tropes underwrite a similar analogical tenor, namely to draw nature and scripture not only closer together but closer to Christ. It is not a coincidence, therefore, that the identification of nature and scripture takes place at the moment of Transfiguration, which Richard Kearney—in terms derived from Jean-Luc Marion—has called a divine saturated phenomenon. As such it involves, in phenomenological terms, a surplus of intuition over intention, or conversely, a deficit of concept vis-à-vis intuition, thereby imposing on Eriugena the need for a sophisticated exegetical hermeneutics.[42] Seen as centered on Christ's Transfiguration, Eriugena's exploration of *natura* perforce becomes deeply involved in that kind of hermeneutics.

A first advantage of the image of nature as vestment over the book-trope is that the former suggests a concrete, more tactile way to pursue the study of nature. For it seems to do so in order to prepare for a live encounter with Christ, who is mediated more directly through texture than text. It is precisely on the point of Christology as an inherent aspect of Eriugena's universe that I find myself most resisting the idealist interpretation, as it seems to lock us once again into a false opposition to realism. Whereas for Moran Eriugena's branch of idealism is characterized by "spiritual imma-terialism," under the influence of what I would like to call the *Periphyseon*'s deep Christology I see Eriugena greatly concerned with the tactility of nature, in part because the element of texture allows him to insert tem-porality into it. This may also help to explain why, for all his ethereal Pla-tonism, Eriugena is so often very concrete and interested in the materiality of creation.

This preference for the tactile and the material over the textual, even if to some extent it involves only a difference in emphasis, reaches a trans-formative apex when Eriugena, again following Maximus, comes to discuss the notion of *incrassatio*, or "thickening," for Christ's incarnation. Not co-incidentally, Eriugena introduces it only toward the end of book V, which contains the eschatological close of the entire *Periphyseon*. Engaging in a discussion of the parable of the Prodigal Son, he sets out to interpret this text as another step in the clarification of nature's return, which is his topic of discussion here; in fact, it is the only matter left to discuss.

To contextualize Eriugena's discussion of the return we should observe that in the *Periphyseon*'s particular scheme the return unfolds in stages. First there is a complex return of all things to human nature, and from there, in a subsequent step, from human nature to God. The return of human na-ture itself, moreover, is a bifurcated one, as it is divided into a general and a special return, with the latter yielding a set of individualized theophanies only for the elect to see. If armed with the knowledge of its eschatological charge we now revisit the parable of the Prodigal Son, we find Eriugena depicting the older son as a stand-in for the world's general return, while the younger represents those who will enjoy the special return. In a rather unfortunate way he maps this same distinction also onto the difference be-tween the Jews and the Gentiles, represented respectively by the older and the younger, Prodigal Son.[43] Eager to press on with the actual completion of return rather than with filling out the parable's detailed structure, Eriugena's allegorical reading does not comment much on either son but immediately zooms in on the sacrifice of the fatted calf, almost conflating this New Testament parable with Abraham's sacrifice of a ram in Genesis 22. Often seen as a prop, like the ram in Genesis 22, the calf turns out to play a surprisingly central role here. For it represents Christ both as inaugurating and fulfilling, even if not yet performing, the return of nature by his own catalytic holocaust:

> And then the fatted calf shall be brought in and slain. And what is that calf? Is it not the man Christ filled with the sevenfold Grace of the Holy Spirit, and heavy with the fatness of the letter and the visible nature? For in these two, the letter and visible nature, the corporeality of Christ is manifest, since it is in them and through them that He is perceived, in so far as He can be perceived. For Christ is the spirit of the Law "and the invisible things of God are made manifest through the things that are made, and his power and eternity are everlasting"; or, in the words of the blessed Maximus when he is explaining what Gregory the Theologian said of the Nativity: "The Word was materialized (*incrassatus est*)":
> 'The Word, Which is simple and incorporeal and Which is the spiritual nourishment of all that comes after It, deigned by His fleshly presence to take from us and on behalf of us and in accordance with our nature, though without sin, material substance for the divine powers that are in heaven.'[44]

For Eriugena, as in Maximus and Gregory Nazianzen, Christ does not just have an isolated capacity to redeem the cosmos but his capacious presence literally fills up the entire universe. Yet for Eriugena, this only becomes fully apparent when Christ is consumed as holocaust at the end of time, for only at that point does the story of salvation come full circle. With the saturated phenomenon of Transfiguration here overflowing, so to speak, and running into the diachronic limits of its surplus of intuition, it does not escape time but reverts back into concretized, material incrassation, an incrassation not just of Christ's incarnation, as indicating one of the four signatory cases of such saturated phenomena—i.e., event, idol, flesh, and the other—but through him of all reality as nested inside *natura*'s own temporality. Only when Christ's incarnation is completed and reinforced by his passion and sacrifice, so Eriugena implies, does he span the totality of *natura*, and will it be possible to halt the treadmill of time by building in moments of irruption and encounter. With theophany edging toward epiphany here at the *Periphyseon*'s conclusion, the novel insight takes hold that creation as a beautiful vestment of the spiritual Christ does not only mediate access to him but fully *stands in for* him, as the eschatological was always lodged in the material.[45]

If one can accept my reading of *incrassatio*, or "thickening," here at the end of *Periphyseon*, it is clear that Eriugena's attention to incarnation does far more than merely prepare us for the union of nature with the divine, pushing us instead toward its actualization. As the idea of nature as majestic vestment succumbs under the fragile weight of the man Christ inhabiting scripture as fatted calf, the embrace of the material which it signals allows Eriugena to puncture the canvas of eternity. As a result the dynamic of nature, no longer moored to the scriptural text, is freed to break out of its discursive constraints, opening up into the malleability of eschatological time. It is as if in retrospect the whole universe can become read as an extended nativity scene, ready at any moment to erupt into Transfiguration. Upon this reading of deep Christology the holocaust of the fatted calf refers no longer to a final union of nature with God as a destination beyond time, which for Eriugena it likely foreshadows, but presupposes such union at the very beginning of creation, as the source of energy from which the first movement of procession was unleashed.

The remaining issue to decide for a new and viable project of natural theology, then—one that does more than revive Paley's project whose functionalist and teleological presuppositions have long been exhausted, and at the same time my point of contention with those following an idealist approach to Eriugena as too subservient to a bicameral view of reality—is to define more clearly where visible nature fits in upon accepting an Eriugenian scheme. Is it ultimately an impediment to the spiritual encounter with the invisible Christ or can we perhaps find traces in the texture and tactility of vestment that beckon us to achieve such union on this side of eternity?

RALPH WALDO EMERSON (1803–82)

Nature's Prophetic Role

It is on the point of the encounter with Christ that the natural theology project of Paley but also of modern intelligent design, as teleological rather than tactile and resting on the use of the book trope as demonstrative rather than investigative, seems to fall short. For my alternative proposal toward a natural theology a stronger foundation, one that generates more synergy, may be derived from the comparison between the heuristically conceived roles of nature in Eriugena and in R. W. Emerson.[46] It is to the latter that I will now turn.

Let me preface this comparison, however, with the following comment. Although Eriugena modified the book trope to accommodate the notion of creation as vestment, we should not lose sight of the fact that his work remained premised on it. The last two books of the *Periphyseon* are written in the shape of a so-called *Hexaemeron* commentary, a standard plot for many treatises on cosmology from Origen's *On First Principles* to Augustine's *De Genesi ad litteram*, and still an operative model, be it less dominant, in William's twelfth century.

A prime reason why the book metaphor no longer holds in the modern as opposed to the medieval period is the so-called eclipse of the biblical narrative, to use Hans Frei's paradigmatic term.[47] As a result of this major cultural paradigm shift, its effect enhanced by the growing importance of science as arbiter of religious truth,[48] the time that natural theology can rely on scripture to give backing to its reliability has passed. Rather than lamenting the demise of scripture as a cultural mainstay, seeing it as yet another deplorable sign of Taylor's "secularity 3,"[49] we can interpret the erosion of the once powerful parallelism of nature and scripture not as the unavoidable result of Enlightenment progress but as a collapse of failing theological and philosophical strategies. Without adequate cultural mediation it is impossible to sustain a tradition of natural theology that maintains a careful intellectual balance, laced with sufficient flexibility of mind, between a groundedness in the Christian tradition on the one hand and an openness toward scientific innovation on the other. I am thinking back here to the medieval rhetorical device of *integumentum*, a popular twelfth-century rhetorical trope, not unrelated to allegory, that allowed for the interpretation of pagan fables as veiling hidden philosophical truths, thereby guaranteeing a seamless integration of Christian and non-Christian truths;[50] William of Conches excelled at this strategy. If we add to the disrobing of biblical language the stripping of other Christological vestments, moreover, such as the concept of sacramentality, it would seem that over and against the scientific paradigm that has been in power since the nineteenth century the saturated phenomenon can only be mediated kenotically, that is, through absence or apophasis rather than affirmation.

The risk of such an apophatic approach, however, defining much of the problem that I have with the contemporary popularity of negative theology, is that it seems aimed at disrupting rather than fostering conversation. While in the era of Dionysius the Areopagite (ca. 500), its intellectual architect, and Eriugena, his prime Western ambassador, negative theology was primarily a method to ward off divine might, geared toward the protection of human identity and human speech, in the current religious and philosophical climate negative theology wants to awake us from false slumber.[51] Preventing the embrace of false security in a cultural situation of divine absence rather than presence, its role is primarily aimed at destabilization, promoting existential unrest rather than relieving it.

Finding himself caught in such existential unrest, Ralph Waldo Emerson turned to nature rather than the Christian God, and, to the extent that his approach preserves its central role as a constructive force of mediation between God and humanity, we have much to learn from his approach. What makes it particularly valuable for my project is that Emerson safeguards nature's revelatory powers not just by emphasizing its functionality as a demonstrative medium (as in contemporary intelligent design) but by having it quietly, yet with great command, assume the prophetic force of divine proclamation. This dimension of prophetic voice, which in an earlier era was conveyed exclusively by the divine otherness of scripture, comes to us in Emerson through the otherness—even if wrapped in familiarity—of nature. While nature may find itself disrobed of scriptural vestments, its newly endowed scientific authority, which Emerson considered friend rather than foe, turns it from speechless into newly speaking.

While one may deplore the loss of scriptural loyalty in Emerson's transcendental approach,[52] and his turning away from institutional Christianity has lessened his theological standing, taking the earlier tradition of theology's double foundation seriously[53] makes it all but acceptable to have nature raise its voice to the level of Old Testament prophecy. Seeing Emerson's nature—in a twist on the Frei thesis—as having absorbed and internalized scripture rather than having abandoned it, we do not need to consider nature's prophetic office as a depreciation of scripture, another sign that the latter's cultural resonance is slowly but surely fading away. Instead, there is much to be said for seeing nature's prophetic role as an attempt at a modern extension of scripture's once universal appeal.

Such a reinvigoration of scriptural appeal seems to be the purport of Emerson's approach in the Divinity School Address. Rather than being contented with the institutional remnants, if not ruins, of what he considers lifeless religion:

I look for the hour when that supreme Beauty which ravished the souls
of those Eastern men, and chiefly of those Hebrews, and through their
lips spoke oracles to all time, shall speak in the West also. The Hebrew
and Greek Scriptures contain immortal sentences that have been bread
of life to millions. But they have no epical integrity; are fragmentary;
are not shown in their order to the intellect. I look for the new Teacher
that shall follow so far those shining laws that he shall see them come
full circle; shall see their rounding complete grace; shall see the world
to be the mirror of the soul; shall see the identity of the law of gravitation with purity of heart; and shall show that the Ought, the Duty, is
one Thing with Science, with Beauty, and with Joy.[54]

"Shall see the world to be the mirror of the soul; shall see the identity
of the law of gravitation with purity of heart." Foregrounding nature's prophetic force seems at least part of Emerson's push for a new Teacher here,
not just an alternate Christ but also a modern Everyman, one whose peda-
gogy is directed toward the future rather than the past.[55] Foregrounding
nature's prophetic force is also what constitutes Emerson's lasting appeal.
After all, he is much more profitably read as continuing and affirming the
earlier nature tradition, dismissed as "Platonic" by Latour, than as con-
travening it, even if for him it includes the explicit desire to incorporate
Kant's Copernican revolution.

Nature's Sacred Affirmation

In what follows I want to identify and highlight two closely related Emersonian elements as important ingredients for a contemporary natural
theology. Not only can they be seen as typical of what I hold to be the
continued innate Christian "coloring" of his thought,[56] but while deeply
informing his sense of nature, in a more explicit and powerful way than
Eriugena they also bring in the self whose role is highly important, given
the absence of hermeneutical stability in the scientific age. Furthermore,
by inserting temporality—another one of my project's concerns—they
avoid the teleological objectification of nature. The elements of Emerson's
thought to which I want to draw attention are the aspect of historicity,
expressed especially in the Emersonian notion of onwardness, and that
of hope, which represents the moral mood or coloring of such onwardness. Below I will first situate Emerson in contemporary philosophico-
theological debate, after which I will draw some conclusions toward the
future of natural theology.

Following the American philosopher Stanley Cavell, one can argue that the prime meaning of the philosophy of Emerson (and earlier of Thoreau) is that he brings us back to the prephilosophical moment in which philosophy, theology, and literature all coincide.[57] In Cavell's reading Emerson's texts encapsulate the philosophical impulse in the moment before its professionalization-cum-sophistication.[58] In this Cavell puts Emerson's thought on a par with that of all major philosophers, whom he sees as sharing the common distinction of being committed to ending the professional, in the sense of overprofessionalized, philosophical tradition.[59] It is against the background of this particular sense of an ending—to paraphrase Frank Kermode's famous clause[60]—that Cavell wants to contextualize Emerson's turn to nature, which he sees as a conscious move which allows him to answer both the Puritan tradition in New England from which he came and the skepticism of Kant.

Labeling Emerson's answer to the Puritan tradition the "sacred affirmative," Cavell characterizes it as an effort, not unlike Nietzsche, not to move beyond tragedy but to move beyond nihilism; that is, beyond the charge of human depravity and its consequent damnation of human beings to despair.[61] By contrast, Cavell finds Emerson's answer to Kant not in a denial of skepticism or the reverse, a kind of wholesale embrace of raw existence, but rather in a subtle acceptance of thinking both as intuition and as reception. As Cavell states in his essay "Thinking of Emerson":

> I may interject here that the idea of thinking as reception, which began
> this path of reasoning, seems to me to be a sound intuition, specifically
> to forward the correct answer to skepticism [which Emerson meant
> it to do]. The answer does not consist in denying the conclusion of
> skepticism but in reconceiving its truth. It is true that we do not know
> the existence of the world with certainty; our relation of it is deeper—
> one in which it is accepted, that is to say received. My favorite way of
> putting this is to say that existence is to be acknowledged.[62]

In light of my earlier analysis, we may perhaps push the interpretation of thinking as reception in a religious sense even further, beyond sound intuition and acknowledgement, to open up into the possibility of effecting self-transformation and self-transfiguration. In terms derived from Marion, one might say that for Emerson it is the prerogative of human thinking to be able to receive and process saturated phenomena, and its specific moral charge to make them both transparent and communicable, all the while guarding their hermeneutical surplus. Earlier in the *Divinity School Address* Emerson calls this a provocation:

> Meantime, whilst the doors of the temple stand open, night and
> day, before every man, and the oracles of this truth cease never, it
> is guarded by one stern condition; this, namely, it is an intuition. It
> cannot be received at second hand. Truly speaking, it is not instruc-
> tion, but provocation, that I can receive from another soul. What he
> announces, I must find true in me, or reject; and on his word, or as his
> second, be he who he may, I can accept nothing. On the contrary, the
> absence of his primary faith is the presence of degradation.[63]

This idea of self-transformation, which Emerson also refers to as metamorphosis,[64] makes it easier to understand why, by way of an answer to
skepticism, Emerson puts his hope on the following of his own Genius,
which seems a sort of transcendental analogue to the caption of the "image of God" so powerful in Eriugena and the Greek Fathers. Following
his Genius allows Emerson to pursue abandonment—rather than Heidegger's settlement or inhabitation—as his specific *telos*, for which purpose
he also devises and collects his own writing(s). To quote Cavell again on
Emerson:

> Whether his writing on the lintels—his writing as such, I gather—is
> thought of as having the constancy of the contents of a mezuzah or the
> emergency of the passover blood, either way he is taking upon himself
> the mark of God, and of departure.[65] His perception of the moment
> is taken in hope, as something to be proven only along the way, *by* the
> way. This departure, such setting out, is, in our poverty, what hope
> consists in, all there is to hope for; it is the abandoning of despair,
> which is otherwise our condition . . . it is our poverty not to be final but
> always to be leaving (abandoning whatever we have and have known):
> to be initial, medial, American. What the ground of the fixated conflict
> between solipsism and realism should give way to—or between subjec-
> tivity and objectivity, or the private and the public, or the inner and the
> outer—is the task of onwardness.[66]

To the dichotomies mentioned by Cavell at the end of this passage (solipsism and realism, subjectivity and objectivity) we may add not only the tension between philosophy and literature, but also between the sciences and
theology. What Emerson, read through Cavell here, confers on humanity
as a way out of their implied stalemate is not a new institutionalized peda-
gogy but rather a care for the moment plucked as if in casual neglect but
with the sacred duty of attention and attunement. The consciousness of
seizing the moment is stamped by an *in*wardness for Emerson that is both
private and public—or universal, if you will—at the same time. Marking

a sort of experience that is intuitive and self-transformative rather than empiricist,[67] it inherently urges the self, and us, *on*ward.

Nature and Experience

In its immediacy and its simultaneous capacity to expand, there is a sense in Emerson that nature, in the words of his recent biographer Robert Richardson, "provides the basic context of our lives and yet is what bats last, is the law, the final word, the supreme court."[68] In the context of this article one might add: nature, coming alive in moments of human self-transformation rather than offering an alternative trajectory, is what provides the final criterion for right religion by providing us literally with common ground. We are not dealing with the closed teleology of Paley here, subjugating creation into silence even before it could speak. Instead, we find ourselves closer to Thomas Paine's move to democratize deism by seeing creation as the Bible of the Deist,[69] however with a nature which for Emerson brings its own voice and concerns to the discussion, a nature which demands to be seen and heard and refuses to be objectified.

Read in terms of the theological program that his reflections set out, as I just did, the unpacking of Emerson's nature, even as it remains enclosed in the author's writings,[70] yields a set of dynamics that is far closer to the incision of divine epiphany than to the stasis of revealed text or the traditional locus of creation in New England Puritanism. Emerson's famous essay on *Nature* from 1836 clearly states as much, holding nature up as the new tableau, if not the new Mosaic divine tablets, whose force he contrasts sharply with his own retrospective age. The problem confronting us as we try to gain access to nature, so we can summarize Emerson, is not the fact that nature's, and by extension God's presence, is forever veiled,[71] but rather that its true face was *once* unveiled, and that we need to recapture our original, incisive relation to the universe by always going in search of that moment.[72]

The only credible way to do so is not by solidifying nature as metaphysical essence, however ecologically responsible—what Latour criticizes about American parks—but by setting it loose, free to erupt in its own unbridled series of revelatory moments. For Emerson our contact with God as tangibly present in nature pivots on a kind of readiness on our part not to unveil it but to allow the divine to become properly "in-carnate" in it in a kenotic-apophatic sense that strikes the mean between excarnation and apocalypticism. Such is the case, for example, in his famous statement that we become transparent eyeballs, as nature's transfigured omnipresence is here made contingent upon the effacement of the transgressive self.[73] Yet like the blinks in the eye of the beholder, we can only monitor the pulse of epiphanic nature by catching its revelation in momentary instances. Only in the punctuated, temporal way of attunement, therefore, will we be able to revitalize nature to ourselves and ourselves to nature. By jump-starting a common conversation that was long overdue—as religion's stifling institutionalism was merely replaced by a scientific one—we can subvert the stasis of monumental physicality:

> Our age is retrospective. It builds the sepulchers of the fathers. It writes biographies, histories, and criticism. The foregoing generations beheld God and nature face to face; we, through their eyes. Why should we not also[74] enjoy an original relation to the universe? Why should not we have a poetry and philosophy of insight and not of tradition, and a religion by revelation to us and not the history of theirs? Embosomed for a season in nature, whose floods of life stream around and through us, and invite us, by the powers they supply, to action proportioned to nature, why should we grope among the dry bones of the past, or put the living generation into masquerade out of its faded wardrobe? The sun shines to-day also. There is more wool and flax in the fields. There are new lands, new men, new thoughts. Let us demand our own works and laws and worship.[75]

The question that we took away from Eriugena about the relevance of the encounter with visible, tactile nature finds an intriguing answer when put to Emerson. Rather than seeing the contact with visible nature as preparing for the spiritual Christ, whom Emerson rather seems to want to revive as a new spiritual Everyman, there is a sense in which, for Emerson, natural theology is not unlike natural science, to the extent that both equally, and jointly, alert humanity to its spiritual vocation. To revive time and again, moment after incarnate moment, our original relation to the universe, and to do so through our own acknowledgement, is what Emerson means when speaking of a religion as revelation to us. What he wants to avoid is the codification of religion, philosophy, or scientific thought beyond the "Whim" on the lintels, as any such preservation would squeeze out the spirit from the revelation and give rise to a triumphalism that is as false as it is lethal. To the extent that it fixates us in the conservation of our retrospective age, Emerson wants to clear History out of the way—not unlike Latour wants to do Science. While Latour's criticism of Science paves the way for his new political ecology, so for Emerson the criticism of history ushers in attention to temporality and incarnation, thereby enabling the encounter of nature and self in concert with their attunement to the divine.

Finally, in his essay on *The Method of Nature* (1841) Emerson gives an interesting analysis of the experience of nature—not its empiricism—as culminating in what he calls ecstasy. Here nature's religious, incarnate force comes fully to the surface in the same way as Richardson describes ecstasy: "not as a technical out-of-body experience but a joyous consciousness of the rich plenitude of existence."[76] Surprisingly, Emerson retains a measure of reserve, as he upholds the distinction between the experience of nature and nature itself, thus leaving room for worship while defying pantheism. This measure of reserve is also why it is important not to confuse Richardson's trope for Emerson's nature as the "supreme court" with Latour's critical depiction of Science—seen there from the perspective of the Platonic Cave from which political ecology should liberate us—as "kidnapping external reality to transform it into an appellate court of last resort." For Emerson, in contrast to Latour, true religion, i.e., religion supported by intuition—whether theological, philosophical, or scientific—would prevent humanity from being put in the Cave in the first place.

In my view, we would do well to embrace Emerson as an original starting point for a contemporary natural theology, one that does not feel the need to constrain the sciences but embraces them without being dissolved into them.[77] Rather than merely allowing an escape from the Cave, the experience of nature empowers humans to soar to ecstasy, where science and poetry become jointly elevated to the transparency of supernatural piety, and in the end nature and humanity fully merge:

> Therefore, man must be on guard against this cup of enchantments, and must look at nature with a supernatural eye. By piety alone, by conversing with the cause of nature, is he safe and commands it. And because all knowledge is assimilation to the object of knowledge, as the power or genius of nature is ecstatic, so must its science or the description of it be. The poet must be a rhapsodist; his inspiration a sort of bright casualty; his will in it only the surrender of the will to the Universal Power, which will not be seen face to face, but must be reconceived and sympathetically known. . . . And because ecstasy is the law and cause of nature, therefore you cannot interpret it in too high and deep a sense. Nature represents the best meaning of the wisest man.[78]

The Challenge of Natural Theology

Why should there be a discussion about nature in a volume about temporality? That was the question with which I started my investigation in this essay. At the end, we do well perhaps to ask the opposite question: Why should temporality matter in an essay on nature? To ask the question is to some extent answering it. As I have tried to argue, the solidification of *creatio ex nihilo* has led Christianity to muffle the voice of nature, as the medieval balance of nature and scripture became replaced by an imposition of scriptural models on nature during the Reformation. Theologically, thinking with nature turned more and more into thinking about nature.

The latter trend became aggravated by the rise of natural science, especially since in the nineteenth century the cultural resonance of Christianity's scriptural narrative began to disappear. Rather than seeing science as merely replacing scripture, however, as if in a preordained swap of external interpreters, the current environmental crisis reveals how there is an unusual underlying convergence of various hermeneutical problems at work, all of which necessitate a rethinking of nature's objectified role. Thus nature's literary role as evoking idyll rather than engagement has been questioned in literary studies, whereas a new ecological awareness has problematized the social-scientific analysis of politics and science as static, mutually opposed entities.

Rather than trying *to turn back* by undoing secularity in one or all of its guises, as is the aim of Charles Taylor, or to retreat into the bulwark of the Christian tradition as by definition antisecular, as is the approach of Radical Orthodoxy not engaged here, this essay takes the position that there is no reason why a contemporary project of natural theology should not be fully secular (and scientific) but that it can only be religious to the extent that it takes temporality into account, as only then can there be a perspective on nature or, rather, can nature be allowed to unfold its own perspective. As a first step, therefore, this article has engaged in *thinking progressively backward* by focusing on the views of Eriugena and Emerson. Seeing Eriugena's Christological attention to transfiguration and incarnation, and Emerson's onwardness and acknowledgement of existence respectively as key themes, I have tried to sketch the contours of a natural theology that draws on the past rather than being beholden to it. Secular in its acceptance of science, it yet wants to reignite the conversation between God, nature, and self that lies behind all scripture. To this aim it will proceed by enlisting nature as a vocal participant in conversation as a prerequisite for its full partnership in revelation.

CHAPTER 5

The Care of the Past:
The Place of Pastness in
Transgenerational Projects

Charles Hallisey

It is not hard to find in different religious communities a concern for trans-generational projects, those human projects that by their very nature assume that many individuals and communities will participate in them, care for them, across time, in different times and places. Transgenerational projects are always ongoing and appear in history as-yet-unfinished projects. They exist only in time—indeed exist at all only in history—through the efforts of persons who do not live in the same time or place but who, by virtue of imagination and self-understanding, are able to join together with each other in a common effort, and in this respect at least transgenerational projects are quite different from merely cumulative traditions. The innumerable efforts of participants in a transgenerational project obviously vary according to the diversity of their agents and to the circumstances in which these agents act. This variation is to such a degree that the common significance of a transgenerational project becomes apparent—even to their agents themselves—only when individual actions and their results are seen within temporal frameworks that are defined by the transgenerational project itself. These temporal frameworks draw attention away both from the immediate context in which actions are done and beyond their immediate futures in which their most obvious results will occur—these are the more conventional contexts to look for the significance of individual actions in the world—to a deep past and to a distant future. Placing individual actions within the temporal framework of a transgenerational project does not, however, put these specific actions into a sequence that allows us to see how specific actions on behalf of a transgenerational project *relate to each other*, and in this regard the understanding of actions within the temporal framework of a transgenerational project is quite different from the temporal frameworks generally invoked in the history of a religious tradition as it evolves in time. At the same time, participation in a transgenerational project seems to confirm in a maximal way Marx's insight that humans make history but not in conditions of their own making,[1] but in striking ways, the temporal framework of a transgenerational project also creates the conditions for generating awareness of the kind of "nextness" that Stanley Cavell sees elaborated by Thoreau.[2]

Just as religions differ in form and character, however, so do transgenerational projects in religions also differ. This is immediately obvious from considering examples like the transgenerational project in Islam of the building of a just society on earth, thematized as "the Trust" in the Quran (Qur'an 33:72),[3] and the perception among Christians of the Church (with a capital "C") as a crucial part of the transgenerational project of the building of the City of God. Of course, self-conscious participation in transgenerational projects is not unique to religious persons by any means, as is obvious from examples like the idea of American democracy as an ongoing and as-yet-unfinished project[4] and to the temporal horizon of "the University" that inflects self-reflection and calls to action in books as varied as John Henry Newman's *The Idea of a University*,[5] Jaroslav Pelikan's *The Idea of the University*,[6] and Louis Menand's *The Marketplace of Ideas: Reform and Resistance in the American University*.[7] Even if transgenerational projects are not unique to religious traditions, they do provide an especially good focus for exploring the place of time in religions because of the self-consciously temporal constitution of such projects by the participants in them.

My purpose in this essay is to use a Theravada Buddhist example of a transgenerational project, the Sasana, sometimes translated as the Buddha's dispensation, to trace one aspect of the place of time in religions, an aspect that might be called the onwardness that is part of pastness in religions. In the case of Theravada Buddhist visions of the Sasana, there is an onwardness in human care as it is received in time, recognized as having been given in the past, and then subsequently given again, precisely because of the care received.[8] This onward motion of human care is revealed when acts of care for the Sasana that were done in the past are perceived in the temporal framework of a transgenerational project, allowing the perceiver of these past acts to see herself, in the framework of nextness, as having already benefited from them and also providing the conditions for new acts of care for the Sasana.

Before looking at this aspect of onwardness in human care for the Sasana as one aspect of pastness in religions, it may be helpful to say a bit more about what a Sasana is. A Sasana is the name given to the ensemble of teachings, practices, and institutions established by a Buddha and handed on by his followers. Clearly, teachings, practices, and institutions in a Sasana can only exist in history if they are embodied in and transmitted by vehicles like books, persons, buildings, and other objects. The current Sasana was established by "our Buddha," the enlightened teacher Siddhattha Gotama who lived twenty-five hundred years ago in northern India. Our Buddha predicted that his Sasana would last for five thousand years, so the finiteness of its temporality is part of its constitution; like all other things that are conditioned by their existence in time, the Sasana has an inherent necessity to change and indeed to decay. This inherent necessity to change and to decay means that the Sasana that we receive comes to us damaged by, as it were, the ravages of time. The fact that the tangible elements of the Sasana come to us damaged—with texts corrupted, buildings in need of repair, practices ineptly learned—is a sign of their *pastness*. It is in the nature of things that whatever comes to us from the past comes to us damaged, and we can see even here that this damage has a connotation of onwardness itself. To receive something valuable from the past is to receive it damaged and thus to receive it is to see that it needs to be cared for, so that it might be "restored" or at least not further damaged.

The men and women who, in the face of this necessity to care for the Sasana, preserve the Buddha's teachings, practice them, and care for the religious institutions established by him by copying texts, studying them, and putting them into practice; by erecting buildings and making other material objects; they care for the Sasana by becoming exemplars for others as they fashion themselves to embody the Buddha's teachings; they strive to achieve the goals of those teachings. All of these can all be called "makers of the Sasana" (Sasanakari). Jacob Carbine's observation about contemporary Burmese Buddhist religious culture applies generally to the religious communities across the Theravada Buddhist world, which historically stretched from South India and Sri Lanka to Southeast Asia: "There are many shades of Burmese Buddhist identity, often related in some way to [one's own participation in] the Sasana."[9] It is important to emphasize that all of these ways of participating in the Sasana, caring for it, represent a way of collective orientation in the religious life that is often overlooked when we focus to Buddhist understandings of soteriologies. To paraphrase Marx, it may well be that individual men and women save themselves, but they only do so in the conditions of the Sasana made by the acts of care and preservation of others. In a sense then, "making the Sasana" "contribute[s] to collective salvation," in the manner identified by Guillaume Rosenberg in another observation about contemporary Burma, but which also applies generally to religious communities in the Theravada Buddhist world, past and present:

> "Making religion" [thathana pyu; thathana is Sasana in Pali] is work-
> ing to consolidate the rooting of this Buddhist ensemble [of doctrine
> ethics, monastic community, institutions, relics, edifices, etc.] in the
> society, which is a determining factor for the well-being and the future
> of the community. In this perspective, society is seen as a space of rela-
> tions and actions whose Buddhist essence must be preserved and rein-
> forced in order to allow as many people as possible to accumulate merit
> and for the most advanced to enter on the path towards salvation.[10]

Assuming such ideas of "making the Sasana" as a backdrop, I will now turn to a few accounts taken from Theravada Buddhist historiographic writing about the Sasana to explore the aspect of pastness in religions that is the central concern of this essay: the onwardness of certain actions in the past. My hope is that an examination of these Buddhist materials, admit-tedly few and admittedly selective, will have theoretical ramifications for the general question about time in religions, ramifications that go beyond these particular sources and beyond whatever contribution their consider-ation can make to our understanding of Theravada Buddhism. This essay will also be concerned with just how it is that a fold of onwardness within pastness is engaged, and I will argue that this happens, at least in part, when the past, as such, is engaged on the model of the application of a "thick concept," to use the philosophical category coined by Bernard Williams.[11] Williams's notion of a "thick concept" has subsequently been elaborated and debated by many others in recent discussions of ethics,[12] but for the limited purposes of this essay, we can accept Williams's basic point without tracking the many important points that have been made in the subsequent elaborations and in the debates.

The basic point in Williams's notion is that a thick concept is a descrip-tion of the world that somehow seems also to bring with it a general course of valuation and action. Thick concepts stand, as it were, between "thin concepts" of description and "thin concepts" of valuation, entangling description and prescription with each other in a single concept. We can see the basic point of the notion of a thick concept if we reflect on the fact that the words "torture" and "strong interrogation techniques" may sometimes describe the very same set of actions done by humans to other humans, but the former, as a thick concept, guides reaction and action in a very different way than the latter does as a "thin concept"; it is not merely a matter of perception, one valuing what the other disvalues, it is more that "strong interrogation techniques" is descriptive in a "thinner" way than "torture" is. At the same time, the thick concept "torture" describes specific actions the world more than the category "evil" can, the latter prescriptive in a "thinner" way than "torture" is. Williams argued that the application of thick concepts "is at the same time world-guided and action-guided."[13] I want to suggest that it is through taking the past in the manner of a thick concept that the onwardness in pastness becomes operative.

Before turning to the specific Theravada Buddhist accounts about the Sasana in time, it should be acknowledged that the orientation toward time of these accounts represents only one way that time has been thought about in Buddhism. In fact, the category of time has been centrally visible in much of Buddhist thought and practice, and it has often been the subject of considerable doctrinal reflection and controversy. It was not controversial for Buddhists, however, to see that the question of the person in time was one that was easy to get wrong, inevitably to considerable unhappiness for the person anyone who misperceived herself in time. To misperceive oneself in time meant that one's intentions would always be at odds with the realities of the world; in many respects, then, time itself becomes a thick concept, in Williams's sense, for many Buddhist thinkers, including the Buddha himself. In one of his sermons the Buddha allowed that it was ordinary for many humans to think back to the past and ask "Was it really us that existed at some point in the past, or did we not exist, what were we in the past, how were we in the past, having been what, what did we become in the past?" and to think forward to the future and ask, "Will it really be us in the future, or will it not be us, what will we come to be in the future, how will we come to be in the future, having been what, what will we become in the future?," but he was quite clear it was equally ordinary for the askers of such questions to get the answers to these questions completely wrong, to answer the questions in the way that they would like things to be rather than the way the world is and these wrong answers, always based on wrong perceptions of the way things are, always lead to misfortune.[14] Given the fact that it is easy to misunderstand how persons exist in time and disastrous to do so, it is not surprising then that Buddhists historically have crafted many "thin" descriptive concepts of time. Coming to an accurate description of time was crucial to understanding the reality of a person in the world, something which itself has clear prescriptive entailments.

Descriptions of time and of a person in time were explored rigorously and with great subtlety by Buddhist philosophers and the conundrums of just how time even "exists" in the world were also noted by Buddhist thinkers. The great Indian Buddhist philosopher Nagarjuna, who can be dated to about the second century of the common era, displayed in four verses of his great work, *The Fundamental Wisdom of the Middle Way* (*Mulamadhyamakakarika*) how he saw a metaphysical incoherence of commonsense notions of time as divided into an interconnected sequence of past, present and future:

> If the present and the future
> Depend on the past,
> Then the present and the future
> Would have existed in the past.

> If the present and the future
> Did not exist there,
> How could the present and the future
> Be dependent upon it?

> If they are not dependent upon the past,
> Neither of the two would be established.
> Therefore neither the present
> Nor the future would exist.

> A nonstatic time is not grasped.
> Nothing one could grasp as
> Stationary time exists.
> If time is not grasped, how is it known?

> If time depends on an entity,
> Then without an entity how could time exist?
> There is no existent entity [that persists as itself over time].
> So how can time exist?[15]

Rather than take up such conundrums to the point of making them philosophical aporias, other Buddhist thinkers instead explored different positive possibilities—especially moral possibilities—that the commonsense notion of time seemed to afford, especially when what might first look like a thin description about time and the world could be engaged in the manner of a thick concept to reveal an appropriate course of action. For example, Buddhaghosa, the great Theravadin commentator from the fifth century CE, engaged the thin description that all things only exist momentarily and that there is no substantial continuity to personal existence in the manner of a thick concept to hint rhetorically at a course of action as part of his instructions on how to remove one's own anger at another person who has done something to you:

> Since states last but a moment's time
> Those aggregates,[16] by which was done
> The odious act, have ceased, so now
> What is it you are angry with?

> Whom shall he hurt, who seeks to hurt
> Another, in the other's absence?[17]

Our examples come from yet another way in which Theravada Buddhist thinkers also explored the moral possibilities that the commonsense notion of time seemed to afford. This was in a tradition of historiographical writing that is a central part of the heritage of Theravada Buddhism. This tradition of historiography is found in the practice of writing history books about monastic lineages and about kings as well as in commentarial practices; historical concerns were also key to Theravada Buddhist commentarial practice, since knowing the context in which a sermon of the Buddha was first given was considered to be a crucial hermeneutic step to discerning its meaning as was knowing the conditions of the preservation of a sermon. Theravadin historiographical writing has received considerable attention from modern scholars, in part for the evidence that it could provide for scholarly reconstructions of Buddhist history, for evidence of "historical consciousness" in an Asian intellectual tradition, as well as for understanding the nature of "ethnohistory" in Theravada Buddhism.[18]

Our first example is an account from one of Buddhaghosa's commentaries. It describes how the Sasana began. The account is found in the commentary on the Mangala Sutta, one of the most important canonical texts in the Theravada Buddhist traditions, and a sign of its importance is the fact that the commentary of this one text includes the account of what happened right after the Buddha died; for almost all other individual sermons, this relatively standard account is only provided at the beginning of the larger divisions of the canon and not for individual sermons.[19] The account explains that at the time of the death of the Buddha, a large number of his followers assembled. Among them was a senior monk, Mahakassapa, who otherwise is not very prominent in the records of the Buddha's teaching career. Immediately after the death of the Buddha, Mahakassapa began to fear that there might be some followers of the Buddha might think that the Buddha's death was also the death of his teaching:

> It is possible that there are bad monks who will come to think that this is the instruction of "a teacher who is only in the past" and who then create factions and soon make the Truth [that the Buddha taught] disappear. But as long as the Buddha's sermons and his instructions for monastic life last, there will still be the instruction of "a teacher who is not only in the past"; the Lord said, "Ananda [the Buddha's 'beloved disciple'], my teachings and my instructions for monastic life that I have shown and described to you will be your teacher after my death."[20]

Mahakassapa then makes a decision to assemble five hundred of the Buddha's disciples to have them recite together the Buddha's sermons and his instructions for monastic life as a way of preserving them. In clarifying this intent to himself, Mahakassapa puts it in terms of a need to do something to make the Sasana last for a long time, but he does not come to this intention through a perception of its practical necessity or its sociological necessity, even though what he does in terms of his own assumption of leadership can easily be explained with the theory of the "routinization of the charisma" of a religious founder, as outlined by Max Weber.[21] The account portrays Mahakassapa going through a process of recollecting how, while the Buddha was still alive, he had been cared for by the Buddha in a variety of ways, from sharing his cast-off robes with him and encouraging Mahakassapa with praise. Mahakassapa then asks himself how this care that he received from the Buddha might be paid back, a question that invokes broad assumptions in Buddhist moral culture of the urge to "give back" is implicit in a sense of authentic gratitude, a sense of knowing what another has done for you. We can see that in the thick concept of gratitude, as it is construed in Buddhist moral culture, a fold of onwardness is key to authentic gratitude. One does not just feel thankful, one must do something commensurate in acknowledgement of what was done. At this point in the account, Mahakassapa re-remembers the gift of used robes that the Buddha had given him. At first, it is just one instance in which the Buddha had helped him, but when he re-remembers it, this gift of the used robes is perceived as something of an anointment, an act that acknowledged him as capable of taking the leadership role in the community that was now required after the Buddha's death. Mahakassapa comes to this re-perception of himself by seeing the gift of the used robes as analogous to a sovereign gifting a piece of his armor to his son as a way of publicly indicating his selection of the son as crown prince. The account tells how Mahakassapa goes on to convene the First Council, which was responsible for the formation of the scriptural canon of the Buddha's teachings, which stands at the headwaters of the history of the Sasana in the Theravada Buddhist imagination.

It is Mahakassapa's recollection of the help that was provided to him that is thematized as the proper stance for anyone looking back at the history of the Sasana. From such a vantage point, the history of the Sasana is a history of help given to us. We can see how this recognition of help given was thematized in the tenth-century commentary to the *Mahavamsa*, a fifth-century work that traced the history of the Sasana in Sri Lanka. According to the *Mahavamsa* itself, its purpose was to generate a feeling of having been taken care of (*pasada*) and also a feeling of fear of the inevitable (*samvega*) in those who heard or read it. The commentary explains what is meant by this as it gives instructions on how to listen to the text:

> May you listen to this *Mahavamsa*, producing a feeling of being taken care of (*pasada*) that is the appropriate emotional counterpart to the splendor of the Buddha when he is described in the text as coming himself to this country, when the coming of his relics here is described, and when the arrival of his teachings here is described; and producing the fear of the inevitable that is the appropriate counterpart to hearing about the death of kings such as Mahāsammata, etc., the passing away of the Buddha and his disciples as described in the text in connection with the First Council.
>
> In those descriptions in the *Mahavamsa*, how the Buddha acted for the welfare of others—by doing actions that were produced by the force of his compassion and the eminence of the enlightenment of the Blessed-One, by actions such as in the coming to the island—is to be seen.
>
> How so?
>
> The Lord came here, having abandoned the foremost delight of enlightenment—a delight that was to be enjoyed by himself—because of having become committed to actions for the welfare of others in a former existence. . . .
>
> It can also be seen that a commitment to action dedicated to the welfare of others also arises in those who hear about actions in the past

on behalf of others and this also arises from the force of the Buddha's compassion.

The splendor of the Blessed-One and the arising of commitment to action for the welfare of others that has arisen by the force of compassion are both occasions for feeling that one has been taken care of. In turn, the Second Council could be convened because the First Council had been convened, and the Third Council could be convened because the Second Council had been convened.[22]

The Councils that are mentioned at the end of this passage from the *Mahavamsa* commentary are paradigmatic ways that monks care for the Sasana. Monks come together in a Council to collectively care for the Sasana, to recite texts together so that lapses in individual memory can be filled and errors removed, and then to write down what is collectively remembered so that the restored books can be passed on to future generations. Each generation benefits from the act of care for the Sasana that was done in the past, but the recognition of that care that was done, as it were, for oneself, generates a recognition of the onwardness within that act of care in the past, that a proper recognition of what was done for one in the past requires one to do something in the present for the sake of the future.

Texts obviously are not the only element of the Buddha's legacy brought together in the Sasana. Another important material element in the Sasana is the bodily relics of the Buddha, which, according to Theravada Buddhist historiography, have often been dispersed around the world by a past determination of the Buddha himself, to confirm the appropriateness of a place as a site for his Sasana to thrive.

Our second account tells of how a relic was discovered in the kingdom of Lanna, in present day northern Thailand. The account is found in a text composed in Pali in Lanna in the sixteenth century, the *Jinakalamali* (*A Garland of Epochs of the Conqueror*; "conqueror" is an epithet of the Buddha). The account tells of how a king named Adicca went to defecate in a field and while he was defecating, a crow flew by and defecated on him. Enraged, the king demanded that the crow be caught and killed. His counselors, however, prevailed on him to find out why the crow had done that. The king followed his advice, and, after finding a way for a human to learn the language of the crows, found out that the crow had been instructed by his grandfather to guard the place where the king had gone to defecate. The grandfather was then brought from the Himalayas, and he explained that while he was still alive the Buddha had traveled alone to this place in northern Thailand and had been fed by the inhabitants of a forest village.

In return for this act of care the Buddha preached a sermon to them, and then when he was finished, he made a prediction:

> After the Buddha has passed away this very place will, in the future, become a great city. A king named Adicca will reign there. During his reign, a relic of the Buddha will become established there.

When he heard this prediction, the king was immediately overjoyed, and he had the place in which he had intended to defecate made into a place suitable for a relic of the Buddha to be enshrined. A relic casket that had been made by an earlier Buddhist king, King Asoka, then appeared and was enshrined by King Adicca and worshiped by all in Lanna in a manner that both replicated the worship given to it by Asoka but also acknowledged Asoka's help in terms of bringing the realization about Adicca to light.

What we see in these two accounts of care for the Sasana is that knowledge about what happened in the past has a dimension to it that is best described as an acknowledgement that what was done to care for the Sasana in the past was an act of care also for the person who is receiving the Sasana in the present. There is in this acknowledgement of what was done in the past a fold of *onwardness*, such that it allows us to see that a motive for caring for the Sasana in the present, for the sake of those in the future, comes from the pastness of the Sasana itself.

CHAPTER 6

Trembling in Time:
Silence and Meaning between Barthes,
Chateaubriand, and Rancé

Mette Birkedal Bruun

This image recalls something of the neglected age and
the hand of the old man: an admirable trembling of
time! Often men of genius have announced their end
by masterpieces: it is their soul which soars.[1]

[Chateaubriand] identifies himself with Poussin dying in
Rome (the city of ruins) and depositing in his last painting that
mysterious and sovereign imperfection, lovelier than a merely
fulfilled art and which is the tremor of time: memory is the
beginning of writing, and writing is in its turn the beginning
of death (however young one is when one undertakes it).[2]

Thus speak Chateaubriand and Barthes about transcending time. Each
steeped in his time, the former lingers with the work of the genius on the
verge of death; the latter with the mystery of the fragmented. Time transcended, time confirmed. Barthes took up this duplexity in his essay "La
voyageuse de nuit" (1965) on Chateaubriand's *Vie de Rancé* (1844), and with
his involvement with the viscount inherited, so to speak, Chateaubriand's
own engagement with the seventeenth-century Cistercian Armand-Jean
de Rancé. Barthes cast Chateaubriand's biographical and autobiographical
volume as a literary masterpiece on a courtier whose monastic profession
became his authorial suicide while providing substance for Chateaubri-
and's authorial vitality.

Roland Barthes (1915–80), François-René de Chateaubriand (1768–
1848), and Armand-Jean de Rancé (1626–1700) are all concerned with
the presentness of the past. With respectively form, memory, and reform
as their primary interest, they reflect upon ways in which communion between present and past exists, can be created or abolished. Taken in their
Sitz im Leben, their endeavors are by and large unrelated, and the con-

nection between the three is arbitrary insofar as Barthes and Rancé come into contact only through Chateaubriand and brush only superficially. As a monk of the most austere mold, Rancé aspired to be dead to the world and for this reason did Barthes discard him. While the Cistercian belonged to the century of Racine, La Bruyère, and La Rochefoucauld, figures who loom large on Barthes's horizon, he had dissociated himself from that world.

But all three are at once readers and writers, and when we read the abbot's works by a light nuanced by Barthes; that is, with a view to the relation between writing and existence as well as to the open and atemporal quality of the topos, it appears that he may have been struggling with seventeenth-century versions of issues addressed by the twentieth-century critic, although the responses differ not only in time but also in tenor. In the following we shall cross between Barthes and Rancé by way of Chateaubriand; between the three authors and between three complexes in which the relation between language, life, and religion is rehearsed and modulated in texts concerned with the bearing of the past on the present and the chiming of the present with the past. While distinct in tone and target, each of these complexes revolves around notions of time and history, ideas of anachronism and tradition, of intersections between religious and aesthetic discourses, and, above all, the function of the topos in mediations across time.

Historia: What Happens?

ROLAND BARTHES: THE POTENTIAL OF FORM AND THE AUTHOR'S QUEST

Barthes's essay on Chateaubriand's *Vie de Rancé* has its place in his diachronic inquiry of the role of form in literature and in his explorations into the existential power of language. His essays on literature circle around the proportions and ambiguous relation between historical fixation and superhistorical connections. On the one hand, the literary function is historical, and literature is thus a sign of history; on the other hand, it cannot be reduced to its historical situatedness and thereby offers resistance to that history.[3] Cohesion is created through a register of literary intentionalities, the similarities of which connect authors across centuries while their dissimilarities separate contemporaries.[4] Form constitutes a repository for such intentionalities. In its gravity, form is a value that transcends history in the same way as the ritual language of preachers, Barthes states with characteristic merger of enigma and revelation.[5] In his brief introduction to *Le Degré zéro de l'écriture* he describes the "sacral Order of written signs" as that which posits literature as an institution and isolates it from history (*l'Histoire*), or which operates most clearly when it rejects history. It is possible to trace a history of literary language that is neither the history of language nor that of style, but the history of the signs of literature, and this formal history manifests its own association with profound history (*l'Histoire profonde*), while potentially varying from history in itself (*l'Histoire elle-même*). One register in this meta- or profound history is the literary pondering of the nature of literature. According to Barthes, Chateaubriand is an early landmark in the establishment of a metalanguage in which literature reflects upon itself.[6] Thus he anticipates, if embryonically, the fundamental What is literature? of the twentieth century; not literature in its time or to its contemporaries; simply literature.[7] It is this landmark quality that paves the way for Barthes's dismantling of the *Sitz im Leben* of *Vie de Rancé* and for its status as a literary masterpiece with a message for today.

The essay on *Vie de Rancé* thus has its place in Barthes's overarching investigation of ways in which language is employed to explore existence. This investigation revolves around the central distinction between the author and the writer. It is a distinction that undergoes development and proliferates in the course of his authorial life but a formulaic identification appears in the essay "Écrivains et écrivants" (1960). The author (*écrivain*) lets the existential "why?" be absorbed, radically, into a question of how to write, striving not for the answer, but for the question about the meaning of things: *Pourquoi le monde? Quel est le sens des choses?*[8] The writer (*écrivant*), however, is not interested in opening new vistas but aims to end all ambiguity, contrary to the project of the author,

> For what defines the writer is the fact that his project of communication is naïve: he does not admit that his message is reflexive, that it closes over itself, and that we can read in it, diacritically, anything else but what he means [. . .]. He considers that his work resolves an ambiguity, institutes an irreversible explanation [. . .]

Apparently, religious metaphors lend themselves to the qualification of the way in which literature relates to existence; in this case "The author participates in the priest's role, the writer in the clerk's."[9] In his essay on Chateaubriand's *Vie de Rancé*, Barthes was to propose that such religious metaphors are not accidental analogies but carry a semantic substance.

ARMAND-JEAN DE RANCÉ: PENITENTIAL AUSTERITY

When Armand-Jean de Rancé (1626–1700) became a Cistercian reformer, he made a radical break with his former life.[10] He was Richelieu's godson and doctor in theology from the Sorbonne and spent life until his midthirties in Paris, among other things as chaplain to Louis XIII's brother Gaston d'Orléans. From childhood, he was commendatory abbot of five monasteries of different observance and demonstrated the lack of interest in their practical and spiritual well-being typical of commendatory abbots of the time. In 1657 Rancé's mistress Marie de Montbazon (born 1610/12) died of scarlet fever or measles. Mme de Montbazon, famed for her beauty, was married to the much older duke of Montbazon. She played an important role in Rancé's early life and introduction in the polished circles of the salons and to the cabale des Importants, which plotted against Mazarin, leading to exile and imprisonment for its members.[11] Her death was one of several impulses that threw Rancé into a conversion process, which lasted six years and concluded with his decision to sell four of his abbacies and enter the fifth monastery. In 1661 he visited his Cistercian monastery La Trappe for the first time. Apparently, the monastery was in ruins, morally as well as materially. Rancé decided to stay and restore it to its proper state. The former courtier underwent the novitiate; he became abbot proper of La Trappe and dedicated his life to an ambitious purging. He purged his monastery, revising the life led there; he tirelessly strove to purge monastic life at the time through treatises and letters, and the spiritual state of his contemporaries, men and women, secular and monastic, through a comprehensive correspondence and reception of visitors.

Conforming to the basic staging of Christian, not least monastic, changes, Rancé's endeavors were couched as a reform. Already at the first day of his novitiate, he wrote to his spiritual mentor that he was going to introduce "*la réforme de saint Bernard*" to drive out the longevous disorder of his monastery. At this point, Rancé had not demonstrated any particularly Cistercian, let alone Bernardine leanings. In fact it seems that one main incentive during his conversion was Jacques-Davy Duperron *Réplique à la réponse du sérénissime roi de la Grande-Bretagne* (1620), a compendium of post-Tridentine ecclesiology, and he gives as a principal aim for his conversion the wish to work for penitence and the glory of God according to, as he pens it, the desires and intentions of the church so clearly described by the Council of Trent.[12] Nonetheless he states that he will dedicate his life to a Bernardine reform. No doubt he had in mind initially the reform of the strict branch of the Cistercians that had sprouted around the turn

of the century. But eventually the abbot took matters in hand more au-
tonomously, and rather than implementing existing mores, he fashioned an
enhanced set, characterized above all by austerity and penitence.

Characteristically for the idea of reform, Rancé's venture hovers between return and modernization, but with a decided leaning towards the
latter. At the time of the *querelle des anciens et des modernes*, the abbot proved
himself something of a religious *moderne;* less interested in harking back
to ancient forms than in making the gist of their ideals come across in a
way that makes sense to contemporaries. This is evident in his handling of
the Rule of Benedict, basis for both Cistercians and Benedictines and the
obvious touchstone for the legitimacy of any reform within these orders.
Rancé's reform manifesto, the bulky *De la sainteté et des devoirs de la vie
monastique* (1683) caused a stir in monastic and ecclesiastical circles and
a yearlong combat, by and large fought on commentaries on the Rule of
Benedict.[13] There was a general agreement that Benedictines and Cistercians should relate to the Rule by way of mimetic adaptation but was this
adaptation to take place according to the spirit or the letter? And if according to the spirit, what was indeed that spirit? In the *Avertissement* to his
commented translation of the Rule of Benedict, Rancé mentions as one of
the preconditions of his works his wish to comply with the desire in a great
number of pious monks for an exposition that is pure and *naturelle* and
does not linger over usages and customs that have been weakened *dans la
suite des temps*.[14] The author states that he has tried to work out his explication of the Rule according to the letter as well as to the spirit, maintaining
its fundamental temper with the greatest diligence. But things must make
sense, and the abbot does not shy away from pruning the family tree of ideals if this means bearing better fruit for contemporaries and in the context
of his reform. Benedict sent out brothers to preach against idolaters: "This
is an extraordinary case from which we cannot conclude anything for our
time [. . .]."[15]

Rancé was no contemplative; he dealt in actions and exterior signs of
penitence. This was provocative in a time preoccupied with the interior
as the main stage for true religious life, resulting in a surge of devotional
literature that brought to the fore notions of interiority.[16] One of the criticisms against Rancé was that he focused too much on the exterior practices, neglecting interior piety.[17] The accusation of exteriority was to be
repeated by Chateaubriand, but on different grounds.

Chateaubriand's charge has its historical roots in the death of Mme
de Montbazon. Apparently the duchess's head was cut off after her death.
Much is made of this severed head, by both Chateaubriand and Barthes.

Rancé's contemporary and devotee Saint-Simon states that the decapitation took place as part of the postmortem, and presumably Rancé ratified this piece of information when Saint-Simon sent him an early version of his memoires in 1699.[18] However, by then an alternative tale had already gained ground. This appeared in a pamphlet against Rancé authored by the young Protestant Daniel de Larroque, who added Gothic horror *avant la lettre* to Montbazon's death. The pamphlet appeared in the aftermath of Rancé's grand oeuvre *De la sainteté*, twenty-eight years after Mme de Montbazon's death. Larroque has his figure Philandre recount how, having been spared the news of his mistress's death by well-meaning servants, Rancé arrives from the countryside to her quarters and is met by the sight of her bloodstained head, which rolls out from beneath the piece of cloth with which it had been casually covered. The head had been severed from the body since, because of poor measuring, the duchess's coffin was too short by half a foot.[19] A striking tale, not least for someone steeped in the spirit of Romanticism.

FRANÇOIS-RENÉ DE CHATEAUBRIAND: APOLOGY, HISTORIOGRAPHY, AND MEMORY

Chateaubriand's last work, *Vie de Rancé* was written at the instigation of his spiritual director, abbé Séguin. Allegedly, he took up the challenge with a *répugnance naturelle*.[20] But in fact the penitential and spiritual assignment develops traits already present in his *oeuvre*. *Vie de Rancé* is related to the apologetic program of Chateaubriand's enchiridion of the dogma and poetics of Christianity, *Génie du christianisme* (written 1795–99, published 1802), which even anticipates the Trappist theme cursorily. In a brief chapter on religious orders, Chateaubriand describes this branch of monastic life as a school of morals instituted in the middle of a world of pleasures, and he lingers over the scenery at a Trappist deathbed fascinated by the thought of the dying monk who, from the gates of eternity, speaks to his brothers and superiors about penitence. The Trappists, he states, only raise their voice to say: *Frères, il faut mourir.* "Not true," retorts Louis Du Bois in his 1824 history of the La Trappe. In *Vie de Rancé* Chateaubriand seeks to meet his criticisms.[21] More importantly, he brings to life the tableau of *Génie;* the life of Rancé.

The portrait of the Cistercian abbot also partakes in an extensive, palimpsestic rewriting of seminal seventeenth-century texts by, for example, Pascal and Bossuet, and Tabet defines this last work as the climax of a long and profound dialogue with the seventeenth century, cherished by the viscount as an age on the boundary between the desert and the court, the pagan memory and the Christian inspiration, the poetical and the holy.[22] In his view, the seventeenth century demonstrates most purely the *génie du christianisme;* morally, stylistically, and emotionally. Chateaubriand blames his own century for having cut off literature from its Christian inspiration; it has left nothing but an empty memory in negligence of the fact that the perfection of this literature stems from its religiosity. The nineteenth century has, he says, reduced the seventeenth century to the genie of the seventeenth century bedizened with the wig of Louis XIV.[23] Finally, the *Vie de Rancé* is also a *Vie de Chateaubriand,* and it enters into an autobiographical and memorial alliance with *Mémoires d'outre-tombe* (published 1849–50). *Mémoires* was conceived as a work to be published posthumously, and, albeit later, *Vie de Rancé* in some ways functions as its prologue.[24]

In *Vie de Rancé* Chateaubriand constructs a frame in which are embedded passages and summaries from earlier lives of Rancé and contemporary documents, stories of his own journeys and encounters and, unsurprisingly, glosses on the Revolution. Links are created by Chateaubriand's memory and the ever-present *vanitas*-motif; *Vie de Rancé* abounds in tombs, ruins, fading love, and beauty in decay; even the monks at La Trappe are but *ruines des religieux* when Rancé arrives.[25] In sum, while carried out under orders and perhaps reluctantly, *Vie de Rancé* is firmly situated in Chateaubriand's grand enterprise; his overarching search for continuities through overlaps between personal memory and cultural memory, intent on continuities that bridge the gap created by the Revolution.[26] To the extent that *Vie de Rancé* has attracted scholarly interest, which is less than Chateaubriand's other works, critics have been keen to stress the autobiographical tier in *Vie de Rancé.*[27] The allusions to the author's own life do indeed constitute a *basso continuo,* which adds a particular tonality to the work, and his authorial point of view features throughout. But the title is in fact a truthful declaration of the substance of the work. This is a text about Rancé. It rests on in-depth historical research, and the narrative is corroborated with a fecundity of references to, and quotations from, the hagiographies of Rancé, contemporary allusions to the abbot, his own works, and exchanges with contemporaries. With its merger of biography and autobiography, *Vie de Rancé* revolves around its author's intense personal engagement: not only with himself but also with his difficult protagonist.

The head of Montbazon plays a crucial role in this. Chateaubriand quotes substantial passages from Larroque's pamphlet; he discusses Saint-Simon's version but gets the gist of it wrong, phrasing it as though the discrepancy is between Larroque's version, which contains a severed head, and Saint-Simon's and the hagiographers' versions, which do not, whereas the difference rests in fact with the causes of the decapitation and with whether Rancé was present when his mistress died.[28] Larroque says he was not, Saint-Simon that he was and even saw to it that she received the final sacraments. This distinction leads to Chateaubriand's statement, in turn taken up by Barthes, that the poets have adopted Larroque's tale while the religious have renounced it. He counts himself a *lecteur indifférent*, allowed the freedom to investigate the case.[29] So he adds other references and opinions on the deceased lady and finds in the abbot's commissioning of, for example, a painting of Mary of Egypt for the monastery a sign of his secret pain. Chateaubriand concludes the section about this painting suggestively: "We must add to these semi-indications Rancé's despair, and it will be for the reader to form an opinion. Human annals are composed of many fables mixed with some truths: whoever has avowed himself to the future has at the core of his life a novel, to give birth to the legend, mirage to the history."[30] The author must add the hopelessness of Rancé to the taciturnity of the man himself; the reader must form his own opinion, add to the silence, create a fuller image.

Chateaubriand's work on Rancé crowned a considerable nineteenth-century literary interest in the Trappists, the popular term for the strict branch of the Cistercian order to which La Trappe formally belonged. This interest rose in the aftermath of the 1830 declaration of Bernard of Clairvaux as *doctor ecclesiae* and the order's dramatic fate during the Revolution, ending with its reinstitution in 1834.[31] The Cistercians themselves met this literary interest with disdain; one abbot compared Chateaubriand's work to a novel by Walter Scott, full of strange tales and foul anecdotes.[32] The abbot was treated as an icon already in his time. Somewhat contrary to its historiographic panoply, Chateaubriand's volume came to augment this tendency and others took his cue. In *Confidence-Man*, Melville described Rancé and Ignatius of Loyola as epitomes of radical conversion.[33] Also to Schopenhauer the Trappist became a primary example of a conversion from mundane desire to repulsion at the world on a par with Raimond Llull; the ideal of *"Verneigung des Willens."* Schopenhauer has his information from Chateaubriand's *Vie*; *"sehr lesenswert,"* he states, its *Geist* comparable to that of Brahmanist and Buddhist books.[34] Nietzsche then offers an engaged portrayal of Schopenhauer before Rancé's portrait.[35] Even when he is invested with radical inclinations and profound gifts, Rancé retains something of the empty shell. Perhaps this emptiness is his own creation; the triumph of his penitence brought about through

silence. To Chateaubriand, Rancé's silence paves the way for both speculation and grandeur. Barthes lets the abbot slide into his own silence, distills
the grandeur, concentrates on Chateaubriand, and, ever keen on fragmentation, lets his exploration of the rhetorical strategy of the work take off
from *la tête coupée*.

Tropologia: What Do They Do?

BARTHES COMBATS ANACHRONISM BY WAY OF FRAGMENTATION

Has anyone ever read the *Life of Rancé* as it was written, as a work of penitence and edification? This is the question with which Barthes opens his
essay on Chateaubriand's *Vie de Rancé*. A few lines below he continues:

> This kind of distortion, afforded by the time between writing and read-
> ing, is the very challenge of what we call literature [. . .] and this anach-
> ronism is the crucial question it puts to the critic: we manage, little by
> little to explain a work by its time or by its project, i.e., to justify the
> scandal of its appearance; but how reduce that of its survival?[36]

The relation between reading and writing is distorted by the anachronism,
scandal even, which separate the two. The challenge for Barthes becomes
to explore what makes Chateaubriand's work relevant for modern readers
whose knowledge of Marx, Nietzsche, Freud, and Sartre separates them
from Chateaubriand and his context. His is a challenge that compares to
Rancé's effort to make the Rule of Benedict applicable to monks in the aftermath of the Tridentine Council, although his motives are aesthetic and
existential rather than spiritual and institutional. Barthes's answer hinges
on Chateaubriand's style and rhetoric, which commend the work to a clas-
sification as a masterpiece and lift it out of the religious context in which it
was written. With his approach to *Vie de Rancé* as a literary work equivalent
to Sartre's *Nausée* despite its Christian attire, Barthes chooses to neglect
two distinct indications of genre inherent in the work. On the one hand
he brushes aside its religious aspirations: *"Dieu est un moyen commode pour
parler du néant"* (*"God is a convenient means for speaking of nothingness"*).[37]
On the other hand, he disregards Chateaubriand's own pretensions to historiography, which compete with the work's literary and autobiographical markers as to generic belonging. It is noteworthy that Barthes does
not relate to, for example, Chateaubriand's comprehensive employment of
sources. His omission of this register is all the more remarkable, since *Vie*

de Rancé seems to represent the kind of historiography that Barthes was to treat two years later in "Le discours de l'histoire" (1967), concerned with the friction between the historian and the time he describes and the temporal fragmentations employed as a rhetorical means in the composition of historical narratives.[38]

The second disregard is related to the first. By viewing Chateaubriand's work as literature rather than historiography, Barthes transposes it from its religious context to a ground where existential fundamentals are explored through linguistic form. In this process, Barthes casts off the figure and oeuvre of Rancé, deciding that the abbot's "[. . .] conversion was nonetheless a writer's suicide; [. . .] Yet to this literary death, Chateaubriand must give a literary life: this is the paradox of the *Life of Rancé*." Presumably, for Barthes, this suicide also paves the way for Chateaubriand's separation from Rancé: "With Chateaubriand, the author begins his solitude: the author *is not* his character: a distance is established, which Chateaubriand assumes, without resigning himself to it."[39] Barthes's essay on *Vie de Rancé* appeared three years before "La mort de l'auteur" (1968) where he was to scrutinize the separation between author and text:

> The removal of the Author [. . .] is not only a historical fact or an act of writing: it utterly transforms the modern text [. . .]. Time, first of all, is no longer the same. The Author, when we believe in him, is always conceived as the past of his own book: book and author are voluntarily placed on one and the same line, distributed as a *before* and an *after* [. . .] Quite the contrary, the modern *scriptor* is born *at the same time* as his text [. . .][40]

The double interest in literary deaths catches the eye. But Rancé's literary death is not that of the authorial figure who lends authority to his text, but that of the author who explores life with his pen. With his conversion, Rancé transposes himself from author to writer and thus writes himself out of Barthes's horizon as someone irretrievably lost to the grand genealogy of authors who, conscious of the potential of form, explore the interrelation and exchange between linguistic and existential ponderings as he slides into the history of penance and edification.

Barthes is now free to treat Chateaubriand's work independently of its *Sitz im Leben*: as a burning book. His exploration revolves around three main topoi. The first is *la région de profond silence*. In Chateaubriand, the region of profound silence is the monastic profession of Rancé, the Trappist obligation to silence, and Rancé's own silence about Mme de Montbazon;

in Barthes, the region of profound silence is Chateaubriand's aging, which alienates him from the world just as Rancé was alienated. With this topos Barthes establishes between Rancé and Chateaubriand a basic and light correlation that does not primarily hinge on religious concerns. The second is *la tête coupée*. Barthes uses the vision of the severed head to introduce the anacoluthon as the fundamental stylistic and rhetorical principle in *Vie de Rancé*. The disrupted rhythm of Chateaubriand's work serves as the basis of a construction of antitheses between Rancé and Chateaubriand and between the before and after of Rancé's conversion. The anacoluthon creates a gap that invites the reader to seek out more meaning. It introduces a poetics of distance. "Such, it would seem, is the major function of rhetoric and its figures: to make us understand, *at the same time*, something else."[41] The third topos is *le chat jaune de l'abbé Séguin*. The yellow cat belongs to Chateaubriand's spiritual director and is mentioned only briefly in the dedicatory preface. But for Barthes, the cat is the essence of the literary quality of Chateaubriand's text. Yellow implies, he argues, that it is a "stray" cat; the word thus points to abbé Séguin's kindness. But it also says less than this, and the silence implied opens into wider complexes of connotations. Barthes states that there are two wavelengths in the figure of the yellow cat. The longest is that of the immediate meaning: that the abbot lives with a stray cat; the shortest does not yield any information except from the sense of literature itself. A lived and read relative of the more technical Iserian *Leerstelle*, the topos opens to experience. But the short wavelength, says Barthes, constitutes a mysterious element that means literature cannot be reduced to a completely decipherable system and that reading is not a purely hermeneutic act. It is this usage of language that makes Chateaubriand an author rather than a writer.[42]

Ever present, the sound of severance resonates not only in the overall stylistic orchestration but also in smaller semantic units; and even if the work follows the chronology of Rancé's conversion, Barthes detects a continuous *brisure du sens* in the stylistically undetermined *unités mysterieuses* "as if Chateaubriand could never keep from suddenly turning his head toward 'something else.'" Even his metaphors, states Barthes, do not bring objects together but separate their different worlds.[43] Taking off from this allegedly split perspective, the critic crystallizes basic thematic tenors of Chateaubriand's *Vie de Rancé* into complex metaphorical units, lifting them out that scandal of apparition, in which they are steeped as long as they are closely connected with Chateaubriand's conversion, thus opening the topoi to a new life in a *livre brûlant*.[44]

CHATEAUBRIAND STRADDLES ANACHRONISMS
THROUGH A CHALLENGE OF SILENCE

Qui suis-je? Chateaubriand's introductory question in *Essai historique* is not an existential but an authorial interrogation. *Vie de Rancé* attests to similar self-reflection. The work is written from a double point of view from which the authorial voice ponders and bridges the gap between his own presentness, Rancé's pastness, and the presence as well as absence of that past. There are Chateaubriand's direct references to his own experiences, as when he mentions Dorotheus of Gaza, whose instructions Rancé translated from the Greek, and adds: "I have seen the desert between Jaffa and Gaza where Dorotheus lived" (a statement then brusquely denied in the editorial note).[45] There are the explanatory commentaries in which he poses as the observing reader, an *lecteur indifférent* who scrutinizes his material with critical acumen and consciousness of historical distance, "The way in which men of that time saw the world did not resemble how we perceive it today. It was never about these men themselves; it was always of God they talked."[46]

He may be indifferent as a reader, but as an author he is profoundly engaged, struggling to come to terms with his Cistercian subject. The abbot leaves much to be desired both as convert and romantic. He shows no sign of *cette passion chrétienne, cette querelle immense* between terrestrial and celestial love, lauded in *Génie*. Why this obstinate silence regarding his love? Did not both Jerome and Augustine draw their mature strength from the weaknesses of their youth?[47] It is a lingering frustration in both the author and the reader Chateaubriand that he is shut out from the interior of the man Rancé;

> Rancé has written much; what dominates in him is a passionate hatred
> of life; that which is inexplicable, which would be horrible if it was
> not admirable; that is the insurmountable barrier which he has placed
> between himself and his readers. Never a confession, never does he
> speak of what he has done, of his mistakes, of his repentance. He arrives
> before his audience without deigning to teach them what he is; the
> creature is not worth the trouble of explaining oneself to it: he encloses
> in himself his history, which again falls back on his heart.[48]

As we have seen, absence of interior displayed was a pique already at Rancé's own time. However, Chateaubriand takes up the challenge. He ponders the gaps of silence, "since the death of Madame de Montbazon,

the name of this woman [. . .] never left his mouth [. . .] Rancé remained
perplexed about himself."[49] He interjects into the narratives gleaned from
earlier biographies of Rancé the emotions, sensations, and reactions that
he finds wanting; as when he imagines the impressions of the courtier who
begins his withdrawal from the world by retreating from Paris to the family mansion Véretz: "The salons were decorated with priceless paintings,
the gardens were exquisitely laid out. It was too much for a man who saw
nothing but through tears." This is not so much a matter of an author who
makes his figure come alive as it is an attempt to make up for the dearth of
that agitation that could have added tragic luster. He moves on to tell how
the converted courtier was advised to follow the missions to India or the
Himalayas. This, Chateaubriand remarks, would have been analogous to
the *grandeur et la tristesse du génie de Rancé.*[50]

Chateaubriand is an avid user of montages and molds his text through
interactions with earlier texts, thus creating the kind of splits that Barthes was to see as anacolutha. These montages add to the *Vie* a distinct
seventeenth-century flavor, which in turn creates a noteworthy tension
when viewed against the backdrop of Chateaubriand's ever present authorial voice, leading to an anachronism of sorts in its adherence to the letter
rather than the spirit. For example, he quotes André Félibien des Avaux's
(d. 1695) depiction of the twelfth-century church at La Trappe, "The
church has nothing substantial but the sanctity of the place: it is built in
a Gothic and very particular way: it has nothing noble or divine [. . .]."[51]
Félibien wrote in a time still ambivalent, and generally negative, toward
the Gothic. When Chateaubriand took over his viewpoint, the attitude had
changed decisively; Gothic had become fashionable, and Chateaubriand
is a man of his time when he writes in *Génie:* "One cannot enter a Gothic
church without feeling a sort of shiver and a vague feeling of the divine."[52]
For all his mediations, *Vie de Rancé* was left with the seventeenth-century
view of Gothic.

Chateaubriand is the reminiscing author. His memories are stirred, not
least, by geographical places. He blends traces of Félibien's portrait of La
Trappe with his own recollections of his family estate, Combourg:

> The abbey had not changed place: it was still, as at the time of the
> foundation, in a valley. The hills gathering around it hid it from the
> rest of the world. I thought, when I saw it, to see again my woods and
> my ponds of Combourg at evening by the sun's dimming lights. Silence
> reigned: if noise was heard, it was only the sound of trees or the mur-

murs of streams [. . .]. Only at the Escorial have I encountered a similar absence of life [. . .].[53]

He sinks into the places connected to Rancé's story, and only with effort does he tear himself away; "Rancé will leave Chambord, and so it is necessary that I too leave this asylum where I fear to have forgotten myself too much"; or rather, remembered himself.[54] Quite the traveler, Chateaubriand makes the most of the abbot's journeys for spiritual guidance during his conversion. Quite the memorialist, he lingers over Rancé's return of two portraits of Mme de Montbazon to her son, "Break with the real things, that is by no means nothing; but with memories! The heart breaks at the separation from dreams; for there is little reality in man."[55] To Barthes, the monastic profession is the suicide of the author, to Chateaubriand, it is the suicide of the reminiscing lover. The biographer pursues his subject into the monastic enclosure, that region of profound silence. His *Vie* takes on a different pace. The unbroken stretches of text become longer, the memorial associations more scarce, Chateaubriand's own memories recede into the background. The abbot takes over, his texts generously quoted and paraphrased; the author is impressed, albeit reluctantly, by the oeuvre's unwavering focus on death, "*C'est toujours dur, mais admirablement exprimé*" ("It is always hard, but it is admirably expressed").[56]

Rancé Champions Silence and Negates Anachronism

Like Barthes's rhetorical topoi, the monastic topoi are employed in a process that is aimed at overcoming temporal friction. These topoi constitute diachronic association within a monastic genealogy, which ranges from the apostles via the desert fathers and the Rule of Benedict to the golden age of the medieval Cistercians. One example is the Cistercian predilection for the wilderness. Right from the first generations in the twelfth century, the Cistercians represented themselves as monks who withdrew into the desert like the Egyptian fathers. It is a mythological topos whose complex relation to factuality need not detain us here. The Cistercian texts abound in wildernesses. They can be thorny thickets, which repel everybody but the Cistercian soldiers of Christ in their ascetical perseverance, or soggy marshland, bad for the health and therefore good for the monks who must always have death before their eyes; it can be a serene remoteness suited for contemplative isolation or a Babylonian chaos of crumbling buildings and flourishing vices.[57] Across their differences each of these examples functions as a Cistercian wilderness and serves the constitution of a monastic site as genuinely Cistercian. With a modulation of Barthes's understanding of the topos it may be argued that the function of topoi such as withdrawal, silence, and penitence within monastic traditions is "to hear, at another time, the same thing."

Toward the end of his life Rancé sums up the ethos of the community at La Trappe as constancy and firmness of spirit, solitude, silence, and seclusion.[58] He called on basic Benedictine topoi to reconstitute monastic purity, legitimize his endeavors, and frame them within the Cistercian mindset, thereby at the same time ensuring that basic Cistercian elements were tinged in Rancéan hues. Like Barthes, Rancé exploits the potential of the topos to refer to something else. With the Trappist reformer, however, this something else is always penitence and abstention. We shall linger over his handling of silence. It is representative and offers an answer of sorts to Chateaubriand's perpetual "Why this silence?" In the monastic tradition silence features prominently as a tool of mortification and is continuously called upon as a means of curtailing verbal sin, from gossip via laughter to quarrels, and as a bulwark against other sins. The distinguishing difference rests with what is negated through silence. Rancé's world cultivates eloquence and adores conversational virtues; *l'honnête homme* has as one of his primary aims the ability to converse well, and lions and lionesses of the salons are judged by their wit. Rancé excelled in the art. Little wonder that the reformer associated silence with withdrawal from the world rather than, as in the medieval context, with composure and guarding of the senses. In *De la sainteté*, the chapter on silence is significantly situated between the chapters *De la retraite* and *De l'abstinence*. His discourse is illustratively structured under three overall questions, with increasingly profound answers. *Is it necessary for the monk to observe the silence with much exactness?* Yes. An exact observation of silence secures the isolation from the world and the harmony within the monastery. In an engaging list of type portraits, the abbot displays the ways in which various characters would take advantage of any liberty with regard to conversation to cultivate their weaknesses and turn the monastery into a microversion of the secular world:

> [. . .] someone rebellious will administer intrigues and parties with a
> diligence as if it was about overturning a state; there will be perpetual
> opportunities for a choleric to be riled, for someone shameless to
> have his evil desires enflamed, for someone malicious to spread his
> venom, for someone anxious to excite divisions and murmuring, for

a conversationalist to spout his tales, for someone obliging to form particular friendships; eventually, each one will follow his own moods and humors. The passions will have changed theatre and will have been compressed within narrower boundaries, but far from being destroyed they will thereby become stronger and more alive [. . .][59]

For once, his premonastic life resurfaces. The description lends itself, perhaps deceptively, to biographical speculation about the characters with whom he then conversed. His monks had parallel sets of experiences. The only way of remedying this disorder is to break off communication. Silence is a crucial instrument in the perpetual withdrawal from the ways of a world preoccupied with intrigues, rhetorical fluency, and critical pursuits; it takes more than a monastic wall to isolate oneself from terrestrial dispositions. Unsurprisingly, Rancé's comprehensive correspondence attests to a more equivocal reality.

Must the silence be perpetual? Yes. Brief conversations are no less dangerous than long ones, and the brothers will soon find out how to say a lot in little time. But with perpetual silence brothers will retain an unaltered esteem for each other, sinful dispositions in one monk will not spread to others, there will be no factions or discontent muttering, and relations between monks and superiors will be straighter. Perpetual silence leads to purer thoughts, more ardent and continuous prayer, and a saintlier intimacy with God. In *De la sainteté*, the strongest contemplative chords are struck in the chapters on silence and other penitential topics.

Would it not be useful for a monk to hear from his brother some words of consolation? Yes, but the evil implied in this consolation is much greater than the good. An opening for conversation is bound to create a slide:

> They will communicate their thoughts, their temptations, their imaginations, their discontent, their trials. They will place themselves in each other's hearts, as toothing stones for future needs and affairs; they will unite with bonds of a peculiar and false love, which cannot exist without the destruction of communal charity.[60]

The abbot resorts to cenobitic arguments, but silence serves to turn the monks into hermits within the community. No one can accuse Rancé of having communicated his thoughts, his temptations, or his imaginings. This passage captures in essence the Rancéan hardness pointed out by Chateaubriand and identifies it as a conscious penitential program. It gives a monastic answer to the challenge that underscores the viscount's conversation with his subject; a conversation that remains a monologue owing to the latter's recalcitrance to reveal those temptations, imaginings, and sorrows that Chateaubriand is so keen to talk about.

Anagogia: What Do They Strive For?

Rancé: The Penitence of Language

Rancé strives for clarity. According to his contemporaries, he did so with striking eloquence. The erudite Gilles Ménage, author of *Observations sur la langue française* (1672–76), declared that he never read works by the abbot of La Trappe without admiration; he called him one of the best writers in the kingdom and praised his style as noble, sublime, and inimitable.[61] André Félibien des Avaux praises the abbot's present rhetorical skills when speaking about the blessings of the afterlife as a saintly parallel of his former eloquence when speaking about the things of the world.[62] His hagiographer marvels that even though Rancé lived in isolation for some thirty years, without study, without effort, without even wanting to, he became one of the finest pens of his age.[63]

Perhaps it is difficult for a modern reader to appraise the tissue of this eloquence. The Cistercian lacks his monastic forbear Bernard of Clairvaux's sense for semantic diversification and rhetorical reconnoitering into ascetic and contemplative terrains. But Rancé and his contemporaries read fire and nerve in his writings; in his *Éclaircissemens* he must defend himself against the charge that he writes with too much vivacity, and in his explication of the Rule of Benedict he anticipates accusations of rhetorical force:

> There may be people who find that in some places the Author has expressed himself too strongly, but this must be attributed to the character of the substance, and the nature of the difficulties and objections to which he responds, for it is hardly possible (when we speak of great truths, when we regard them with an attentive gaze, when we love them, and when we see that they are neglected by a large part of those who ought to attach themselves to them and follow them) that the interior sentiment does not pass over into the word: it is difficult, I say, to express oneself in a soft and languid way, when the heart is deeply touched by what one says; one talks with an indifferent air of indifferent things; but when dealing with that which is sensitive, the expressions are always intense, and there would not be the least of reason in attributing to mood or passion that which is but the effect of the love we have for the truth and the justice.[64]

It is hardly possible that the interior sentiment does not spill over into language, the penitent argues. Any interior sentiment concerning Montbazon has been silenced, the love of truth and justice having taken its place.

Rancé had the split perspective cherished by Barthes at his disposal. The monastic and, further down the line, Patristic tradition have a predilection for intertwinement of writing and existence and employment of metaphorical open-endedness as a means to explore the meaning of text for life. The split perspective drives the typological *figura* and parabolic figures apt to reveal as well as to shroud. Also the urge to overcome anachronism lingers with this tradition. Evidently Rancé's climate is not that of the allegorically charged Middle Ages. But it is not simply a question of eras; his friend and contemporary Bossuet took up the legacy which he himself dismissed.

In Barthes's universe, the meanings alluded to tacitly in the topos distend its semantic range and decipherable character through the idea of a mysterious surplus. In this surplus rests the utterance about existence. For Rancé, the slightest reference to worldly matters among the monks will only call to mind everything that ought to have been forever effaced from their memory.[65] Contrary to his medieval ancestors, he wants to purge the monastic minds and memories of former lives; his own above all. This takes place through, among other things, a linguistic purging. The abbot seems to, as it were, drain his language of any hint of a semantic polyphony that might open to memories and associations. He condensates a variety of topoi, each with its own potential, into figures of one and the same thing: penitence and abstention. As we have seen, the chapters of Rancé's main work *De la sainteté* are structured around questions such as "Must silence be perpetual?" Most of them may be answered with a simple yes or no—in fact, generally a simple yes.

CHATEAUBRIAND: THE LANGUAGE OF AGE

Chateaubriand strives to pin down the wisdom embodied in the withdrawn penitent; less his penitential wisdom than that which pertains to a life remembered or obliterated. If Chateaubriand is vexed by what Rancé does not say, he is impressed with what he says; especially with the way in which he says it. His is the language of a man of his age; redolent of a precision shaped by the seventeenth century and the serenity that comes with growing old. The language of Rancé's time, states Chateaubriand, offers force, precision, and clarity to the author, while allowing him the freedom of phrase and the impress of his genie.[66]

Rancé was in his midthirties when he withdrew from the world, but to his biographer he becomes fixed in old age from that point on. The hot-spurred verve that the abbot admits to in his own style finds no resonance with Chateaubriand, whose understanding of Rancé as withdrawn, silent, and old permeates his view on the Cistercian's language. Book 3 begins momentously: "Here begins the new life of Rancé: we enter the region of profound silence. Rancé breaks with his youth, he chases it away and does not see it again."[67] This severance affects his style, which "is never young, he has left his youth with Madame de Montbazon. In the works of Rancé, the breath of spring lacks in flowers; but instead: what autumn evenings! How beautiful they are, these sounds of the last days of the year!"[68] Penitentially speaking, Rancé and his monks had one foot in the grave. Chateaubriand retains this position but charges it aesthetically and existentially. Not only has the *Frères, il faut mourir* of *Génie du christianisme* been replaced by more elaborate statements, it has also been invested with an air of melancholic sophistication, owing to Rancé's permanent autumnal age. Chateaubriand finds a resonance of his own situation in the tonality of this language. The biographer furthermore posits an amorous *leitmotif.* He can relate to the motif but not follow the way in which it is played out. The main penitential motif, however, he identifies with diligence. As a historian he stays painstakingly close to the Cistercian, his time, and his writings; as an author he can only wonder from afar.

Barthes: The Language of Ethics

Barthes strives to overcome anachronism; the broken relation between one time and another, the distortion between writing and reading. The means by which a work may transcend its own time—that of its creation as well as its inherent time—is a literary form that carries significance beyond that of the words themselves. This semantic transcendence hinges on a double notion of time; existential and literary time. Barthes divests the biography of its own time and replaces this with a new temporal mode created by the dynamic between time condensed and time distended. The motto of the essay is a sentence from *Vie de Rancé*: "I am no longer anything but time." In Chateaubriand, these words are enunciated by the corpse of Louis XIV when his coffin is broken open during the Revolution.[69] Barthes transfers the phrase from its narrative context and its association with the king and opens it to a repersonification. Chateaubriand is the new "I," weighed down by his age, having passed over into pure time. *Vie de Rancé* is a work written from the point of view of memory, which turns existence into destiny and thereby recasts life as essence rather than lived life. Chateaubriand creates a literary time in which the extension of Rancé's conversion in its own time is condensed into a poetic moment; only thus can it become relevant to us.[70] Rancé's own story is turned into a literary topos wherein the biographical disruptions do not take place in the course of time but are condensed into a complex, internally antithetical iconic figure.

But condensation is only the first step in the establishment of the temporal mode that makes the work that white-hot book in which a modern reader may discover problems of his or her own. The condensation abolishes the temporal registers inherent in the work. In order for the work to reach beyond its own time, it must have openings toward a different time; a time that could be ours. Barthes deposits this potential with the charged fragmentations and disruptions, the anacolutha. The meaning these fragmentations yield to modern readers is neither the penitence of Rancé nor Chateaubriand's *génie du christianisme*. Nonetheless, it is a meaning that apparently calls for religiously flavored notions, although, unsurprisingly, Barthes does not take over their religious content. He evokes Kierkegaard's association of the universal (*det almene*) and language in *Fear and Trembling* (*Frygt og Bæven*). In its origin, this association is closely related to Abraham as the knight of faith, but in Barthes it becomes a matter of mediating between the individual, amoral existence of the author and a universal, ethical universe. The aim of this mediation is to diminish suffering.[71]

Is this, then, all there is to it? To suffer less? Barthes's finale is in chiming with his ideals for the author; the aim is not the answer but the inquiry. Barthes concludes with a register of openness in Chateaubriand. This is an openness related to that of the topos and the potential that lies in the tension between the power and the powerlessness of language.

[. . .] although Rancé himself is indifferent to us, we understand the power of a useless language. Certainly calling old age *the nighttime traveler* cannot continuously cure the misery of growing old; for on the one hand, there is the time of real miseries [. . .]; and on the other, some metaphor which explodes, which enlightens without acting. And yet this explosion of the word affords our wretchedness a shock of distance [. . .]. This distance, established by writing, should have only one name [. . .]: *irony*. In relation to the difficulty of being, of which it is a continual observation, the *Life of Rancé* is a work of sovereign irony (*eironeia* means *interrogation*); [. . .] is it not a certain "detachment" applied by the excess of words [. . .] to the tenacious will to suffer?[72]

Rancéan autumn, Chateaubriand's examination of life as it draws to its closure has been burst open.

Epilogue

At once presence and absence, silence is a constant force in the three-plied complex examined. The silence of Rancé about his loss of Mme de Montbazon, which at once vexes Chateaubriand and opens the abbot's history to the viscount's engagement. *La région de profond silence,* a land of infinite and no extension; the Trappist silence that muzzles the voices and instincts of the world. Johannes de Silentio, the pseudonym that Kierkegaard chose for *Fear and Trembling,* passed over by Barthes. The silence of Johannes de Silentio, who can speak of faith only through the silence of Abraham, passed over, too. The silence within the topos that opens it to interpretations. The silence created between author and reader by Rancé's reluctance to surrender himself to his reader or the anachronism constituted by the temporal or spiritual distance. Silence as a deficit of meaning and a repository for surpluses of meaning. If the topos provides the matrix for a transposition of meaning across time, it is its inherent silence that enables each reader to reach for the deep questioning invested in it. Some topoi have more of this silence than others. The monastic ones have just enough to make them pliable, not so much that they lose the firmness needed within the institutional context of regular life. The topoi gleaned by Barthes from Chateaubriand have more. It is the silence of the yellow cat, the sense hinted at by the author, the sense of the reader.

PART III

Time and the Ordinary

CHAPTER 7

The Literary Comfort of Eternity: Calvin and Thoreau

Ernst van den Hemel

> In eternity, there is indeed something true and sublime. But all
> these times and places and occasions are now and here. God himself
> culminates in the present moment, and will never be more divine
> in the lapse of all ages. And we are enabled to apprehend at all what
> is sublime and noble only by the perpetual instilling and drenching
> of the reality which surrounds us. (. . .) Let us spend our lives in
> conceiving then. The poet or the artist never yet had so fair and
> noble a design but some of his posterity at least could accomplish it.[1]

Calvin's theology has a peculiar relationship to the comfort that eternity
can bring. In Calvin scholarship, a polemic has ensued between those who
believe that there is a clear break between Calvin and the later Calvinists
who transformed his Calvinist theology into an orthodox and overly philosophical Calvinist doctrine,[2] on the one hand, and those that uphold that in
fact there is a straight line from Calvin to the writers of the Westminster
Confession of Faith and the Puritans.[3] In this article I will argue that both
sides of the debate make implicit claims about the ambivalent status of the
comfort of eternity in Calvin's theology, and that a focus on the way in
which Calvin's language communicates comfort might offer a new perspective on this debate.

For the difference between Calvin and the Calvinists might not be located solely in the doctrinal content but also, to an important degree in
a particular "literary" voice. Without taking sides in the debate, one can
state that this "voice" changed over time. There is such a thing as a Calvinist voice that sets Calvin apart from someone like Theodore Beza. To
bring to the fore the relevance of this particularity of Calvin, in the debate
on Calvin's theology I will discuss two voices that make a claim on how

Calvin's notion of faith can offer assurance for the believer. After clearly locating the two sides of the debate, I will put forward a suggestion about how the relation between eternity and reassurance in Calvin's theology can be thought of as not only doctrinal content but as a linguistic *charge* to theological language as well. For an example of such a "charge" that is important in interpreting a text, I propose taking a look at Henry David Thoreau's *Walden*. By reading *Walden* as a project that attempts to communicate the charge of eternity that can be read in a text, we can perhaps see how the notion of the literary voice can help in reading theological texts that grapple with the double danger of dogmatism and self-referentiality that lay in emphasizing under the slogan *Sola fide*, faith, and faith alone.

Calvin on Faith and the Reprobate

The debate between the "Calvin against the Calvinists" side and the side that emphasizes the Calvinist orthodoxy of later Reformed writers, originates in what many describe as an unclear element of Calvin's theology: In the thinking of John Calvin there is an unsettled issue around whether or not, and under what modalities, the believer can have certain knowledge that he is saved. The communicability of faith is highly problematic. This has given rise to such diverse disagreements as the Arminian-Gomarus debate, as well as to matters pertaining to the difference between Puritan strands of thought and Calvinism as Calvin was supposed to have founded it. It is argued that already with the work of Calvin's successor in Geneva, Theodore Beza, a change was made in Calvin's theology that emphasizes communicability and thus "philosophized" a tension that was left unsettled in Calvin. But let us start with what gave rise to this confusion, by examining the definition of faith that Calvin himself gives:

> We shall now have a full definition of faith if we say that it is a firm and
> sure knowledge of the divine favour toward us, founded on the truth of
> a free promise in Christ, and revealed to our minds, and sealed on our
> hearts, by the Holy Spirit.[4]

"A firm and sure knowledge," we see here that in Calvin there is, for those who have faith, a firm and sure comfort that results from having faith. True faith, reserved for the elect, is part of the regenerating work of the Holy Spirit in the heart of the believer. In the process of sanctification, the believer receives an unfoundering faith and assurance of the "divine favor toward us." However, there are some problems with this definition of faith as far as the assurance is concerned. In keeping with the imperfections of man, the work of faith is in man always, to a certain extent, "implicit":

> We grant, indeed, that so long as we are pilgrims in the world faith is implicit, not only because as yet many things are hidden from us, but because, involved in the midst of error, we attain not to all.[5]

This does not mean that faith is not true, nor does it mean that faith is not "firm and sure," it means only that faith remains incomplete, the work is never done. As an example, Calvin discusses the disciples of Christ that erred even though they had faith: "They had therefore a true but implicit faith, having reverently embraced Christ as the only teacher." Faith, as a firm and sure knowledge, is then a *process* toward full faith. The words that Calvin uses to describe faith are frequently associated with a *process* that is *open-ended:* obedience, trusting with undoubting confidence,[6] irradiated,[7] explicit recognition,[8] assurance, a security to make peace follow from it,[9] receiving,[10] and passive: "For, in regard to justification, faith is merely passive, bringing nothing of our own to procure the favor of God, but receiving from Christ everything that we want."[11] All these characterizations are part and parcel of faith as a form of knowledge that is open-ended, receiving. The form of knowledge is not so much "firm and sure," as the evidence of experimental knowledge, but, as Calvin describes it, a process in that we receive a feeling of assurance that lies beyond human capacity. In this sense, doubt remains a part of the work of faith:

> When we say that faith must be certain and secure, we certainly speak not of an assurance which is never affected by doubt, nor a security which anxiety never assails, we rather maintain that believers have a perpetual struggle with their own distrust, and are thus far from thinking that their consciences possess a placid, quiet, uninterrupted by perturbation.[12]

Already we see that doubt can be part of the work of faith, and that the reassurance lies predominantly in the things that "we lack." Things become even more complicated with the idea that a temporary faith exists, a faith given to the reprobate that can be very hard to distinguish from the true faith of the elect:

> For experience shows that the reprobate are sometimes affected by almost the same feeling as the elect, so that even in their own judgment they do not in any way differ from the elect.[13]

So, with faith lying beyond human reasoning, and with a simulacrum of
faith that tricks people into believing that they are saved, what does Calvin do with the idea that the believer might doubt his election? That the
believer might think his sense of security is actually a simulacrum of faith?
What does Calvin say of anxiety? What is left of the assurance if doubt can
be part of the faith process? Calvin seems to have addressed this problem
of the believer's anxiety (of the believer) about election:

> Should it be objected, that believers have no stronger testimony to
> assure them of their adoption, I answer, that though there is a great
> resemblance and affinity between the elect of God and those who are
> impressed for a time with a fading faith, yet the elect alone have that
> full assurance which is extolled by Paul, and by which they are enabled
> to cry Abba, Father.[14]

Faith as such brings a confidence that the ones who possess it will recognize; there is a certain circularity in the description of faith in Calvin's
theology. The "implicit faith," and the impurity of even the elect, prevents
works from becoming the tell-tale sign of election. Although good works
are linked to the practice of being sanctified, there is no security to be derived from these works, nor even from the emotional security they offer,[15]
since even the reprobate, acting under the impression that they are saved,
can show the signs of being elected. Yet at the same time Calvin suggests
that believers can be sure of their election: There are clear signs that a
person can form knowledge of his election:

> Therefore, as those are in error who make the power of election depen-
> dent on the faith by which we perceive that we are elected, so we shall
> follow the best order, if, in seeking the certainty of our election, we
> cleave to those posterior signs which are *sure attestations* to it.[16]

Calvin continually sets up a sort of palimpsest that enforces the need of security, and assures its attainability, yet immediately after he defers describing this attainability. "A certain and secure knowledge" turns out to consist,
at least partly, of doubt, enforced by the assertion that the reprobate can
possess almost the same knowledge, yet the assuring foundation is absent
from this almost-similar knowledge. Similarly, the signs that are "sure attes-
tations" to election are differentiated from forms of knowledge that linked
the human "depraved desire of inquiring after it out of the proper way":

> By inquiring out of the proper way, I mean when puny man endeavors
> to penetrate to the hidden recesses of the divine wisdom, and goes back
> even to the remotest eternity, in order that he may understand what

final determination God has made with regard to him. In this way he plunges headlong into an immense abyss.[17]

So the security offered in Christ oscillates between being capable of being expressed in "posterior signs," and the undermining of their value because their ground lies beyond human grasp. It is this apparent incongruity that created division among the inheritors and commentators of Calvin's theology. On the one hand election lies to an important extent out of reach for the believer, and as such the believer has a more passive position with regards to faith. Yet on the other hand Calvin indicates that there are clear signs that the believer is elected, opening up to a worldly morality in which he or she can base a firm knowledge of election. The first position characterizes Kendall and will be discussed in the next paragraph; the second position is defended by Helm and will be discussed in the third paragraph.

Kendall: Westminster Calvinism?

In his *Calvin and English Calvinism to 1649* (1979), Robert Tillman Kendall makes a bold claim: the descriptive uncertainty in Calvin's concept of faith was molded into forms of voluntarism that Reformed orthodoxy and Puritanism took on,[18] and as such Beza and the strands of thought he inspired departed from Calvin to such a degree that they "hardly deserve to be called Calvinistic."[19] It is because Calvin did not pay enough attention to the dimension of insecurity in his conception of faith that, soon after his death, Beza would reformulate the notion in the direction of a clearer, reassuring description of the signs of faith.

From Beza onward, Kendall states, Calvinist theology was modified on two important points. First, the universal atonement of Calvin was changed into limited atonement in Beza. As a result of Christ dying only for the elect, atonement became a process that was reserved for said elect. As a result, the second important change in Calvin's theology followed logically: Faith becomes the result of the experience of union with Christ. According to Kendall, the result was that these later strands of Calvinism could focus more on the signs of being elected, thus generating an attitude toward knowledge about election that comes close to voluntarism.

In basing themselves on Calvin's theology, with such central notions as predestination and election of true believers, such Westminster theologians and Puritans as Perkins and Ames actually based themselves on the adaptation that Beza made to Calvin's thinking: "Perkins's main problem apparently was that he could not see that Calvin and Beza were not alike. He may have assumed that Beza was but an extension of Calvin, and that Beza merely stated Calvin's theology better."[20] As a result, the theology of the Westminster Confession was based more on Beza than it was on Calvin: "The architectural mind of Westminster theology, however, is Beza's."[21] The result is faith following assurance, whereas Calvin consistently maintained the hiddenness. The result of this is an inward turn, wherein "it is only the persevering believer after all who can be certainly said to be elected."[22]

For Kendall, the comfort in Calvin lies beyond language, or beyond proof; Calvin fails to give a further description of what faith is and how it can be differentiated from temporary faith:

> Therefore if we want to know we are in the number of the elect, we
> must be *persuaded* that Christ died for us. We know this by a direct act
> of faith. This is why Calvin can affirm: "If Pighius asks how I know I am
> elect, I answer that Christ is more than a thousand testimonies to me."[23]

The image of faith that Kendall sketches consists largely of discouraging the believer from grounding the notion of faith in all too easy definitions. As to what the comforting notion is, Calvin necessarily points to that which lies beyond his capability to express. The result of this problematic unclear notion, for in Kendall's image it is a serious blank spot in Calvin's theology, is that it became possible, perhaps even necessary, for future theologians to fill in this blank spot with the notion of limited atonement, and with a more reassuring definition of faith. "While Calvin's doctrine of sanctification can be seen as thankfulness, Westminster theology lends itself to making sanctification the payment for the promise of salvation."[24] Whereas Calvin would use notions that emphasize passivity, reception, and process, all rolled into his notion of knowledge, the Westminster Confession uses more active terms:

> Instead Westminster theology manages consistently to use voluntaris-
> tic words: accepting, receiving, assenting, resting, yielding, answering
> and embracing. There is no hint of man's will being effaced; it is rather
> renewed.[25]

Kendall states that this process came with a price: "But such insurance to protect the Church from Antinomianism and to preserve godliness costs, the cost that Calvin warned against—endless introspection, the constant checking of the spiritual pulse for the right "effects," and, possibly, legalism."[26] The price that was paid then, for filling in the blank spot of faith in

Calvin with terms like "assenting," "answering," and "embracing" was that faith became an "endless" introspective testing of signs. Between the lines, we can see a critique forming that sees Reformed orthodoxy as facilitating a rigid and moralistic form of piety that lacked the universal, but ambivalent, open-ended assurance that Calvin's theology contained.

What I have focused on here is the image of comfort in Calvin that Kendall proposes. I will briefly discuss Helm's book, *Calvin and the Calvinists*, largely written as a reaction to Kendall's *Calvin and English Calvinism to 1649*, from the same perspective. I will briefly discuss Helm's position before I go on to the figure of comfort that Helm sees in Calvin.

Helm: Continuation and Comfort

So, in Kendall's reasoning, there are two pillars of the image where the followers of Calvin departed from Calvin's theology: (1) From a doctrine of universal atonement, which Calvin allegedly taught, Beza, Perkins, and the Westminster Confession of faith transformed this doctrine into a doctrine of limited atonement. Christ died for the elect only. (2) Calvin defended a notion of faith that focused on passivity, on doubt, and on an extralingual affirmation, and in the work of the inheritors of Calvin's theology, according to Kendall, this view was transformed into a view on faith that amounts basically to voluntarism, where faith can be "proven" through an investigation of the signs of assurance. In this way Calvin's followers separated assurance and faith, whereas, again according to Kendall, for Calvin faith and assurance are in fact one. Now these two boundaries that separate Calvin from his followers, namely limited versus universal atonement and passive versus voluntaristic faith, are according to Paul Helm based on a gross misunderstanding. Although Helm recognizes the "seriousness of the charge that Kendall levels against Puritanism," Helm is of the opinion that Kendall is wrong on basically all counts.[27]

The charge is that the Westminster Confession uses legalistic terms to such a degree that Westminster theology comes close to voluntarism: In the Westminster Confession, Kendall argued, good works are indeed referred to as meritorious and as preceding faith. But Helm counters with the argument that this would mean an unwarranted departure from Calvin's theology as follows: "The Westminster divines were quite prepared to follow the apostle John and to say that *knowledge* of justification, and assurance of salvation, are grounded in works."[28] Here Helm cites the Westminster Confession:

> These good works, done in obedience to God's commandments, are
> the fruits and evidence of a true and lively faith: and by them believers
> manifest their thankfulness, strengthen their assurance

Helm continues by stating: "But these good works are not in any way meritorious. The question of merit does not arise. They are the visible evidence
of the regenerating work of the Holy Spirit at work in the hearts and lives
of men."[29] Helm argues that even though the word "evidence" is used, even
though the descriptions of works comes close to seeing them as meritorious, this position is actually incorrect: The Puritans revert straight back to
the source of any meritorious affirmation of works: Christ. Helm says: "[I]t
is quite false to suggest that the Puritans taught salvation by human merit,
to suggest that they almost did so, or that they should have done so. They
were perfectly aware of the danger of such views, and their over-all position was thoroughly clear and consistent."[30] In this "clear and consistent"
position, Helm argues again and again, that the Puritan strand of thought
is actually a continuation of Calvin's thought.

For Calvin, according to Helm, even though he goes to great trouble to
keep faith from being a logical or work-based exercise, does nonetheless
allow affirmative knowledge of faith:

> There are *signs* of true, as opposed to false and temporary faith, "signs
> which are sure attestations" of it. The signs that Calvin mentions
> include divine calling, illumination by Christ's Spirit, communion with
> Christ, receiving Christ by faith, the embracing of Christ, perseverance
> in the faith, the avoidance of self-confidence, and fear.[31]

The confusion is caused, according to Helm, by the "ground of assurance";
of course, Calvin like all reformers made it clear that "a person's salvation is due solely to the work of Christ," but "he is equally emphatic that
the evidence of personal salvation is found in a person's own spiritual and
moral renovation."[32] Calvin then expresses that even though faith is not
the believer's to acquire, it can nonetheless be experienced that one is able
to have faith: "While the believer has not to trust in himself for salvation—this would be salvation by human merit—nevertheless he may find
in himself evidence that he has trusted in Christ for salvation."[33] As Helm
states, "It was monstrous to teach that such assurance was impossible. But
he recognized that saving faith is often accompanied by periods of doubt
which eclipse assurance, and that even assured faith is never totally free
from doubt."[34] If Calvin's position is viewed from this perspective, many
of the differences between the Puritan teachings and Calvin's own writ-

ings disappear. The Puritan theology states, according to Helm, that even though there might be doubt, there is a form of assurance that can be experienced and communicated. And inversely, though there is a form of assurance that can be experienced, this does not mean that there will not be any doubt. This position, says Helm, is inherently Calvin's. Calvin's and the Westminster Confession's are "virtually the same voice":

> Once it is allowed that assent is an act of the intellect by means of which the truth of certain statements is acknowledged, then it becomes clear that Calvin and the *Confession* speak with virtually the same voice.[35]

What Helm does not answer, though, is why the Puritans used expressions such as "good works" and "the evidence" that they are of "true and lively faith," when Calvin expressly and almost consistently refuses to use these terms. What is it in the language of the Puritans, and of Beza, that enabled this renewed affirmative language? It seems that to be able to prove that the Puritans and Beza in fact were not setting up a voluntarist notion of faith, the scholastic charge of their language needs to be investigated along the axis of the doctrinal content of the language. If "evidence" does not in fact mean "evidence," why is the word, with its forensic connotations, used?

For it is interesting to note that Paul Helm, throughout his refutation of any gap between Calvin and the Calvinists, keeps giving examples that are at the same time convincing examples of how there is a deeper continuation between Calvin and for instance the Reformed orthodoxy, and of a profound linguistic difference between Calvin and other theologians. For even when the doctrinal difference might not be as clear and decisive as Kendall might have argued, for Helm launches quite an effective critique of Kendall, the change between Calvin's thinking and Reformed orthodoxy could still be thought of as a linguistic change.[36] For Helm's argument could be read as stating the following: Even though Beza, Perkins, and the Westminster Confession sometimes use linguistic categories that would *seem* to lead to legalistic or voluntaristic roads; in fact, at the center of their theology lies the unfathomable work of faith that rests entirely in the hands of Christ. Even though Kendall and Helm fully disagree on the accessibility of this faith, they both affirm the centrality of the affirmative dimension of the Calvinist theology. This affirmative dimension has, for both Helm and Kendall, a certain unspeakable dimension: Helm also affirms that even though election can be ascertained through signs, this knowledge is not the knowledge that can be proved or easily arrogated. The "evidence" of which the Westminster Confession speaks is in fact an indirect evidence whose source lies in the mysterious communion with Christ. Just as in Calvin the words "firm and sure" are framed by a deeper sense of insecurity, words like "evidence" in the Westminster Confession function in the same way: In both strands we see the importance of affirmation as a limit concept that we should trust, while the parameters for this trust continue to lie wholly in the hands of Christ. What Helm is arguing is in fact that Calvin and the Westminster Confession both grapple with the same problem: expressing the assurance of faith. Helm affirms that the terminology might be different, and hence he opens up, yet does not explore, the singular voices at play in both documents.

Therefore, and I propose here a thought that I cannot fully develop, would it not be possible to write the history of the passage from Calvin to the Calvinists as a passage of subsurface-current of assurance, passing from one voice to the next? If the structure of Calvin's language, as Kendall argues, can merely point to the limits of its own description when characterizing faith, and if the Puritans, as Helm argues, equally use limit concepts that point to the descriptive limits of assurance, albeit in different terminology, would it not become an interesting question to see how the passage between these different voices can be mapped? The absent center of Reformed textuality is what is at stake here. To write theology, as both Helm and Kendall stress, albeit each in their own way, means to create, to embody these limit concepts with firm and sure knowledge while guarding against unwarranted solidification. If this hunch is correct, it would become possible to study the modalities of this absent center; to what extent is the language capable of sustaining this tension? And to what extent does a language close back upon itself?[37] Such a study would be interesting from the viewpoint of the stereotype of rigid Puritan thought.[38] It would also be beneficial to study fundamentalist forms of political agency derived from Calvinism.

Let us conclude by reflecting a little further on this notion of the limit concept. What could it mean for an interpretation of Calvin to see the word faith as such a limit concept? What could this absent center be if it stands, to a certain degree, apart from, or passes underneath, doctrinal definitions?

Doubt and Assurance: Thoreau

Should it be objected, that believers have no stronger testimony to assure them of their adoption, I answer, that though there is a great resemblance and affinity between the elect of God and those who are impressed for a time with a fading faith, yet the elect alone have that full assurance which is extolled by Paul, and by which they are enabled to cry Abba, Father.[39]

As we have seen, for Calvin there exists a believer who is not part of the elect yet nonetheless not only displays the signs of being elected but also believes in his or her election. The elect are set apart from this group of simulacric believers by "full assurance" that enables them to cry "Abba, Father." Now, since the simulacric believer is also, in any case physically, capable of crying "Father," the true, fully assured crying must be of a different nature.

It is in Henry David Thoreau's *Walden* that a reflection is at stake that is remarkably similar to Calvin. For *Walden* centers not so much around whether one should live, as Thoreau did, for a while next to Walden Pond, but about the status of its own textuality as such. It is this self-reflexive element in Thoreau's *Walden* that Stanley Cavell underlines in his *The Senses of Walden*:

> I assume that however else one understands Thoreau's topics and projects it is as a writer that he is finally to be known. But the easier that has become to accept, the more difficult it becomes to understand why his words about writing in *Walden* are not (so far as I know) systematically used in making out what kind of book he had undertaken to write, and achieved.[40]

Cavell suggested reading Thoreau's book as a book that is fully conscious about its own language, "it means every word it says, and (. . .) it is fully sensible of its mysteries and fully open about them."[41] Viewed from this perspective, it becomes obvious how certain apparent incongruities in *Walden* become clear. For in spite of all the praise for living in solitude in nature, one can say that Thoreau's book is not about nature. The narrator in *Walden* is advocating the benefits of living in "splendid isolation," but when we take a closer look it is not necessarily the isolation in nature that makes the project of *Walden* splendid. The isolation that Thoreau seeks is not as radical as one is at first tempted to believe: In the chapter "Visitors" it becomes apparent that there is not only a village at a short distance, but that Thoreau often receives visitors. At multiple moments in the book, when images of isolation are conjured up, they are more often than not interrupted by the sound of church bells, trains, or the bustle of the nearby village.

When one reads *Walden*, at the suggestion of Cavell, as a book that attempts to communicate its own foundational gesture, and the foundationality of writing as such, we can see that the value of his stay at Walden Pond lies not in Walden Pond, nor in the purity of his isolation. The purity of his isolation is undermined by the constant proximity of civilization. Similarly, the act of living in isolation is without doctrinal value:

> One young man of my acquaintance, who has inherited some acres,
> told me that he thought he should live as I did, if he had the means. I
> would not have any one adopt my mode of living on any account; for,
> beside that before he has fairly learned it I may have found out another
> for myself, I desire that there may be as many different persons in the
> world as possible; but I would have each one be very careful to find
> out and pursue his own way, and not his father's or his mother's or his
> neighbor's instead.[42]

Thoreau emphasizes that a follower of his should not so much copy his exact style of life but should "pursue his own way," clearly steering away from any thoughts the reader might have of copying the direct style that Thoreau elsewhere in the book so clearly advocates. The aim of the project, the goal, it becomes clear, is then to communicate just one of the ways in which one can pursue one's own way. At the end of the book, Thoreau muses over the value of his work: Even though, through "an infirmity of our natures," we are "for the most part not where we are, but in a false position."[43] The challenge is not to think that there is a mode of living that is superior to the other but that in each form of life there lies a reflection about the way things are that can offer an affirmation: "However mean your life is, meet it and live it; do not shun it and call it hard names. It is not so bad as you are."[44] Even though we cannot control how we live, when reflected upon it in the right way, there is solidity that can be found: "So will help you God, and so only. Every nail driven should be as another rivet in the machine of the universe, you carrying on the work."[45] And, even more concisely: "There is a solid bottom everywhere."[46] The book *Walden* in its entirety then can be read as an attempt to bring this solidity under words, for as far as this can be done.

> Books must be read as deliberately and reservedly as they were written.
> It is not enough even to be able to speak the language of that nation by
> which they are written, for there is a memorable interval between the
> spoken and the written language, the language heard and the language
> read. The one is commonly transitory, a sound, a tongue, a dialect
> merely, almost brutish, and we learn it unconsciously, like the brutes,
> of our mothers. The other is the maturity and experience of that; if that
> is our mother tongue, this is our father tongue, a reserved and select

expression, too significant to be heard by the ear, which we must be born again in order to speak.[47]

The book *Walden* then, is, departing from the mother tongue, pointing to the existence of a father tongue, a language that is exactly the same as the mother tongue, except for that it is "the maturity and the experience" of the normal situation in which people speak, live, and read. For this language, "we must be reborn again in order to speak."

It is the existence and effectivity of this "father tongue" that *Walden* is about: it is the "father tongue" that is connected to the written text, to scripture, to the founding knowledge that places both the negativity of everyday life, "we are for the most part in a false position" as well as the "solid bottom" that can underlie this existence, in a right experiential framework for those who "are reborn."

Now it is this notion of the "father tongue" that charges the "mother tongue" with religious affirmation, with which we can return to the problematic of the textual center, as we have seen in John Calvin. For just as in *Walden* the idea is not so much to offer a doctrinal assurance, a manual for living, but to point to that which contains both insecurity on the level of the mother tongue and security on the level of the father tongue, the problematic for Calvin consists of explaining affirmation that lies beyond the hands that write. We were left with the question of what the difference could be between those that merely convince themselves that they are saved, and that show all the signs of being part of the elect, and those that are truly saved. Calvin says that it is only with the "full" assurance of the truly elected that one can cry out "Abba, Father." The charge with which this "Abba" has to be powered, which distinguishes it from its simulacrum, cannot be expressed in the "mother tongue"; it can only be hinted at.

Whereas in the discussion between Helm and Kendall the doctrinal elements remained central, the idea of a linguistic charge that dominates the doctrinal categories in both Calvin and his successor can turn the question not to whether Calvin taught universal or limited atonement, but to a question about assurance as a literary limit-concept. Just as Thoreau's project started from his framework (society, isolation, Walden Pond), and moved to the underlying notion of affirmation, characterized by the "father tongue," we can see Calvin's use of the word "faith" as a process whose affirmation can only be understood from a sort of arrogation of affirmation. Similarly, for the Westminster Confession, it becomes not so much a question to decry the use of words like "evidence" as a deviation from Calvin's theology, but as a different form to arrogate an affirmation, which ultimately lies at the limits of what can be expressed. Both Helm and Kendall, in spite of all their differences, employ an implicit notion of Reformed textuality that emphasizes an absent center. Their differences can be viewed from a more productive viewpoint if the discussion could be geared toward the modalities of interacting with this absent center. It could very well be that to demonstrate that Calvin and the later Calvinists have a form of continuation, this voice has to be taken into account: How does the use of the word "evidence" in the specific literary voice of the Westminster Confession relate to the arrogation of the "ground" of faith that lies at the center of Calvin's voice?

However, new problems arise. Just as Thoreau was forced to write from his example, and encouraged his followers to find their own voice, one can wonder whether it is actually possible to set an example that separates itself sufficiently from the simulacrum: Does Calvin's father tongue succeed enough in keeping at bay a solidification of a center? Is it thinkable, within Calvin's parameters, that, just as with the temporary faith of the reprobate, there is a theology that resembles faith but is in fact a simulacrum? It is a question that would entail more space than is available here, but perhaps it is a new starting point; instead of claiming doctrines, to gauge theology's resistance to the solidifying of assurance.

CHAPTER 8

The Past and History in Ordinary Language Philosophy

Asja Szafraniec

An attempt to address temporality from the point of view of ordinary language philosophy may appear to be self-defeating—so elusive is the topic in the work of its major exponents, Ludwig Wittgenstein, J. L. Austin, and Stanley Cavell. This elusiveness fosters the idea that ordinary language philosophy is generally hostile to historical approaches. For example, when addressing Cavell's attitude to the history of philosophy, Richard Fleming attributes to Cavell treating the latter "as that which is in tension with the ordinary," and treating "the history of philosophy as a flight from the ordinary."[1] At the same time, Fleming hints at his sense that there are motifs in Cavell's work that are in tension with such characterization (or at least with a too straightforward reading of it). The latter is also my conviction. While Fleming is right that an attitude to time and history is somehow defining for the concept of the ordinary, this attitude goes beyond a simple rejection or exclusion and must hence be more complex than it at first sight appears. In fact, Cavell himself tangentially indicated as much by questioning the alleged a-historicity of Wittgenstein. In a forthcoming article[2] I have already drawn attention to the moment in *The Claim of Reason*, where after considering the objection, that "the call upon history [introduced by Cavell into his own interpretation of Wittgenstein—A. S.] might seem uncongenial with Wittgenstein [who] seems so a-historical," Cavell replies: "He is a-historical the way Nietzsche is a-theistical," and adds parenthetically: "call these desires for awakening."[3] He suggests here that the respective rejection of history and God by Wittgenstein and Nietzsche is not a wholesale rejection in favor of some kind of static or secularized way of thinking. Rather, it is a strategy, *a way* of choosing a particular stance so as to combat the possibility of being misunderstood.[4]

The strategy of putting into question or avoiding the notions of history or God reflects those thinkers' conviction that the strange pull exercised by history ("the before") and transcendence ("the beyond") distracts us from the present of our ordinary lives. Cavell characterizes an important aspect of Wittgenstein's work as a "theory of the origin of the metaphysical, of the human restlessness in the ordinary and *its attraction to the beyond, not to mention the before* (. . .)."[5] This aspect of Wittgenstein's work expresses his sense of the proneness of human nature to perpetuate what Cavell refers to as "the dream"—a fixation within a received and unexamined perspective, whether narrative, conceptual, psychological, perceptual, or a mix of those, that functions as an excuse for not attending to the real (and no less spiritual for that—the ordinary must not be confused with the brutish or the matter-of-factly) needs of the present. In the case of Wittgenstein and Nietzsche this fixation is exemplified by the approaches to history and God that are subservient to a particular conceptualization of these notions, a conceptualization out of touch with ourselves as human subjects and the world in which we are embedded. When facing the problems of such fixation, Cavell suggests, it is preferable to appear a-historical or a-theistical, the way Wittgenstein and Nietzsche respectively do.[6] This indicates that the attitude to time in the ordinary language philosophy is more complex than is usually assumed. The accusation that we might be tempted to direct at the ordinary language philosophy—that it is indifferent to history and that it therefore privileges some timeless and static present—is perhaps unjust. It is even strangely similar to what Cavell says this philosophy turns against: the state of mental fixation. The well-known goal of the ordinary language philosophy, described often as the undoing of this state of fixation, is in fact an effort to make us receptive to another sense of the present, to reveal to us the sense of its unexpected depth that makes escapes into "the beyond" and "the before" unnecessary. But to say this is to get ahead of my argument.

Even though Cavell says that "the idea of pastness threads through [his] books," it is certainly not immediately obvious that an attitude to time is a defining feature of his work. It assumes the form of few, scattered, and often tangential remarks that are likely to escape the reader's attention. For this reason I'll begin by gathering three significant instances. In response to Ricoeur's address "The Eclipse of Event in Modern French Historiography,"[7] Cavell defended his own notion of a historical event (distinct both from Ricoeur's position and from that of the historians of the *Annales* School) as requiring a community of speakers who treat it as such.[8] Some years later, Cavell addressed Derrida's attitude to history of philosophy by insisting that this attitude marks a "sublime difference" between his own thought and Derrida's: "The difference may be read in that strain or moment of philosophizing when philosophy does not recognize itself as having a history."[9] These two remarks already introduce a certain amount of tension, by juxtaposing on the one hand Cavell's (qualified) acceptance of the notion of a historical event (qualified, because in the last instance, Cavell will insist that the ordinary is "uneventful") and on the other his reservations with respect to the notion of history (be it with respect to philosophy). Some light can be thrown on the above by looking at Cavell's earlier *The World Viewed*, in which he addressed some of those issues head on, stating: "I speak of 'a world past,' and the idea of pastness threads through my books, as does the idea of presentness and of futurity. But I do not say that this is *the* past, that it is history. I do say that in viewing a movie I am 'present . . . at something that has happened.'"[10] While I'd for the moment suspend the question of the meaning of "being present at something that has happened" (different with respect to film, theater, and the past), the latter statement presents most clearly Cavell's suspicion of an essentialist aspect in the notion of history: history as an independent space of sequenced events to be consulted at will (referred to by Cavell as "*the* past" or "narrative history").[11]

At first sight those statements make an impression that Cavell aims at a debunking of the myth of history: There are events, to be sure, but their being perceived as such is dependent on the ordinary as the uneventful that shapes our agreements in the light of which we are able to call something an event in the first place. The sense of Cavell's a-historical position is only made stronger if we realize that if historical events are dependent for their existence on a community of speakers, then once the community is dead (or even merely diverted or disinterested), so is the event. It is for this reason that Cavell says that philosophy does not have a history—that it cannot, for example, be seen as a history of ideas. At the same time, any dehistoricizing stance must become a problem in the context of ordinary language philosophy: Calling something "history" is, after all, part of our ordinary language, another word we have to address our past. History in this sense is not a "sublimed notion" (to speak with Wittgenstein), but an integral part of our form of life. A rejection of the word in the name of its fairly academic and technical usage must be seen, at worst, as a departure from the procedure of the ordinary he himself advocates, and at best, as a defiant invitation to the readers to share the sense of the meaning of the word with Cavell, to see it in a different way. We cannot hence but see Cavell as just as a-historical as he depicts Wittgenstein to be—of having a way of being a-historical.

It is equally difficult to answer in a straightforward manner the question of whether this attitude to history leaves room for a sense of the past. In the strong sense of Cavell's rejection of history, philosophy exists only in its practice, in the current discourse of its current community; whatever philosophy fails to preserve in its practice, it fails *tout court* by failing to acknowledge it, hence relegating it to silence. (This is how we can read Cavell's attitude to the past in his early essay on Beckett: The past is seen there as a flood of meaning that must be absorbed in the present. The extent to which we relegate it to silence, by failing to absorb it, is exactly the extent to which we silence ourselves.[12]) On this reading, our sense of the past must be illusionary, for "the time is always now."[13] Cavell likes to quote Thoreau on this subject: "When that ancient Egyptian or Hindoo philosopher first lifted the veil from the Goddess, it was me in him . . . And it is him in me now that reviews the vision."[14] Generally, Cavell's heroes of thought (not only Thoreau but also Emerson) have in common that as Cavell himself puts it, in their work "narrative history is under inces-sant attack": "When a thought of Plato becomes a thought to me—when a truth that fired the soul of Pindar fires mine, time is no more."[15] In its weaker sense, Cavell allows more explicitly room for the past as a succes-sion of events. He merely casts into doubt whether "there is such a one thing as a history of philosophy rather than a succession of responses that, as Thoreau pictures things (. . .) disperses the veils called, among other things, history."[16] In the latter sense, the past or what has happened is not necessarily history, though: It may be myth, or a dream or a film; and for Cavell its being one of these does not make it any less important; after all, the coordinates we seek bear on our own life, not on some independently existing system of reference. In our present, we are inheriting (or refusing to inherit) something that has been, but not so much in a historical sense as in a mythical sense, or in the sense of a collective unconscious. Cavell's attitude to the past oscillates between these two senses. This ambiguity of attitude (not only with respect to history or the past but also with respect to skepticism) has to do with the fact that Cavell, rather than in straightforward rejection or acceptance of the phenomena he studies, is interested in tracing the true extent to which rejection and acceptance variously penetrate our lives.

History and Theater

This analysis does not yet address the stakes of this attitude to history and does not yet make clear in what way this problem is interwoven with the core of Cavell's philosophical project; to wit, his preoccupation with the problems of skepticism. I am turning to it now. In order to fully appreciate the centrality of Cavell's attitude to time to his overall project we must pay attention to his statement in "The Avoidance of Love": "This is what a historian has to face in knowing the past: the epistemology of other minds is the same as the metaphysics of other times and places."[17] Cavell's saying this is equivalent to admitting that a certain attitude to temporality goes hand in hand with his focal investigation of other mind skepticism. But what, then, is the analogy between the historian and the epistemologist, between envisioning ourselves as spectators of our past and the attempt to penetrate the privacy of another mind? Their common fault, Cavell suggests, is the result of our "all but inescapable temptation to think (. . .) in terms of theater";[18] i.e., to our temptation of either behaving like spectators or like having spectators. Cavell's love for theater was constantly accompanied by incessant critical preoccupation with theatricality in human lives (often addressed by means of concern with what Cavell calls turning the human into stone, analogous to Sartre's concept of "reification"), exploring the necessity and the ways to resist it. When in *The World Viewed* Cavell writes that "like religion, art had to learn to defeat theater,"[19] the necessity he speaks of can also be projected on historiography. What Cavell glosses as "thinking in terms of theater" is in fact a whole complex of attitudes based on one presupposition: that we have available to us *a point of view* from which to assess respectively the past event or the state of the mind of an other—analogously to the way we assess natural phenomena (Wittgenstein would say ostensively; Cavell prefers the notion of "ocular proof"). To presuppose such a "natural" point of view is to fail to understand the requirements of the particular situation the historian and the epistemologist are in. Cavell: "[F]rom what position are we imagining that we can see it? [i.e., the past or the soul of another] One there or one here?" "There is no *place* from which we can see the past."[20] This already points in the direction of the deeper reason for Cavell to dehistoricize the past. He is of the opinion that our attempt to envisage ourselves as the spectators of past events forces on us the assumption of a type of vantage point that precludes any access to those events. The alternative, nontheatrical type of vantage point, that would permit such access, would have to be constructed in terms of the conditions not of verifiability but of judgment, hence not in terms of theater or spectatorship but of reflection on the reach of our concepts. Most of the time, this reach is determined indirectly, by means of the conceptual coordinates we ourselves are prepared to assign to situations we encounter in our everyday lives. Once we realize the importance of each time "uneventfully" doing so in our conversations with others we can begin to reflect on the way past events or other humans appear to us through the prism of the ordinary. They are given to us through this prism or not at all, and always with our subjective participation—so that we, as subjects have influence, without being aware of it, on the way they will be given to us. As such, it can be defined only indirectly, by discovering the conceptual coordinates we ourselves are prepared to assign to other positions in speaking about them with others; i.e., in judging them. It is here that the radicality of ordinary language philosophy announces itself once more: by insistence on the primordiality of those casual judgments; by taking seriously Heidegger's claim about the fundamental status of the world of casual conversation, *Gerede*. (It often needs reminding that Heidegger does not treat *Gerede*, or "idle talk," as a disparaging term. And the formulations in the paragraph on *Gerede* are strikingly close to the spirit of ordinary language philosophy. Compare, for example, "The way things have been expressed or spoken out is such that in the totality of contexts of signification into which it has been articulated, it preserves an understanding of the disclosed world [. . .]. In language, as a way things have been expressed or spoken out, there is hidden a way in which the understanding of Dasein has been interpreted."[21]) It is because of this fundamental status of what we take something to be, of what we are inclined to say about it, that from Cavell's point of view, any kind of pure self-reflection, or a solipsistic examination of our inner self before we pass on to the assessment of other minds or other times would be quite misplaced. On the contrary, Cavell insists that we not only owe it to both (others and past events) to make their present "theirs," but that it is a requirement for gaining any determinate sense of our own present. But making their present "theirs," again must not be conceived in terms of spectatorship. Where the past or the state of mind of a human other is concerned, the relevant aspect of our position cannot be defined in any directly spatio-temporal terms. "[O]ur position" is something that must be "discovered," "pieced out"—hence must be constructed by adding or patching the implications of our casual acts of judging (it is not of a piece, harmonious, consistent) and this process of discovery demands of us that we abandon the position of a spectator, or as Cavell provocatively puts it, that we "repudiate our perception altogether."[22] The central requirement of Cavell's thought is thereby that we cease to seek a spatio-temporal point as a condition of verification. This does not mean that to find our position, our vantage point on Cavell's terms we must eliminate time, but that we must revise the role we assign to it.

(This contestation of theatricality in all its aspects must affect not only the perception of the past but also that of the future. Should we want to address any kind of messianism in Cavell's thought, it will have to be seen as directed at the present rather than at the future [it seems to me that it cannot, for example, express itself in posture of waiting]. As Russell B. Goodman plausibly argued, analogously to Wittgenstein, who distinguished two sorts of eternity, the eternity of infinite temporal duration and the eternity as "living in the present" ["If we take eternity to mean not infinite temporal duration but timelessness, then eternal life belongs to those who live in the present"[23]], Cavell distinguishes two sorts of the future. While we generally tend to conceive the future as that which comes later, as the future successive, Cavell approaches it instead as an altered relation to the present. The "new yet unapproachable America" in the title of one of Cavell's books is "new because it has never happened before," but "unapproachable" not because it is endlessly deferred but "because we are already there."[24])

The same framework of thought, projected on the American thought, is also the deeper reason for Cavell's saying that "no American philosopher plays off history."[25] Instead, he says, "philosophy approaches me, like a conversion" (ibid.). This suggests that the correct attitude to the past is in a sense not an (active) attitude at all and certainly not an unmediated attitude. The past only makes its claim upon us in the guise of an experience akin to the phenomenon of the Proustian involuntary memory, set into motion by our engaging in, and attending to, present and shared forms of human interaction. The past is only real to the extent that it reveals itself in our present, and the only proper way to attend to the historical past is to absorb it in an orphic mode, with our back turned, without looking. The sustained attention to the present is the absolute precondition of any archaeology of the past: "[T]he time is always now."[26] Cavell likes to return in this context to the famous quote from Wittgenstein's *Philosophical Investigations*, "[I]f a lion could talk, we could not understand him,"[27] implying that any ability we may have to understand the events of the past depends on the shared forms of life or on the extent to which we find them share-able. Failing this the past must recede into silence.

Wittgenstein and the Grammatical Present

Cavell's critique of theatricality forms the background of his radical at-titude to the past. To what extent does this critique have its roots in Witt-genstein's thought?[28] To answer this question it is useful to begin with Wittgenstein's passage in the *Philosophical Investigations*, where the latter also writes about the misconception of our attitude to other times and other minds: "[W]e feel as if we had to *penetrate* phenomena."[29] (Cavell himself prefers to speak of the desire to grasp phenomena, as a result of which they "slip through our fingers then when we clutch hardest."[30]) It is this assumption that we must penetrate or grasp phenomena that forces us inevitably to recognize that, should we fail to have a vantage point from which to assess them, those phenomena must prove immeasurable, leav-ing us no other option but skepticism.[31] As a result, our examination of a past moment must lead to the skeptical conclusion that whatever we think happened perhaps had no place at all. The past, just like the soul of an-other, withdraws when we try to approach them under their presumed phenomenal aspect. While the tendency to do so is an ineradicable part of our humanity, in his readings of Shakespeare's tragedies Cavell repeatedly examined the outcomes of the fixation on this way of approach. Those analyses repeatedly point to another aspect that is not seen, even though it is "in plain view."[32] What is this other aspect?

An important characteristic of gestalt switch examined by Wittgenstein in the major section of the second part of the *Philosophical Investigations* (ad-dressed often by him as "seeing aspects") is that we cannot see both aspects simultaneously—that a fixation on one aspect prevents us from seeing an-other. That switch, I take Cavell to suggest, operates on aspects belonging to the same cognitive level but also on aspects belonging to different levels (e.g., the phenomenal and the transcendental). This is what I take him to mean when he says that in the whole field covered by the "duck-rabbit" he chooses to focus on one specific problem: "a *categorical* difference between different objects of sight."[33] We have, then (or in any case can cultivate), the possibility of switching between the phenomenal (sensory, verificationist) inflection of our minds—the desire to grasp or penetrate—and an inflec-tion of "the ordinary." If this is the case, the aspect of visibility that makes a phenomenon possible, will hide the non-phenomenal, grammatical aspect, in the case of other times and other minds precisely the one we are seeking to see. It is to foster our ability to see the latter aspect that Wittgenstein proposes to direct our investigation not at phenomena but "towards the possibilities of phenomena." He does so explicitly during the discussion of the notion of time.[34] Those possibilities of phenomena are themselves decidedly not of phenomenal but of grammatical (or logical—perhaps Cavell would even be inclined to use, in this particular sense the word "phenomenological"—) nature. The transcendental aspect is expressed in Wittgenstein's statement, that this investigation

> explores the nature of all things, it seeks to the bottom of things and is not meant to concern itself whether what actually happens is this or that.—It takes its rise, not from an interest in the facts of nature, nor from a need to grasp causal connections: but from an urge to understand the basis, or essence, of everything empirical. (. . .) We remind ourselves, that is to say, of the *kind of statement* that we make about phenomena.[35]

What we ordinarily say (the line along which the world meets our ideas of it) is the trustworthiest source for exploring the conditions of the understanding of those phenomena. Here the sensory perception we are accustomed to use as an instrument of verification, must be restrained. Instead, it is with our statements that we measure and assess our world: Our words are another (distinct from our senses) instrument of knowledge, assuring on a different level the matching between the world and our ideas of it.

Here we come to the core of what Cavell calls the "repudiation of perception": Unlike the physical phenomena (facts of nature, causal connections), the sincerity of the other and the reality of the past moment require a grammatical rather than a verificationist approach, an approach in terms of conditions rather than in terms of proofs. In preparing ourselves to pass a judgment, we will have to abstain from seeking an "ocular proof." In Cavell's reading of Shakespeare's *Othello*, the latter's pursuit of such proof obliterates the other aspect that is nevertheless in plain view. Instead, we will need to consult criteria that are available to us but which of themselves are not able to determine our judgment.

This particular conception of the opposition between perception and grammar explains why the doubt about an other occupies such an important place in Cavell's thought. Understanding it requires in itself an important shift in philosophical perspective. The examples of doubt on which Cavell's discussions are centered are all too often seen as "merely" contingent facts of human life (e.g., jealousy, an arguably philosophically marginal issue of psychological insecurity is seen as opposed to the realm of philosophical necessities). Instead, quite on the contrary, those questions of another's sincerity in love or pain should be seen as precisely the ones that reverse this pervasive philosophical order: They are not examples of mere facts but examples of situations in human lives that absolutely require engaging in the realm in which verification will not do and is not what is called for. We might call it the domain of the transcendental of grammar, or of criteria (the realm described by the question what we take something to be)—even if this in turn will need further qualification. This realm is by no means marginal: As Cavell puts it, skepticism about external objects is not inevitable. But skepticism about other minds and ability to "live it" is part of our human sanity.

It has been said about Wittgenstein's *Tractatus* that it displayed a "temporal solipsism"—in the sense that the matching between the world and our ideas of it (expressed in propositions) was assured by its verification in the present. As Jaakko Hintikka put it, in that work the "interface between language and reality lies entirely in the present"[36]—the present is the only point of verification. But in the *Philosophical Investigations*, this matching function seems to be performed primarily by the grammatical criteria: The function of verification is subordinated to the much more extensive function of appeal to grammar. As Wittgenstein puts it, "Asking whether and how a proposition can be verified is only a special form of the question 'How d'you mean?' The answer is a contribution to the grammar of the proposition."[37]

In context of the ongoing debates regarding the turning points in Wittgenstein's work we might ask to what extent the above signalizes a turning point between the *Tractatus* and the *Investigations*. Does the present disappear as the focal point of verification when we turn our interest to meaning? In his *Philosophical Remarks* (first post-Tractarian manuscript Wittgenstein gave to Russell in May 1930), Wittgenstein returns to his examination of the present.

> Our propositions are only verified by the present. So they must be so constructed that they can be verified by it. And so in some way they must be commensurable with the present; and they cannot be so *in spite of* their spatio-temporal nature; on the contrary this [spatio-temporal nature] must be related to their commensurability as the corporeality of a ruler is to its being extended—which is what enables it to measure. In this case, too, you cannot say: "A ruler does measure in spite of its corporeality; of course a ruler which only has length would be the Ideal, you might say the pure ruler." No, if a body has length, there can be no length without a body—and although I realize that in a certain sense

only the ruler's length measures, what I put in my pocket still remains the ruler, the body, and isn't the length.[38]

Wittgenstein is addressing here the question he formulated explicitly about a year later (in the so-called Big Typescript) of how temporality expresses itself grammatically.[39] By then he had already come to the conclusion that only as a "custodian of grammar" can philosophy "describe the essence of the world."[40] And his preliminary answer to this, still in the framework of the conditions of verification (a framework that will interest him less and less), is that in many of our sentences their present, the present of their verification does not have to be the moment to which they refer but may be the moment of their being uttered. He is saying, in effect, that the criterial reach of the sentence (its being extended, which is to say its ability to account for the world, to measure the world like a ruler) cannot do its work on its own: It must be incarnate at a certain fixed point in time (identical with the moment of its performance, of my saying, e.g., "I do"). So a momentaneous verification of an event still plays a role at this point of Wittgenstein's thought. But already in the *Brown Book* (the preliminary study for the *Investigations*) the problem of incarnation itself turns grammatical—this is to say that this last remnant of the measurable present as the condition of verification is itself put in question:

> If someone talked to me with a kindly play of facial expressions, is it necessary that in any short interval his face should have looked such that seeing in it under any other circumstances I should have called its expression distinctly kindly? And if not, does it mean that his "kindly play of expression" was interrupted by periods of inexpressiveness?—We certainly should not say this under the circumstances which I am assuming. (. . .) Just in this way we refer by the phrase "understanding a word" not necessarily to that which happens while we are saying or hearing it, but to the whole environment of the event of saying it.[41]

Here "the present" of verification becomes diffuse, is no longer in any way punctual: It becomes "the whole environment of the event" that expresses itself grammatically. It is "what we should say" that is the basis of judgment, not a phenomenon at any measurable point in time. The insistence on the grammatical perception of time is very well visible in Wittgenstein's remarks on Augustine in the *Philosophical Investigations*: "So, too, Augustine calls to mind the different statements that are made about the duration of events, about their being past, present or future (these are, of course, not *philosophical* statements about time, the past, the present and the future).

Our inquiry is therefore a grammatical one."[42] To hint at a possible answer to the question of continuity of Wittgenstein's thought posed above, we might say that the present remains its focal point, but while the *Tractatus* investigates it from the point of view of factual verification, the *Philosophical Investigations* addresses the transcendental aspect—the conditions of our understanding of time.

Time, Subjectivity, and Thoreau's Discovery of the Present

But "the whole environment of the event of saying it" still lacks in this discussion its central point. Without it, the grammar of what we ordinarily say must turn out to be insufficient. (This insufficiency is addressed by Cavell when he speaks of our "disappointment with the criteria.") The criteria are the criteria for something's being *so*, not for its *being* so. They do not assure the matching between language and reality without our subjective agreements. The idea of the "environment of the event" and the problem of deciding its limits and nature brings up the human subject as the ultimate responsible for their respective range and definition, hence the one who is responsible for the limits of the grammatical present. In this way the question of the grammatical present becomes the question of the subject as the measuring instrument of this present; the "me" that is not metaphysical, phenomenological, or psychological but grammatical (to the extent that it is not available but must be discovered, pieced out). This is the proper meaning of the grammatical present: as the articulation of my place within the grammar surrounding me. It is not enough that we are privately attuned to the present around us: We must (to speak with Cavell) "show the time"—publicly demonstrate our individual implication in grammar, our present. This publicness is very important for Cavell— the grammatical present is not something felt or available for introspection; it is publicly manifested. In *The Claim of Reason*, Cavell compares our public expressions to the turning of the hands of the clock and then considers a situation in which, while the clock is working properly, the hands, its "superficial characteristics," are gone—so that the clock is showing the right hour, so to speak, in private. This allegory of the private grammatical present is directed against the idea that this knowledge of our present (the knowledge equated by Cavell to our conscience[43]) does not have to be displayed, that we can keep our "sense of time" to ourselves. "Would a conscientious clock think of its hands as mere conveniences, essentially for others? Only if it thought of itself as essentially a thing for others."[44]

Cavell finds a paradigmatic instance of such grammatical present in Thoreau's *Walden*, the work of which he says that all of it is an "experiment [in] the discovery of the present."[45] This experiment is at the same time addressed by Cavell as Thoreau's (and ours, if we are prepared to accept its terms) "moulting season," the process of abandoning his "larval state," a "metamorphosis"[46]: It is clear that the experiment in the discovery of the present is nothing less than an experiment in transfiguration. It culminates in *Walden*'s closing parable about a man who defeats time by creating his own system of measurement or proportion: an "artist from Kouroo" is driven in his pursuit of perfection to make for himself a staff—an object uncannily resembling Wittgenstein's yardstick. The very process of making the staff turns out to defeat time, opening up a "new system" and "a world with full and fair proportions."

> There was an artist in the city of Kouroo who was disposed to strive after perfection. One day it came into his mind to make a staff. Having considered that in an imperfect work time does not enter, he said to himself, It shall be perfect in all respect, though I should do nothing else in my life. He proceeded instantly to the forest for wood (. . .). As he searched for and rejected stick after stick his friends gradually deserted him, for they grew old in their works and died, but he grew not older by a moment. (. . .) As he made no compromise with Time, Time kept out of his way. Before he had found a stock in all respectable, the city of Kouroo was a hoary ruin, and he sat on one of its mounds to peel the stick. Before he had given it the proper shape the dynasty of the Candahars was at an end, and with the point of the stick he wrote the name of the last of that race in the sand, and then resumed his work. By the time he had smoothed and polished the staff (. . .) Brahma had awoken and slumbered many times (. . .). When the finishing stroke was put to his work, it suddenly expanded before the eyes of the astonished artist into the fairest of all creations of Brahma. He had made a new system in making a staff, a world with full and fair proportions.[47]

Projecting this story on Thoreau's striving, we may say that it is a particular kind of presentness he is after. Cavell calls it a "presentness that admits eternity."[48] But what is the way of attaining it, and how does it relate to Thoreau's book? The discovery of the present, the parable suggests, takes place in the process of the production of the measuring instrument to gauge reality (called by Thoreau the "realometer"[49]). The parable says as much; but, more important, its very surface, its epidermis (i.e., the words in which Thoreau clothes himself in his transfiguration) is a demonstration of this, shows how it can be done. The parable speaks of notching but it is also itself notched; it is itself a measuring rod. Or rather, to be more precise, the words that Thoreau dons, his new skin, are notched—he has himself become a measuring rod, through the specificities (notching points) of his pen. It is not a "mere" question of style, however (although it is how a style may originate). To see that it is not we must take into account not only the concepts of measurement (notching, marking, cutting) but also of the double meaning of that which does the notching: the blade. It's not just a pen making marks on paper. It is the acuity of a pen articulating the world. (Cf. Cavell's explanations: "the sword is words"—they are "Thoreau's words as they sink" and they have "power to divide one through" [*Walden*, 17, 11, 12].) It is in this context that we should read the famous fragment of *Walden*:

> If you stand right fronting and face to face to a fact, you will see the sun glimmer on both its surfaces, as if it were a cimeter, and feel its sweet edge dividing you through the heart and marrow, and so you will happily conclude your mortal career.[50]

The transfiguration, the experiment in the discovery of the present is then one of shedding the words in which one was clothed (where the meeting of language and world is unquestioningly inherited, hence always approximate and provisional), and assuming the garment of words in which the language meets the world: "to write standing face to face to a fact, as if it were a scimitar whose sweet edge divides you, is to seek not a style of writing but a justness of it, its happy injuries, ecstasies of exactness. (. . .) A fact has two surfaces because a fact is not merely an event in the world but the assertion of an event, the wording of the world."[51] Each just wording of the world is a notch that contributes to the coming to be of a new Thoreau transfigured in a standard of measurement that assures the matching of the world and our ideas of it. Thoreau turns himself, from an object measured, into a principle of assessment and thereby itself beyond assessment—a presentness that admits eternity.

It needs to be stressed that while attaining this personal present "admits eternity," it is not the same as eternity. In the grammatical "perception" of time, the point of view is human finitude: the fact that our criteria must reflect the transitory nature of our judgments. It is through those transitory judgments and criteria that we discover, piece out our own position, our grammatical present. This means that the present from which we speak is always under construction, a lifetime project, and it also provides another reason why our present cannot be pieced out finally. While "something in me" is pursuing this position, seeking the grammatical present of others and thereby my own, perfectioning myself as a most versatile measuring instrument—this something, while at work, continuously undergoes measurement (recounting) by the statements of others.

It is for this reason that Cavell insisted on a redefinition of a historical event as something filtered through and acknowledged by the consciousness of a community. Cavell describes it when speaking of Thoreau: This experiment, consisting of "building a habitation," is, again, not so much to be conceived spatio-temporally as Thoreau's literal act of building a house in the woods (also this act is from the beginning overshadowed by its meaning, hence "transcendental, an attempt to live the idea"[52])—as "the writing of his book." This writing process is equivalent to the formation of a new epidermis, displaying Thoreau's new grammatical present (that otherwise would stay "hidden and silent and fixed"), hence which makes this present available to him as the grammatical present and makes the latter available for others. So we might say that in writing a book, Thoreau produces his present by making it available as on a cinematic screen—for himself and for others, and for further recounting. But with every new reading, every time a reader measures him in turn, Thoreau may be forced to quit his present and reenter time.

It should be clear by now that history and the past are not so much denied by Cavell as revaluated. We would do better and show more insight pursuing our grammatical present understood as that which shapes our personal inflection towards reality (cf. "Call it our history; it is our present"). The present is our conceptual habitation, the measuring instrument we apply to reality. What then remains of Cavell's casting doubt on Wittgenstein's a-historicity, about which I spoke at the beginning of this article? In the end, history is that from which we can awaken, hence it is conceived as an aspect of our present (un)consciousness responsible for failure of seeing in a certain way. History is distraction, a failure of concentration. It is the condition in which we find ourselves before we are transfigured into our present.

PART IV

Time and Lateness

CHAPTER 9

From Past to Present and from Listening to Hearing: Final Indefinable Moments in Bach's and Stravinsky's Music

Rokus de Groot

Without Applause . . .

On May 15, 1999, the main organizer of Indian music concerts in Amsterdam, John Eijlers, decided to launch a completely different approach to music performance.[1] At the beginning of a recital at the Theatre of the Royal Tropical Institute he declared that the time had come to end applause from the public, even as the last musical sounds are still moving through the hall. To Eijlers, Indian classical music was not a common form of art. It meant to him the manifestation of cosmic vibrations presenting themselves through the finest musical sound waves. Listening to it would offer the listener the opportunity of fine-tuning his/her soul to those vibrations. In view of this, Eijlers considered the conventional hand clapping in Western music practice a shame: The chaotic, rough percussive behavior was nothing less than the destruction of this rare opportunity. So he emphatically enjoined the public in the hall to keep quiet after the concert and to leave their hands where they were. He had, however, forgotten to inform the performer.

The musical star of that evening was no one less than Hariprasad Chaurasia, the great Indian *bansuri* (bamboo flute) player. Chaurasia, in his introductory words, had seemed only to confirm Eijlers's message. As a musician, he stated, he was nothing but a servant of God. In eloquent expressions, Chaurasia depicted that his flute was actually Lord Krishna's elusive instrument. The more a musician forgot about himself and surrendered to this divine flute player, the more his music would seduce the listeners to the Lord's feet. The public had also been prepared for Chaurasia's view by a quotation in the program booklet:

> When we make music, we first assume a meditative state of mind. We
> listen to the *tanpura* [a lute providing the main pitches as a drone] (. . .),
> and concentrate on that. As soon as we are absorbed in the sound, our
> consciousness turns inward. And what we do then . . . it is actually
> not us who are doing anything. Someone acts through us. There is a
> shadow behind us which uses us. And we are like puppets. Someone is
> pulling the strings and we dance according to his will. There is a power
> behind us, which guides us, dependent on the degree of our practice.[2]

After an enchanting concert that evening, the public remained silent, as requested by John Eijlers. It took some time for Chaurasia to digest what was happening. But then it became clear how hybrid spirituality in art is. True, Chaurasia was quite sincere when he presented himself as a servant of Lord Krishna. However, at the same time, he was a musician and a "diva" in his own right, very much enjoying appreciation from earthly beings. So he stood up, went to the edge of the stage with a bewildered expression on his face, expanded his arms, and with eyes wide open more or less demanded his well-earned applause. At that very moment the public broke into a thunderous clapping and cheering, which made the hall resound longer than usual. The happening was quite amusing. Yet John Eijlers had a serious point. He showed awareness of an extraordinary experience: At the end of a performance the musical ordering of time is fading away, and the order of the daily activities is not yet in effect. It is a moment with an indefinable nature, especially when at some point it cannot be decided whether the music is still resounding or has stopped doing so. It is a moment of singularity.

Eijlers was right to point out that the concert public quite often does not have the patience to endure this precious moment. On the contrary, the listeners are usually quite prone to prematurely end the moment's singularity by seizing their "right" to become audible in their turn. It was an important moment for Eijlers: It was his last season of concert organization before his retirement, and he wanted to impress a final message on the public. In his personal life, he was in a situation similar to the ending of a composition, the moment that musical ordering wanes.

How to End a Musical Composition

We may be sure that composers are well aware of the literally extraordinary moment when the musical ordering of time stops and the daily ordering of affairs has not yet started. I shall call this "the final indefinable moment." But I add immediately that I use this expression only provisionally, because this indefinability can be called initial as well, as we will see later, or could be taken as defying initiality or finality. The end of a musical composition is only one instance of becoming aware of this experience. Also I mention here that the word "moment" does not imply any definite length of time for me, because also in terms of duration it is indefinable.

All musicians have to deal with the final indefinable moment when they plan the closure of their compositions. Western composers of the eighteenth and early nineteenth centuries present the listener with elaborate possibilities to prepare themselves for the music's ending. They bring the principal musical themes into the main key, and they often attach a coda that affirms and reaffirms (elements of) these themes as well as the main key. Often this is described in a colloquial way that "the music is coming home." In this phase, composers make ample use of conventional finalizing melodic, metric, rhythmic, harmonic, and dynamic patterns called cadences. The listener "falls," so to speak, into the end. In this way there can be no doubt as to when the musical order stops.

Especially during the nineteenth century, composers not only press the music's ending on the listener, they also tend to pre-compose their applause as well. By using all kinds of techniques of increasing the pressure of sound acoustically and psychologically, like *crescendo*, rising melodic lines, *accelerando*, repetition with diminishing pattern length, and so on, they "warm up" the public so that at the music's final culmination, immediate applause becomes almost unavoidable. These composers seem to want to own the applause by coercion and leave no time for a singular moment of indeterminacy, a final indefinable moment. Of course, performers quite happily exaggerate the composed culmination in order to appropriate the public reward in *their* favor.

It is only fair to add here that, on the other hand, music of the classical-romantic periods may take other courses. Such music may, for instance, present a chain of cadences, with several of them being a *"Trugschluss"*

("false ending"), which postpones the final ending and makes its actual occurrence as the final one uncertain. In this way, in the listener's experience,
musical ordering may extend beyond the final sound: She or he is left in
doubt whether what was heard last is indeed final. As to performers, there
are many who do justice to the final indefinable moment by dwelling on it
beyond what the notation requires. So a conductor may embody the cessation of sound by "freezing" his final movement, keeping the public in awe
and the applause at bay.

Yet there is usually uneasiness in the public about the singular moment
between musical and other ways of time ordering. We have just noted several ways of shortening or even abolishing its happening. Climactic composing and applause are principal among them.

It is quite likely that this uneasiness has to do with the indeterminacy
of that moment. Generally we have no time for it, as the moment "has no
time." We have really no word for it, though we use such expressions as entering into silence, the now, infinity, eternity. It is a moment of transition,
of passage into the unknown. While for some time there was a constant
coming and going of sounds, now at this critical final moment, sound is
ebbing away. The import of this experience can be told from verbal expressions related to it. While music in progress is often heard as a narrative
around a subject, as if it were a life story in sound, its ending is commonly
described as "dying out." Indeed, it is not improbable that music's ending
is felt as a premonition of dying. Just like in dying, the order of time as we
know it is fading away, to make place for something unknown.

Initial Indefinable Moment

Conversely, the beginning of a music composition offers similar challenges
to composers, performers, and listeners. It is here that a moment of singularity has to be created between a daily ordering of time and a musical one.
From various music traditions there are many examples that emphasize this
phase of initial indefinability as the very subject of musical composition:
the ample use of moments of silence, melodic and/or harmonic instability,
loose rhythmic ordering, absence of a definite meter, relatively free improvisation instead of strict composition, etc. Examples are the *âlâpa* before
the compositions (*gat, bandish*) in Indian classical music; the *taqsim* before
a suite of compositions in Arabic and Turkish music; Johann Sebastian
Bach's preludes, toccatas, and fantasias before fugues; Louis Couperin's
préludes non-mesurés to the *ordres* of well-measured dances; the slow intro-

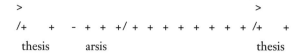

Figure 1. W. A. Mozart, Symphony no. 29 in A Major, K. 201, beginning of the first movement. The + denotes sound and the – denotes the absence of sound; > indicates accent; / refers to the bar line.

duction to the emphatic first theme of first movements in symphonies since Joseph Haydn; Debussy's well-composed "inarticulate" openings to a more defined phrasing, and so forth. The typical incidental moments of absence of sound involved imply the appropriation of silence by the music: These absences are destined to differ fundamentally from the premusical silence, first of all because sound has broken it and second because of the creation of musical syntax, with its concomitant implications and expectations.

As an alternative, especially eighteenth-century European compositions may begin in a quite articulate way, with a cadence. Later examples are the second *Nachtmusik* of Gustav Mahler's Symphony nr. 7, which repeatedly (re)starts with a cadence—the figure of opening is topical here—and the beginning of Stravinsky's *l'Histoire du Soldat*. Related to this is a well-known way of definite opening: to start with the *end*, that is the thesis component, of an arsis-thesis pattern. Among countless examples, listen to the first movement of Mozart's Symphony no. 29 in A Major, K. 201. See Figure 1.

Also here it is worthwhile to listen more closely. The initial cadence or the thesis component immediately give rise to the question: To what do they build a closure? In both cases the finalizing musical gesture takes the preceding nonmusical time into its fold. The perception of the daily order is transformed at the very entrance of musical sound. It seems as if in hindsight—in "hindhearing"—there had been going on all the time an "unheard" music, to which the present cadence or thesis builds a conclusion.

So in both cases the music does not start with the first sound. It is either in the process of beginning or has already started.

Drawing Silence into Musical Ending

It is quite striking that around the beginning of the twentieth century, composers begin to draw the final indefinable moment into their music. This is first and foremost the case with Claude Debussy, the master of the articulation of dying out. I should like to mention here the ending of *Pré-lude à "l'Après-midi d'un Faune"* (1892–94) and *Nuages* (1899). It is not only the dying out of sound, but the dying out of music itself that is *composed* here. The musical ordering of time established earlier is now gradually broken down and taken away. Fewer and fewer sound events are presented; what was a phrase earlier becomes a fragment now; the dynamics become ever softer, up to the limit of our hearing. It is not clear when the music ends. And when it has ended, it is sensed as to have been ending for quite some time.

Epochal is the giving back of music to silence at the ending of Mahler's Symphony no. 9 (1909–10). This ending has made Arnold Schönberg and Anton Webern hesitant to break the silence in their epigrammatic compositions of those years. One of the most impressive performances is Leonard Bernstein's: Conducting stops several times, as, for example, in response to a *fermata*[3] notated over the bar line—already denoting a moment beyond the musical time order—to be resumed temporarily, well before the final sound.

I should like to consider here how some compositions deal with the final indefinable moment. I expect to find in those musical compositions striking cases that are related to the very theme of "time and death," since this theme seems so closely involved in the experience of the dying out of sound. Therefore I have been examining requiems and musical obituaries.

Johann Sebastian Bach: Trauerode

The first example is an extraordinary composition by Johann Sebastian Bach. It is the fourth movement of his Cantata BWV 198, "*Laß Fürstin, laß noch einen Strahl*," the so-called *Trauerode*. The cantata is dedicated to the memory of Christiane Eberhardine, queen of Poland and Kurfürstin of Saxony, who had passed away in 1727. The text of the *recitativo* movement speaks of death bells, whose terrifying sound should go to our very core.

> *Der Glocken bebendes Getön*
> *Soll unsrer trüben Seelen Schrecken*
> *Durch ihr geschwungnes Erze wecken*
> *Und uns durch Mark und Adern gehn.*
> *O, könnte nur dies bange Klingen,*
> *Davon das Ohr uns täglich gellt,*
> *Der ganzen Europäerwelt*
> *Ein Zeugnis unsres Jammers bringen!*

[Let the vibrating sound of the bells
Awaken terror in our downcast souls
With their tolling bronze,
And pierce through marrow and veins.
O, if only this dreadful sound,
Resounding in our ears all day,
Could bear witness to our grief
To all of Europe!][4]

Bach presents us with a time machine in sound, consisting, not by chance, of twelve individual instrumental parts.[5] An alto voice is singing the text to it. The instruments suggest bells of different sizes, the ones playing faster presenting the higher sounds, and the ones playing slower the lower ones.

When we take as a unit the shortest sound duration used (in this case the sixteenth note), the flutes have a cyclicity of 1 (that is, in this case the periodicity of repetition in terms of pitch is one unit). Violins I and II, viola, as well as lutes I and II also use duration unit 1, but grouped in a melodic cyclicity of 4 at the time. These strings play *pizzicato*, to emphasize the quality of a clock sound. Viole da gamba I and II, also *pizzicato*, employ pitches of 2 units in length, with a larger melodic cyclicity of 2 (totaling 4 units). The bass part uses pitches with a duration of 4 units each, and a melodic cyclicity of 2 (totaling 8 units). Unlike the other instruments, the bass is not playing continuously but in groups of 5 elements at a time, interspersed with rests, which adds to the impression of large "bell" size. Also oboes I and II are involved; they are not participating in the time machine but play long-held tones articulating the harmonic structure.

This musical time ordering is appearing gradually, as the instruments enter one after the other (the order of appearance is flute I, flute II, oboe I, oboe II, violin I, violin II, viola, viola da gamba I, viola da gamba II, lute I, lute II plus bass [violoncello, double bass]).[6] This ordering is geared to produce an overwhelming effect.

While the music, in the rhythmic sense, portrays the mechanism of a clock, audible as "bells," it is through the harmonic setting that we are confronted with the emotional quality of that clockwork. Most of the chords employed are dissonant, and when they are not and serve as temporary tonal centers, they keep a highly dissonant relationship with neighboring centers. In this way we pass from D major to C minor to F-sharp minor. The latter relationship counts especially as the most dissonant one in tonal music (the tritone). Finally, in the last bar but one we hear a terrifying clash between the upper voices and the bass: *A* in the bass against a dominant

seventh chord on *C#*, including *G#*. Bach has strongly underlined the relationship between the passing of time and grief.

Now let us pay attention to the ending of this piece. Similarly to their
entrance in the beginning, the instrumental parts leave one by one (in order of *dis*appearance flute I, then II, oboe I, then II, violin I, violin II, viola,
the two viole de gamba, the two lutes). Moreover, the last time when the
bass pattern is presented, it is lacking its first note within the group of
five current until then. And finally, after all the other instruments have
stopped, we hear a single isolated sound by the bass. The last written sign
in the score is a rest (a "nonsound").

In this course, the time ordering in sound is broken down step-by-
step, to make way for a final rest, which fuses with the nonordered time
before the next movement starts: The *recitativo* is followed by a moment
that is not specified in the score other than by a space on the page before
the following aria in print begins. In a sense, the final indefinable moment has been included by Bach, as a notated rest, as part of the *recitativo*'s
composition.

Within Bach's theological frame of thought, we may venture an interpretation here like the portrayal of the evanescence of time, the pain of
time-bound life on earth, and the dying out of the time order as we know
it, calling for contemplation of what is beyond that order.

The listener is invited to such further contemplation—about "the arm
of death being arrested"—during the next movement of the cantata, an
aria for alto voice, two viole da gamba, two lutes, and continuo:

> *Wie starb die Heldin so vergnügt!*
> *Wie mutig hat ihr Geist gerungen,*
> *Da sie des Todes Arm bezwungen,*
> *Noch eh er ihre Brust besiegt.*
> [How contently the heroine died!
> How bravely her spirit struggled
> When she arrested death's arm
> Even before he had vanquished her heart.][7]

Bach provides an opportunity for contemplation in a striking way. At both
the words "*starb*" (died) and "*besiegt*" (conquered, arrested) he prescribes
tones for the alto voice, that are to be held far beyond what was usual (except for the end of compositions), a period of total cessation of melodic
activity. "*Starb*" is extended on a lower pitch, "*besiegt*" on a higher one.
Complementary to the final indefinable moment/movement into silence

at the *recitativo*, the aria invites the listener to totally concentrate on an unmovable single tone, while in the instruments a complex activity is going on: *another indefinable moment*. The alto voice, especially at "*starb*," transcends the current melodic-rhythmic order into a world beyond both clock and musical time.

Stravinsky's "Ecstatic" Endings

Turning to the twentieth century, I should like to consider some of Igor Stravinsky's work, and again in particular its endings. The way he dealt with the final indefinable moment in his compositions attracted the special attention of a number of scholars.

This is how Pierre Suvchinsky commented on the issue, as reported in Robert Craft's *Chronicle of a Friendship*:

> The Postlude to the *Requiem Canticles* is one of those endings, like that of *Les Noces*, which do not end, or end in infinity. And this is where Stravinsky adds a dimension to Western music, beyond the classical composers. Think, for comparison, of the ending of a Beethoven or Brahms symphony, which simply thumps more loudly with each repeat.[8]

Testimonies in the same vein about Stravinsky's musical endings have been written by Joseph Straus:

> In truth, the most characteristic kind of ending for Stravinsky, in his late music as in his earlier music, is the extended, rapturous coda in which the concrete concerns of the preceding work seem to melt away in a sense of timeless ecstasy. *Introitus, A Sermon, a Narrative, and a Prayer, Requiem Canticles,* and other works conclude with solemn, devotional chorales. These chorales engage the substance of the music that precedes them, but only in an abstract, insubstantial way. Rather than offering any kind of recapitulation, they serve to open the piece out, to point beyond the boundaries of the piece, to refuse closure at the ultimate moment.[9]

The same source observes about the role of the coda in Stravinsky's work:

> In a *Stravinskyan* coda, time seems almost to stop. Rhythmic activity suddenly slows almost to the point of cessation. A principal motive from earlier in the piece is repeated in a radically augmented and fragmented form. In the rapturous conclusions of *Les Noces, Symphony*

in C, Symphony of Psalms, and *The Fairy's Kiss,* we gain a glimpse of the infinite, of a time beyond time.[10]

Furthermore, Louis Andriessen and Elmer Schönberger, in *The Apollonian Clockwork* of 1983, characterize the bells of *Requiem Canticles'* Postlude as the clocks of the end of times.[11]

All these comments point to an experience of singularity such as we are studying here. Such expressions as "not ending," "refusing closure," "ending in infinity," "the end of times," "a glimpse of the infinite, of a time beyond time," and "a sense of timeless ecstasy" deserve special attention in relation to the final stages of Stravinsky's compositions.[12]

Apollo (Apollon Musagète)

An eloquent example of the waning of musical ordering into a final singular moment of indeterminacy is the last movement of *Apollo* for string orchestra, a composition for ballet (1928). Called Apothéose, this movement, though not literally related to death, obviously refers to a fundamental ontological transition, since it is here in the choreographic plan that Apollo, followed by the Muses, ascends to Parnassus. The last six 4/2 bars present a process of gradual cessation of rhythmic activity. After a preceding *Steigerung,* the main motif arrives at a fixed position in pitch and register and is stated six times. Each time its entrance is postponed by one quarter note (its overall duration progressing from 5 to 6, 7, 8, and 9 quarter notes, respectively, and finally to an indefinite length, due to a *fermata,* so that step-by-step inactivity enters the music. This slowing-down process is backed up by the accompaniment, which first moves in quarter notes, then twice as slow in half notes, and then four times as slow in whole notes.

The process of cessation of activity is compositionally speaking a largely mechanical affair. Everything in the music keeps its course with utmost precision and inevitability, while the *ostinato* patterns in the different synchronous musical layers constantly shift in relation to each other and produce ever new harmonic combinations. Indeed, at first listening it gives the impression of a petrification into an inhuman condition—after all, it is an "apotheosis"; that is, a reification into deification. Yet this is not my experience as a listener. Certainly, there is something nonhuman in this ending, with its cyclicities, and systematics of retardation and of shift between layers, a nonhumanity that only humans can devise and experience. At the same time the transition from the slowing down of rhythmic activity into (almost) complete cessation of it and finally into silence provokes a rare acuity of listening: Each new sonorous event increasingly becomes a surprise—one does not know what to expect when, but keeps yearning for sound—while each new sound becomes ever more precious. This listening in wonder continues for some time even after the last physical sound has ebbed away.

It is like the act of listening to a loved one between life and death: Is she still breathing? What can be experienced at this final singular moment is the death of the listener, in the sense that the music does not provoke any (pro)active listening intervention in terms of the subjectivation of music or the identification with it. In offering the opportunity to become increasingly conscious of the preciousness of sound and the receptivity of silence, the final moment now opens up the possibility of sheer hearing in fascination and abandon. Indeed, is this music a preparation for dying?

Les Noces (Svadebka)

As a further illustration, I should like to discuss another example from Stravinsky. It is the ending of *Les Noces* for vocal soloists, chorus, four pianos, and percussion (1917, final instrumentation completed in 1923). The Russian title of the composition is *Svadebka*, "little marriage," a Russian diminutive which in this case implies nothing sweet or cute. See Figure 2.

The final stage of *Les Noces* is based on a strict beat: a time measurement by means of a constant unit of duration (1 quarter value).[13] It is moreover based on a constant meter, the 3/4 bar, a grouping of 3 quarter beats. It is the bass, singing the bridegroom's address to his new spouse, who establishes this 3/4 meter. Because of this connection, I propose to designate 3/4 here as "the time of the individual" or "lyrical time."

Very prominent in the ending of *Les Noces* is the tolling of bells. They are played by a bell, two *crotales* (antique cymbals), to which are added later piano chords. Their sound may be taken as church bells, markers of rites of passage. In a sense they are also bells of death, heralding the consummation of the marriage, in which both individuals "die" into union.[14] The bells are connected with a different time periodicity, of 8 quarter values (though notated within the frame of 3/4, and not in 8/4). I shall refer to this periodicity in the case of the ending of *Les Noces* as "ritual time." (Eventually something extraordinary will happen to the ritual bell time, about which I comment later.)

There is a tension between the two time orderings, the vocal one of the individual (bridegroom's voice) and the instrumental ritual one (the bells). Is it possible for us to hear this tension, even though it seems a matter of

Phase 1

group 1 (3 bars)

bass

*   *   *

B G# B C# B G# B C# _____

(a) + (b)   (a) + (b)

B   **B**

group 2 (3 bars)

bass

*   *   *

B C# B C#B C# B   G# B C# _____

(b el.)   (a) + (b)

                              B

group 3 (3 bars)

bass

*   *   *

B C# B G# B C# B C# _____

(b)   (a) + (b el.)

                    B

Phase 2

group 1 (4 bars)

bass

*   *   *   *

 B   C# EDC# B C#   EDC# B G# B C# ____

 (b var.)   (b var.)   (a) + (b)

                    B

group 2 (5 bars)

bass   chords by pianos

*   *   *   *   *   *

____ *B   C# EDC# B   C# B C# B C#* _____

   (b var.)   (b el.)

                                                  B G# B C#   B

                                                  (a) + (b)

        B   **B**   **B**

Figure 2. Structure of the ending of Stravinsky's *Les Noces*, rehearsal numbers 133–34, m. 8. Capitals in italics denote pitches. The (a) and (b) refer to the first and second halves of the melodic motive; el. means "elaboration." **B** refers to the bells (bell, pianos, antique cymbals). The * denotes the first beat of the 3/4 bar.

notation? Indeed, it is. Stravinsky belongs to a literate music tradition. So his work comprises both score and sound. At the performance we become visually aware of the tension by the conductor's behavior in relation to the bell sounds: He conducts in 3/4, against which the bell sounds every 8 beats. But also without visuality we can tell the tension between the periodicities of 3 and 8. There is a difference between the performance of the bells from the actual notation in Stravinsky's score in 3/4, and from a score in which their part would have been notated in 8/4. The former requires a much higher degree of alertness from the musicians than the latter one, since they are playing against the prevailing meter; this usually results in a greater intensity of sound.

Let us look now at the bass part. It proceeds in 2 phases, each of 9 bars in 3/4 time. Phase 1 is composed of 3 times 3 bars. The first group of 3 bars contains two times the same melodic pattern. The first pitch of the melodic pattern's first occurrence, as well as the last pitch of its second occurrence stress the first beat of the bar, in the sense that these elements coincide with it.

The second group of 3 bars elaborates the second half of the melodic pattern and then states this pattern in full. The first as well as the last pitch of the pattern's elaboration coincide with the first beat of the bar. Differently from the first group of 3 bars, both beginning and end of the ensuing pattern's full statement avoid beat one.

The third group of 3 bars starts with the second half of the melodic pattern and then gives that pattern in full extended by an elaboration of its second half. The first pitch of this complex as well as its final one stress beat one of the bar. In this way, during the whole of phase 1, the 3/4 meter is established.

Things become quite different in phase 2, which also presents 9 bars. First of all, these 9 are not divided in 3 times 3, but in 4 plus 5. So the cyclic order is undermined by asymmetry. In the first group of 4 bars, containing three melodic statements (twice a variant of the main pattern's second half, and its full statement), the first beat of the bar is stressed only once by the final element of one of the pattern's statements, while in the second group of 5 bars, presenting an extensive elaboration of the pattern's second half, the first beat of the bar is not even touched. So the musical ordering of time in terms of 3/4 meter, the "time of the individual," is waning step-by-step and is ultimately taken away. Moreover the melodic pattern's statements become less and less clear-cut. No new order is established by the voice: On the contrary, it frees itself increasingly from melodic patterning, metric confines, and beat.

What is taking over here is the ritual time, the order of the bells, running in a periodicity of 8 quarter values. This final process of the composition's ending starts when the four pianos take over the melodic pattern of the voice, each statement finishing with the bell sound (only the beginning of this is depicted in Figure 2). The piano patterns are continuously displaced in relation to the predominant constant 8 quarter cycle of the bells. The former lyrical time of the individual in 3/4 is definitely gone. The relation between the shifting piano patterns and the constant bells is so capricious that we cannot derive a regular time ordering from it.[15] In ballet performances the transitional character of this passage is theatrically emphasized by the direction "*Le rideau se baisse lentement durant toute la musique suivante*" / "The curtain is dropped slowly during all of the following music."

Then something remarkable may happen to the listener. While we get less and less support in the actual sound for the time of the individual, and the ritual time gets involved in unpredictable relations with the piano patterns, our hearing may become more open to the acoustic actuality. We may grow aware that each stroke of the bell is different in sound. Something subtle is going on. Our sense of acoustic actuality is engendered by the continuous sound differentiation in the composition. Each bell stroke is colored by the piano patterns preceding it, because the piano tones are allowed to die out (by the use of the right pedal). Since none of these piano patterns has actually the same pitch makeup, their sounds transform the ensuing bell strokes differently each time. Moreover the time position of the piano patterns in relation to the bell strokes is different throughout: The distance between the final element of the piano pattern and the bell strokes is, respectively, 3, 1, 2, 4, and 12 eighth notes. So in cases where there is little time between the bell sound and the preceding last piano attack, the aftermath of piano sounds dying out has a strong effect on the bell sound, whereas in cases with larger time intervals between the two, the effect is weaker.[16]

During this phase something really extraordinary takes place in the mechanical ritual time ordering of the bell. The bell will eventually be struck 16 times. Now the tenth entrance of the bell is delayed by one extra bar of 3/4, so that the cyclicity of 8 is broken. A singularity makes itself manifest, as once a time interval of 11 instead of 8 quarter notes between bell strokes is observed. It could be called, literally, a preemptive delay, as silence interrupts the ritual bell time. The final indefinable moment has thus already broken into the musical ordering of time long before the ultimate dying out.

An amusing story is connected with this unusual moment. Once Stravinsky was almost convinced to delete it, but fortunately refrained from doing so. Robert Craft reports:

> During this visit [Los Angeles, March 1965] Stravinsky was being filmed in his home, and Boulez had been invited to lunch. After the meal, he opened the score of *Les Noces* to the last page and tried to convince the composer that the two bars of rest between [rehearsal numbers] *134* and *135* were a mistake; one, according to Boulez's calculations, was correct [that is, Boulez did not accept the singular time interval of 11 quarter notes between bell strokes, but insisted on having them all 8 quarters]. Stravinsky, slightly inebriated, agreed. All of this can be seen in the Liebermann film. In Dec.1965, at a recording, Stravinsky restored the second bar.[17]

Finally this interaction between piano patterns and bell strokes also stops, without any conclusive moment. The last vestiges of the time of the individual have vanished, or in other words, the individual has freed himself from time constraints (entering the ecstasy of nuptial union). What remains is the sounding of the bells, with its ritual time, but as we have heard, this time has also become uncertain by the singular intervention of silence.

However, in our listening, while the bells keep tolling, we do not know whether and how long new sound events will arrive. This keeps our listening acute, as we pass into the final indefinable moment, when musical ordering is waning and a new order has not yet announced itself. Our attention remains wide open, even if we are coming to accept that the music has finally died out.

It is here, in this dying out, that a transition is possible from listening to hearing.[18]

Requiem Canticles

Let us end with the final movement of *Requiem Canticles*, which bears the name of Postlude. Stravinsky composed the piece in 1965–66, when he was well into his eighties. The choice of this composition has a poignancy in this context, since it is also the ending of a life's oeuvre. It is Stravinsky's last major piece. Robert Craft, the composer's assistant, reports that Vera Stravinsky, while they were planning the funeral, said to him: "*He* and *we* knew he was writing it for himself."[19] In fact it was performed at his funeral in Venice, in the basilica Santi Giovanni e Paolo, on April 15, 1971.

When we investigate the Postlude's elements and the way the music proceeds, we find as a first element a widely spaced chord for four flutes (1 piccolo, 2 grand flutes, 1 alto flute), piano, harp, and horn. Robert Craft calls them "chords of death."[20] There are 3 single occurrences of such chords. They last 4 beats each (quarter values), in the very slow tempo of 40 beats per minute, together 12 beats. These chords open the consecutive sections of the movement. Each of the single chords is followed by the tolling of bells, played by celesta, tubular bells, and vibraphone, over the sustained horn-tone remaining from the chord—and then by silence. This order of events is repeated 2 times (sections I through III).

Then, as a conclusion, in section IV, 3 final chords of death are sounded immediately after each other, without intervening bells. The first two of them last 3 beats, the last one 6 beats. Together they also count 12 beats, just like the single chords of death together before.

The number 12 is found to determine the total number of silent beats within the movement, too.[21] This recurrent number of 12 may be taken as a symbol of the fulfillment of time.

At the same time, there are processes at work which articulate the increasing breaking down of the musical order. Part of this is a process of deletion, in a course of emptying. See Figure 3. Before going into the emptying process, let me observe that during the whole movement we are already confronted with the breaking down/*brokenness* of the musical ordering of time. The mechanical presentation of time units, which is so characteristic for the human ordering of time, is presented by the bells. Their tolling proceeds with a fixed time interval between the strokes. However, this tolling is not continuous and not regular: The bell strokes appear intermittently in groups of unequal length. Each sequence of bell tolling is interrupted and followed by silence. In this way the final silence already creeps into the musical ordering of time.

Let us inspect the music more closely. The first two sections of the Postlude are structured in the same way as far as timing is concerned. But there are at least three factors which keep our hearing alert:

the intermittent presentation and interruption of the mechanical time ordering in the bells,
the irregularity in the number of bell strokes within each section, namely 6 and 5, and
the bars of silence.

Section III undermines to some extent our conceptual grasp of the course of events. This time the sequence of bell tolling does not bring

Section I

C (1)	B	R	B	R
4/4	(1/4 **R**) 6/4	(3/4)	5/4	(3/4)
H_____		(1/4 **R**) _____		

Section II

C (2)	B	R	B	R
4/4	(1/4 **R**) 6/4	(3/4)	5/4	(3/4)
H_____		(1/4 **R**) _____		

Section III

C (3)	B	R	B	R
4/4	(1/4 **R**) 4/4	(3/4)	6/4	(3/4)
H_____		(1/4 **R**) _____		

Section IV

C (4)	C (4)	C (5)+B
3/4	3/4	6/4
		H_____

C: 'Chord of Death'; **B**: 'Bells' (Celesta, Tubular Bells, Vibraphone)
R: Rest; **H**: Horn

Figure 3. Structure of I. Stravinsky: *Requiem Canticles* (1965–66), Postlude.

groups of 6 plus 5, but groups of 4 plus 6 strokes. One stroke is missing, and the order of groups (in terms of longer and shorter ones) is reversed.

Section IV continues the breaking down of the musical order. It opens with a chord of death played by widely spaced flutes, piano, and harp. As noted earlier, however, the tolling of bells is lacking now. Moreover, the chord is shorter than before (3 instead of 4 beats). And also different from before, the next chord is exactly the same as the one preceding it.

Then the final chord arrives. For the first time it coincides with a stroke
of the bells (that is,—one could say—the one "missing" from section III).
This final chord is a terrifying one. Up till now a process was going on
between the single chords of death of an increase in compass, register, and
complexity. The first chord has 8 tones, with 7 different pitch identities,
and the third one has 12 different tones and 8 different pitch identities
(which means that there are multiple occurrences of certain pitch identities at different octave positions). At first hearing, the final chord seems
to embody the culmination of this process. This is because it is combined
with the bell group, for the first—and last—time. But as it dies out, it
turns out to be much poorer in pitch content. In fact it contains 8 tones
and no more than 4 different pitch identities; that is, several of them are
doubled in various octave positions.

Furthermore, the last chord is diatonic, while all the others were chromatic. All these factors account for the impression of nakedness of the last
chord. Joseph Straus observes about this process:

> One can imagine the progression of the five chords of death as leading
> from large, complex, chromatic chords of five, six, seven, or eight dif-
> ferent notes [pitch identities], to this relatively simple diatonic conclu-
> sion, a process of gradual simplification and clarification. The diatonic
> emerges from the chromatic, and the contrast of the two links the *Re-
> quiem* Postlude to that rich expressive tradition in Stravinsky's music.[22]

To explain just briefly the tradition that Straus is referring to, in Stravinsky's work, from as early as the *Firebird* of 1910, we find a polarity between
the diatonic and the chromatic. The latter is related in the composer's great
ballets to the domain of the supernatural, whereas the former has to do
with everyday life of "normal" humans, or humans in a "normal" state of
mind. The fact that the chromatic-diatonic opposition has been such an
important expressive topic throughout Stravinsky's oeuvre is the base for
Straus to attach symbolic weight to the course of events in this Postlude
to his work:

> As in *The Rake's Progress* and *Agon*, the diatonic ending of the *Requiem
> Canticles* comes as an awakening from a rich, complex dream of life into
> the bright, hard reality of death.[23]

The interruption and eventual dispelling of a conceivable musical ordering
may bring our listening to a state of rare acuity. As it loses foothold, it may
become more open to the nuances of sonorities, the fading away of sound
and the taking over by silence. The final undefined moment may invite a

singular hearing attention, which is gradually transformed into surrender while retaining the intensity of openness.

Invention at the Limits: From Listening to Hearing

We have investigated some musical compositions related to the human measurement of time as well as its demise. In this context we have spoken of the final indefinable moment, maybe similar to dying, when the musical ordering of time is fading away, while no new order is presenting itself, and when we are invited to enter a nonorder, a moment that has been likened in the musicological literature to the ending of time, infinity, eternity. We have observed that this liminal moment has been conducive to the innovation of composing and listening. Apparently the representation of dying (out), no less, or maybe even more than that of vitality, induces the development of musical sensitivity. Indeed, just as in life, the moment of a final good-bye may raise a profundity of awareness that is rare in current life.

The composers involved have investigated the mechanics of clocks and bells, a nonhuman sound world of human invention, as well as the breaking down of this mechanics. The musical exploration related to the final indefinable moment seems to lie, in the cases studied, in the realm of sonority. Bach, in his *Trauerode*, composed a unique time machine of twelve individual instrumental parts, and, apart from the alto voice, of at least seven different timbres. In Stravinsky's *Les Noces* we find the continuous sound coloring of bell strokes. For the first time in his whole oeuvre, he uses the vibraphone in the Postlude of his *Requiem Canticles*. Apart from this, at the end of his life, he arrives at the composition of chords in a new way, compared to the serial techniques current at that time.[24] Finally, it is quite peculiar that even though Stravinsky took great care to have mistakes in the score of *Requiem Canticles* meticulously corrected by assistant composer Claudio Spies, he left various strange lapses in the pitch ordering of the Postlude alone. Also in that sense, the strictness of musical ordering is passing away at the ending of Stravinsky's last great work.[25]

Also as listeners we are invited to innovation. These musical endings urge us to develop a particular acuteness of attention. At some point it is no longer possible to exert cognitive control over the musical course of events, as the basis of the order one has used to exert that control, is waning. In that sense the first adjective in the expression final indefinable moment could well be replaced by "initial": A new orientation is called for, to which these musical endings may serve as an initiation. I suggest the initiation to be the shift from listening to hearing. Listening is bound up with intentionality, while hearing involves a nonrestricted openness of attention. It is significant that the recurrent admonition in the bible is not "Who hath ears to listen, let him listen," but "Who hath ears to hear, let him hear."[26] Especially the ending of *Les Noces* is a magnificent occasion for the emptying of listening and the opening of hearing.

Hearing as the heightening of sensitivity to the slightest sounds—is she still breathing?—up to the acceptance of the eventual absence of audible sound, expectation being transformed into surrender: This is clearly not a moment for the explosion of applause. If we have become nonlisteners, let us assume the way deaf people express their appreciation for music at performances: by waving their hands in the air.

Theodor Adorno, in his *Philosophy of Modern Music*, has strongly objected to Stravinsky's composing. His criticism is that the listener is left to the mercy of the music; she or he is prevented, in Van den Toorn's paraphrase, from "forming metrical patterns, and hence from anticipating and assimilating displacement. Their engagement with the music is interrupted." According to Adorno, this is the more painful as it happens through "convulsive blows and shocks," as he calls it. He goes so far as to attribute to Stravinsky's music "sadomasochistic strains," noting the composer's "perverse joy in self-denial."[27] True, as we have seen, the means of conceptual grasp are taken out of the listener's hands while the final/*initiating* indefinable moment is unfolding. And indeed, the possibility of an empathetic dialogue between listener and the course of music is not evident. Adorno was a fervent listener, not a hearer. What his listener's aesthetics seems to *miss* in Stravinsky's music may actually turn into a gift: the opening of a literally extraordinary acuity of hearing.

Music is no less a lesson in dying than it is in living. This is not a plea for the rejection of listening in favor of hearing, but to investigate them as complements. What is it that remains when the final/initiating indefinable moment arrives, when we indeed refrain from defining it, even in terms of infinity, of eternity, of the "now," or, for that matter, when we even do not call it "indefinable" or "final"? Though the final/initial indefinable moment in music cannot be simply equated with a religious experience, it may have a resemblance to it: the unveiling of time as pastness—the unknowing of the present.

CHAPTER 10

Late Style Messiaen

Sander van Maas

At the end of his life, when [Seneca] has the whole world before
his eyes—its sequence, and its sorrows and its splendors—thanks
to this great view from above that ascent to the summit of the
world, in the *consortium Dei*, has given him through the study of
nature, the sage will then be free to choose whether to live or die.

MICHEL FOUCAULT[1]

Religious Art and the Question of Time

What is the role of time in the work of a religious artist? This question
shall guide my ruminations in this essay.

For most religious artists some relation with the eternal—that is, it
seems, with the square opposite of time—appears to be part of their creative program. Religious works of art often aim to express, symbolize, al-
legorize, or perhaps even capture some aspect of the timeless realms of
nirvana, the heavens, mystical union, or else. In a stronger sense one could
argue that religious art is dependent on eternity by definition and that,
therefore, temporal aspects should have no real say in religious art. What
is decisive, it seems, is the relation to the eternal.[2]

From this perspective it is surprising to find that some religious artists show a fascination for time and temporality. The French composer
Olivier Messiaen is a case in point. He regarded himself a "rhythmician,"
a manipulator of time, rather than a *"compositeur de musique."* He spent
several volumes of writing on theories of rhythm (accent, meter, modes,

etc.) and philosophies of time (from Bergson to Bachelard and beyond). As his point of entry into the history of twentieth-century music he regarded his work on time and rhythm, developing their concepts even further than did such predecessors as Debussy and Stravinsky. In his music, Messiaen developed a number of original devices for the enhancement of temporal and rhythmical plasticity such as the added values (*valeurs ajoutées*), *personnages rythmiques*, and symmetrical permutations.

If we accept Messiaen's profession that the ultimate goal of his art was the illumination of the theological truths of the Catholic faith—that he regarded himself as a religious artist—the question then becomes how his work is related to eternity.

To answer this question I shall take a different route than is usually taken. The standard account of Messiaen's relation to eternity and time-lessness is that his work manages to convey a sense of temporal arrest by using an abundance of symmetrical and homogenizing devices (e.g., additive rhythm based on homogeneous counts) or by frustrating the linear sense of time by means of temporal blocks and sudden breakthroughs.[3] There is, however, another level on which artworks, time, and eternity interrelate and which is often overlooked as field of inquiry; namely, the privileged position of old age and "lateness" with regard to the diaphanousness of time.

Since Adorno's writings on this subject this is referred to as *Spätstil*, or late style. More in particular this concept expresses the idea that works of art belonging to the final period in the creative life of an artist, such as Bach's *Kunst der Fuge* or Beethoven's so-called third period, often exhibit a character of their own—one might even say, they exhibit character per se. The concept of late style expresses the notion that this expression of character is somehow reducible to a (musical) content that calls for interpretation in terms of virtue, such as profundity, wisdom, freedom—or exile.

What do we notice, at first sight, in Messiaen? Does his work display a specific late style? It seems not. For few composers in the twentieth century have expressed a fully developed style as early in life as Messiaen, who wrote in his early twenties a specific kind of music, elements of which return in his very last works as though they had been written in that very same period. Although being diverse in many respects, Messiaen's style is remarkably stable and, on a deeper level, appears to be resistant to periodization. On the other hand, as some have observed, things did seem to change in his work after he finished his opera on Saint Francis in 1983. Such a change appears even more intriguing in religious than in allegedly secular artists. For what could such a marked expression of temporality entail with regard to the relation to the eternal?

The questions to answer seem, first, in what respect his later work (from about 1983 to 1984 until his death in April 1992) started to differ from the works of earlier periods; second, what the nature of this difference is; and finally, how this difference can be assessed with regard to late style and eternity.

The Topos of Late Style

Adorno first articulated his theory of late style in the 1934 essay "Beethovens Spätstil," published in *Moments musicaux* from 1964. In this essay he criticized the usual view of Beethoven's third and last creative period according to which his works can be read as a function of the composer's biography. In contrast to what classical theories would predict, these late works do not display a sense of harmonious accomplishment, organic maturity, and serene resignation. Rather they appear to be fissured, inaccessible, difficult, and, as Adorno writes, they show more traces of history than of growth. The usual explanation is that these works are products of "a 'personality' ruthlessly proclaiming itself, which breaks through the roundedness of form for the sake of expression, exchanging harmony for the dissonance of its sorrow and spurning sensuous charm under the dictates of the imperiously emancipated mind."[4] The effect, then, is that these works are reduced to documents in which the composer's biography is made to resound.[5]

As might be expected from Adorno, he argues that late works obey a "formal law" that makes them resist the reduction to mere biologico-biographical expression. The formal law materializes as (and in) the late *style* that Adorno discerns in the later works. What is late style? As a concept it appears to center around the dissociation of musical conventions and (the composer's) subjectivity—and also around the enigma of the late work as it holds the two together in their in commensurability. Explaining his concept Adorno argues that Beethoven in his middle period made subjectivity appear by twisting and turning the conventions of the genre. In the Fifth Symphony, for instance, Beethoven "absorbed the traditional trappings into his subjective dynamic by forming latent middle voices, by rhythm, tension, or whatever other means, transforming them in keeping with his intention."[6] The late works, by contrast, exhibit the purest conventionality. "They are full of decorative trills, cadences, and fiorituras. The convention is often made visible in unconcealed, untransformed bare-ness."[7] Hence Adorno contends that, in the late style, the "conventions become expression in the naked depiction of themselves."[8]

This nakedness results from there being no subject in the work to appropriate the conventions as its medium for the production of (its) presence and fullness of sense. In the late style, Adorno contends, subjectivity is only present in a gesture of absenting. "The force of subjectivity in late works is the irascible gesture with which it leaves them. It bursts them asunder, not in order to express itself but, expressionlessly, to cast off the illusion of art. Of the works it leaves only fragments behind, communicating itself, as if in ciphers, only through the spaces it has vacated. Touched by death, the masterly hand sets free the matter it previously formed."[9] Thus, balancing between the "empty phrase" of pure conventionality on the one hand and the "caesura" of absenting subjectivity on the other, the late work (in the late *style*, for not all works exhibit late style) has both the character of an allegory and of an enigma. Adorno tends to contrast this allegorical force of the late style to the symbolic power of the classical symphonies. Elsewhere he describes the "individual element" in the late works as severed from the dialectics of the whole, thus symbolizing the individual as conscious of its own insignificance. "Late style," he concludes, "is the self-awareness of the insignificance society.[10]

Late Messiaen

Let us now turn to Messiaen. As mentioned above, there seems to be a late style in his oeuvre as well. In order to affirm this impression the first question that would seem to need answering is at what point in time the late period should be said to begin. This is a difficult question to answer. For some commentators, like Arnold Whittall, everything Messiaen wrote from 1969 onward is like a series of "alternatively grand and unassuming epilogues to the achievements of his earlier years."[11] For others, such as Luke Berryman, an important change in Messiaen's language occurs only in the *Livre du Saint Sacrement* from 1984. After finishing *Saint François d'Assise* in 1983 and feeling creatively exhausted, Messiaen announced to his intimates that he considered himself finished as a composer.[12] Within a year, however, he resurrected from his creative death and produced his largest organ cycle ever. In his analysis of the *Livre*, Berryman reaches the conclusion that, rather than being a mere product of late style synthesis, or "a garland of mementoes" as Paul Griffiths has put it, the work shows Messiaen struggling with—and ultimately accomplishing—the reinvention of his own musical language after its apotheosis in *Saint François d'Assise*.[13]

The years after *Livre du Saint Sacrement* give an even more explicit clue as to significant changes in style. In 1985 Messiaen wrote a series of short, virtuosic birdsong piano pieces called the *Petites esquisses d'oiseaux*, which he did not think of highly himself, but which Yvonne Loriod welcomed warmly, saying that they were "finding in their sparseness a completely new style."[14] Commenting on the work's "exquisite transparency" Hill and Simeone touch upon the first of what are arguably *three main features* of the later works: transparency, warmth, and recycling. The transparency announced in the *Esquisses* would be elevated to a new high point in the orchestral work *Éclairs sur l'au-delà* . . . written between 1987 and 1991. Here the hard-edged and direct language of Messiaen makes way for a much more resonant and subtle play with orchestral nuance. As can be clearly heard in the fifth movement of *Éclairs*, "Demeurer dans l'amour . . . ," this work introduces a new sense of texture and luminous timbre, allowing Messiaen to create a sense of unending openness. This *sens du flou* (sense of vagueness) which he so admired in Debussy but had never been able to realize himself, finally seems to have come to him, albeit in a very different fashion than found in his predecessor.

The second main feature of the later works—warmth—ensues in the year after the *Petites esquisses*, when Messiaen accepted a commission to write an examination piece in the style of Mozart, which became *Chant dans le style de Mozart* for clarinet and piano. With this piece, which is highly remarkable for the fact that Messiaen decided to emulate the historical and individual style of a distant colleague, a new or *renewed* chamber musical melodicism and warmth erupts in his oeuvre. Peter Hill and Nigel Simeone see a decisive role for Mozart in the late Messiaen. "The flowering of melody in *Éclairs* stems from the renewal of Messiaen's love for the music of Mozart."[15] This love for Mozart materialized in the following year (1987), when Messiaen had a volume of analyses of Mozart's integral piano concertos published. Also, in the same year, he accepted a commission to write a piece for the Mozart bicentennial.[16] In this work, *Un sourire* and in his unfinished *Concert à quatre*, we hear a remarkably pronounced role for the solo oboe, an instrument Messiaen had not foregrounded in his earlier works and which adds a warm resonance to the sound of his later works.

The third and final feature of these works is recycling. This aspect has been frequently commented upon and has often—too hastily—been identified with the later work as a whole. Berryman mentions several authors who, according to him, appear to accept the "[Richard] Strauss model" of lateness for Messiaen, emphasizing the leisurely, synthetic, and retrospective elements even to the point that, for example for Christopher

Dingle, listening to the late work requires one to "simply sit back and be charmed."[17] Certainly, works such as *Un vitrail et des oiseaux* and *La Ville d'en-haut* from 1986 and 1987 respectively represent revisitings of the original works Messiaen composed in the early and mid-1960s (notably *Couleurs de la cité céleste* and *Et Exspecto resurrectionem mortuorum*). The mechanical quality involved in the "empty" repetition of this style outside of its context of origin adds to the impression that late Messiaen has either become a victim of the toolbox approach to composing or that he regarded this rigid return as holding the promise of something beyond itself—a virtualizing effect of sorts, as I have argued elsewhere.[18]

If we now try to answer whether Messiaen's later works evidence a late style in Adorno's sense, we should note the following. It may be said—and surprisingly so—that *all* of Messiaen's music falls into the category of late style, that is, if we accept Edward Said's suggestion that the aesthetics of negativity, fragmentation, caesura, the empty phrase, and so on, which we find in late Beethoven has set the stage for Schoenberg and the ensuing development of musical modernism.[19] Messiaen emphatically embraced the modernist primacy of the aesthetically negative.[20] His music is full of cuts, "empty" formulas, and enigmatic *ciphers*, as it is perhaps best exemplified by the works of the 1960 and their recurrence in *Vitrail* and *Ville*. However, these works' ritualism remains substantially different from the "empty phrases" created by Beethoven's bare conventionalism in the late piano works. Rather, they invoke Adorno's remark on the *Missa Solemnis* being a "late work without late style"—a work from which the composer's subjectivity appears to have been eliminated clear and simple.[21] *Vitrail* and *Ville* remain clearly signed by Messiaen's style, but their attempt to make us forget this signature and raise itself to the level of anonymity (a phenomenon which Messiaen admired in Gregorian chant) should make us think about the difference between (1) the sublime vacation of subjectivity in late Beethoven, (2) the lack of subjectivity which makes "bad" compositions vulnerable to the criticism of not being a composition at all, and (3) the elimination of subjectivity from ritualistic musics such as the *Missa* or *La Ville d'en-haut*.

Given these echoes of ritualism and anonymization it is all the more surprising to find that Messiaen's late works appear to actually bring a new dimension of subjectivity *into* his oeuvre. This new dimension differs, for example, from the subjectivity surfacing in the lyricism of the Tristan period (e.g., *Harawi*) in that it is close to the spirit of devotion found in *L'Ascension* and *Quatuor*. Yet while in the latter works a certain tone of inwardness appears to direct the devotional mood—an effect that, in the first movement of the orchestral *L'Ascension*, is attained by the restrained but expressive dynamics in the solo trumpet melody—in *Éclairs* there appears to be no such inwardness left. The transparency of the timbres carries over to the texture of the whole work, relaxing in the process the hard demarcation between the invisible and the very (in)tense aspiration toward it that is so typical of Messiaen. Indeed, it seems that he is playing here on a note of synthesis, not just in the sense of integrating everything that he accomplished in his past compositions, but also in the sense that, on a musical level, he appears to have to come to terms with the painful *distance* between the visible and the invisible. Rather than simply erasing this distance the music of *Éclairs* seems to refract it, to make it indirect. It also makes it produce a reverberation, an encompassing resonance—or, placing it in a more subjective register: an intimacy without center, open toward all sides (including the innermost ones).[22]

The Eternity of Late Style

Up to this point I have been focusing on the questions of what late style is and what evidence there is for late style in Messiaen. This discussion, however, has only taken one criterion into consideration; namely, the supposedly unique character of "late" music as it is expressed by late style. What needs further questioning is to what extent this phenomenon—or, as Joseph Straus has shown in a survey of qualities associated with late style in various commentators, this loose complex of very diverse and often contradictory phenomena—can be related to time and eternity.[23]

If we continue our reading of Adorno's ruminations of late Beethoven, we are informed that late style is defined by a boundary. "A theory of the very late Beethoven," he writes, "must start from the decisive boundary dividing it from the earlier work. [. . .] The boundary is doubtless marked by the Piano Sonata op. 101, a work of the highest, of inexhaustible beauty."[24] Leaving this latter qualification of late style aside we are struck by the notion of a "decisive boundary." What could such a boundary be? Evidently, the decisive boundary is the boundary that inaugurates the late style; that is, beyond which something really different, profound, and challenging begins. Adorno does not however intend to refer to just any radical change in a creative output; for him, the late style remains a (however indirect) function of the notion of age: of "lateness" in life. Where is such lateness to be found? Well, it appears that old age as such gives no guarantee for anything of the quality Adorno associates with late style. Late works may also prove to be superficial, repetitive, or nostalgic, as may be suggested by the late works of Richard Strauss.[25]

The qualification "late" is a mobile one that may also be applicable to very young composers, such as Mozart, whose later works are often thought of in terms of "difficult" late style.[26] His example makes one wonder if we should consider that Mozart's life had been cut short; that is, if he had been ripped away from a life that was not yet accomplished. In that case it would be difficult to ascribe its late works any real lateness—they all would in fact have been middle period works. In light of the commonplace that Mozart was a precocious musician, however, we could also consider that he had indeed traversed much more of "life" than most of us will in eighty years. The assessment of "early" and "late," then, poses serious problems. In music, this problem may be worsened in that signs of maturity can easily be emulated by very young people. As Hegel observed, "Musical talent generally announces itself in very early youth, while the head is still empty and the heart has been but little moved, and is capable of attaining to a very considerable height in early years, before mind and life have experience of themselves. And again, as a matter of fact we often enough see very great expertness in musical composition, as also in execution, subsist along with remarkable barrenness of mind and character."[27]

Late style, then, turns out to be a category that can be applied to any period in the creative output of an artist that appears under the aegis of the *end*, in particular of the *announcement* of the end. The end, generally speaking, may be caused by internal circumstances, such as reaching maturity or reaching the point of exhaustion of a style or the compositional material; or by external circumstances such as the debilitation of conditions that favor the production of (a particular form of) music. These may include writing for instruments that no longer exist, or for an audience that has perished, or in a musical language that is largely experienced to be dead (a case in point being Beethoven's *Missa Solemnis*). Messiaen, too, has been in such a position when around 1952 he all of a sudden gave up his role as mentor of the European musical avant-garde and started to focus exclusively on bird-song. In the eyes of many, this choice simply meant that he allowed himself to be overtaken by the younger innovators and sought refuge in a musical language (e.g., his previously invented system of modes) that did not seem to point the way forward for anyone other than himself. More important, however, the announcement of the end (as well as of the End itself) has a special ring in Messiaen in that it functions as the key theme of *everything* he felt to be important in a religious sense.

The announcement of the End is most colorfully related the Apocalypse of John, the book of visions that Messiaen found to be the most important and beautiful of all the Bible. Indeed, according to philosopher Jean-Luc Nancy, Christianity essentially consists in the (infinite) announcement of the end.[28] To compose and live, as Messiaen apparently did, with the Apocalypse before one's eyes can only imply that everything—from the very first second and even before that—falls under the aegis of the end— and hence, takes part in "lateness." In Messiaen's oeuvre the grand theme of the End surfaces in early works such as *Dyptique* ("*essai sur la vie terrestre et l'éternité bien-heureux*"), the song cycle *La mort du nombre* (which deals with the end of time), and, most conspicuously, *Apparition de l'Église éter-nelle*. What is the structure of the End in Messiaen? First of all, it appears to take on the form of a *desire* for plenitude and fulfillment. The object of this desire is projected along the axis of time in such a way that the original scene of plenitude (Eden) is completely forgotten. Messiaen never uttered a word on the subject of Paradise. Everything is projected forward into the future and beyond the future into eternity. This (arguably one-sided, luminous) Apocalypticism is painted in dazzling multicolor and birdsong, the symbols of the resurrected—and, in Freud, symbols of consummation, that is, of the release of energy and the return to a state of relaxation.[29] Messiaen's aspiration toward the beyond often results in a highly tense fo-cus on the object of desire rather than the infinite feeling of desire as such (cf. romantic *Sehnsucht*). The birds occupy a special place in this regard.

Fulfillment, as the End of all ends, is only attainable through radical finitude; that is, through the end of life and through the ends (or endings) of the works.[30] Although Messiaen's music is full of cuts and interruptions, the endings often represent gestures of infinity, such as the dazzling choirs of *La Transfiguration* (parts 7 and 14) and the final scene of *Saint François*, or the minimalistic birdsong that appears at the end of the *Méditations sur le mystère de la Sainte Trinité* (parts 2, 5, and 8). When toward the end of his life the structure of Messiaen's music becomes more organic and less sec-tional, it seems that the distance between finitude and infinity decreases, absorbing, as the music does, the "beyond" into its fabric and lowering the *intension* (Nancy) of anticipation.[31]

In an interview from 1987 Messiaen relates that he is awaiting the be-yond with "great curiosity"—which bespeaks a very different attitude to-ward the Last Things than found in his earlier work.[32] Like an actor who feels his nerves calm down in the seconds before going on stage, Messiaen, on the basis of the *theobiological* certainly of imminent death, no longer seems to feel the need to proclaim the End in the combatant fashion of his earlier works. There appear folds in his works: Time is not only treated in strictly linear sequences (lines, melodies, blocks) but now also tends to produce complex temporalities in which the past folds into the present or in which it appears that a certain movement of infinitization becomes part of the finite musical moment.

The Point of Indifference

Messiaen, then, seemed to attain a point in time—a point in existence one may say—where the language of *folds* and (double) *edges* seems more fitting than the language of creative periods and Adorno's "decisive boundaries." This point in time, which may be construed as a point of *indifference*, is referred to by Michel Foucault in his lectures on the hermeneutics of the subject.[33] In one of these lectures Foucault reconstructs the reasons why Seneca, the author of the *Natural Questions*, found the study of nature an important undertaking for himself as a writer of old age. The answer Seneca gives is that the study of nature allows one to traverse the world, to see what world we live in, and from there to see what the life is we are offered to live. Only then, Seneca argues, are we in a position to say yes or no to life, to make a choice between entering life or dying—that is, only then are we in a position to actually live in the full sense of the word. In Roman times suicide was considered more honorable an option to choose compared to the taboo that came to rest on it in Christian times. But the logic of what Seneca discusses here is quite clear. What we need to do, he argues, is make an ascent—like a bird—and see the world, and the tiny space we occupy within it, as it were from above. As Foucault paraphrases, "you would see 'a city . . . shared by gods and men,' you would see the stars, their regular course, the moon, and the planets whose movements govern men's fortune. You would admire 'the accumulated clouds,' the 'the jagged lightning and the roar of heaven.' Then, when you 'lower your eyes to earth,' you will find many different and wonderful things; the plains, mountains, and towns, the ocean, sea monsters, and the ships which cross the seas and ply their trade."[34]

In a similar fashion Messiaen had toured the natural world: its landscapes, starry heavens, lakes, trees, and birds in order to see, from a distance, from a high point in the vicinity of God, the totality of the cosmos he lived in. Messiaen regarded many of his works as "reports" (and even picture albums) of his studies of nature across the globe: from the canyons of Utah to the isles of New Caledonia, from the deserts of Israel to the landscapes of the Languedoc. This cosmic approach has served him to find material for his compositions, which then function as "maps" of his life. In *Éclairs sur l'au-delà* . . . , his final large-scale work, this is no different: We hear Australia in all its splendor, the Superb Lyre bird, the constellation of Sagittarius, and, looking higher up, we see the Elect with their seals, the seven angels and their trumpets, and the resplendent Christ. At the same time, Messiaen weaved a temporal thread into this fabric by referring to the great movements of his earlier works such as *Turangalîla, Quatuor* and, through these works, to the very early melodies of *L'Ascension*. As Griffiths has it, *Éclairs* "is [*Quatuor*] raised to its apotheosis;" it seems that in both works, written amid war violence and at old age, respectively, Messiaen had been faced with the imminence of death.

Although it appears that Messiaen, unlike Seneca, categorically excluded death and suffering from his music, here in the seventh movement of his last major work, the gaze is suddenly turned downward and mankind is addressed in almost subjective terms. The movement is called "And God wiped every tear from their eyes . . ." Suffering, which Messiaen had always responded to in "naïve" terms, foregrounding flowers, birds, and colors, finally seemed to have received explicit recognition.[35] It is from the point of indifference only—balancing as it were on the edge between life and death—that Messiaen can say yes to it all (and Yes is all he wanted to say). Is this a sad position, framed by a sense of impotence and melancholy, as one might expect from looking at life from some fold outside of it? No, not at all. For the bird that carries him toward this point and allows him to hover above and affirm life is also the symbol of the pure vitality, of the *libidinality* of his music. The birds are the *trait d'union* between this vitality and the flight away from this life—perhaps into the next, perhaps into a blissful oblivion . . . They are the Janus-faced figures that lift up toward the interspace between life and death that, in Seneca, is the prerogative of old age (and which, one might say, had already entered Messiaen's music from the very moment birdsong became his point of focus). In Messiaen, then, late style is ultimately the synthesis of life, (eternal) Life, and death in the obscure light, the *clair obscur*, that had always been the signature of his most illuminated and most liberated and birdlike music.[36]

PART V

Time and Oblivion

CHAPTER 11

Of Shakespeare and Pastness

Brian Cummings

Shakespeare, it is often said, is a writer neither of the past nor of the future but of the continuous present. From his first posthumous entry into the world in the complete works edition of 1623, he was described (in an epigraph to the First Folio by his own contemporary Ben Jonson) as a poet who transcended time. He is a monument without a tomb, and lives on, as long as his books do live. To sing his praises properly we must call the ancient tragic poets of Athens back to life to witness our modern poet on the stage and pay him homage. This being Ben Jonson, he can't resist the slur that Shakespeare did not have enough skill in ancient languages to understand the compliment, but he praises his fellow poet, all the same, as fulfilling the oldest dream of poetry, to achieve immortality:

> And though thou hadst small *Latine*, and lesse *Greeke*,
>   From thence to honour thee, I would not seeke
> For names; but call forth thund'ring *Aeschilus*,
>   Euripides, and Sophocles to vs,
> Paccuuius, Accius, him of Cordoua dead,
>   To life againe, to heare thy Buskin tread,

And shake a Stage: Or, when thy Sockes were on,
   Leaue thee alone, for the comparison
Of all, that insolent *Greece*, or haughtie *Rome*
   sent forth, or since did from their ashes come.
Triumph, my *Britaine*, thou hast one to showe,
   To whom all Scenes of *Europe* homage owe.
He was not of an age, but for all time!
   And all the *Muses* still were in their prime,
When like *Apollo* he came forth to warme
   Our eares, or like a *Mercury* to charme![1]

Jonson, addressing Shakespeare as "not of an age, but for all time," was
indulging in a rhetorical figure of speech, a hyperbole. He did not perhaps
mean it. Poets are always creating this kind of figure. *Exegi monumentum
aere perennius*, says Horace most famously of all in *Odes*, 3.30, "I have built
a monument more lasting than bronze":

> *Exegi monumentum aere perennius,*
> *Regalique situ Pyramidum altius:*
> *Quod non imber edax, non Aquilo impotens*
> *Possit diruere, aut innumerabilis*
>
> *Annorum series, & fuga temporum.*[2]

> (I have completed a monument more lasting than bronze
> and higher than the decaying Pyramids of kings,
> which cannot be destroyed by gnawing rain
> nor north wind, or by the unnumbered
>
> procession of the years and flight of time.)[3]

Shakespeare wrote his own version of this ode in Sonnet 55:

> Not marble, nor the gilded monuments
> Of princes, shall outlive this powerful rhyme.[4]

The counting of the years and the passage of time itself will not compre-
hend him, he will outlive even the death-god himself.
   Yet there is something other than poetic boasting at work here. The
Horatian trope is expressing something about the nature of writing. It is at
once a material and an immaterial trace. It is in these terms that Derrida
composed a sense of the "temporalization" of writing:

> *Ces précautions étant prises, on doit reconnaître que c'est dans la zone spéci-*
> *fique de cette empreinte et de cette trace, dans la temporalisation d'un vécu qui*

n'est ni dans le monde ni dans un « autre monde », qui n'est pas plus sonore que lumineux, pas plus dans le temps que dans l'espace, que les différences apparaissent entre les éléments ou plutôt les produisent, les font surgir comme tels et constituent des textes, des chaînes et des systèmes de traces.[5]

(These precautions taken, it should be recognized that it is in the specific zone of this imprint and this trace, in the temporalization of a *lived experience* which is neither *in* the world nor in "another world," which is not more sonorous than luminous, not more *in* time than *in* space, that differences appear among the elements or rather produce them, make them emerge as such and constitute the *texts*, the chains, and the systems of traces.)[6]

In this immaterial sense, once called into being, writing never strictly disappears. And yet writing also brings with it the implication of repetition, absence, loss, and death. *Verba volant, scripta manent.*[7] Once iterated, writing exists beyond its author and lives in its own time and space, even though it also brings with it the mortality of the author, and therefore also of the reader. It remains ambiguously, in the words of Sonnet 55, "The living record of your memory."

Indeed, within the concept of pastness, we could place *literature* alongside religion as a cultural trajectory that challenges a linear conception of history. Every time we open the page in a work of literature we cross a boundary between past and future, as we read the work in the singularity of our own moment, as if for the first time. And we at the same moment predict our own death. This is one of the first paradoxes of literature: However old a work is and however much we construe it as a product of a particular moment in history, it nonetheless appears completely anew, afresh. And yet each reading also disappears just as quickly into its own past. Each time any one of us reads, it is as if the words were writing themselves in front of us for the first time and simultaneously disappearing. On the roof of Atreus's palace a watchman appears every night at the same time and cries again in the same inflection:

Θεοὺς μὲν αἰτῶ τῶνδ' ἀπαλλαγὴν πόνων
φρουρᾶς ἐτείας μῆκος

(O gods! Grant me release from this long weary watch.)[8]

Two and a half millennia after Aeschylus's *Agamemnon* was first performed at the Dionysia of 458 BCE the watchman's words still speak as if spontaneously. Each instantiation of the words composes a newly realized singularity. Moreover, they are not any longer Aeschylus's words: The text speaks for itself. Indeed, when *I* read these words, I temporarily inhabit these words as if from my point of view and make them my own.

Shakespeare, as the author of authors, possesses this function *a fortiori*. He stands as a figure for the timelessness of poetry, of writing itself. However, as well as serving this general purpose, he is also figured as transcending the bounds of his art in a special sense. Shakespeare, as well as manifesting the aspiration of all writing to achieve immortality, stands outside of his own historical time in a peculiar way. Jonson, his contemporary, is forever condemned to be just that: Shakespeare's contemporary. Jonson is bound by time. He has been admired and read for four hundred years, but he is admired as a great writer of the past. Shakespeare, by contrast, seems to have escaped his own pastness altogether. He has come to represent his own age: the age of Shakespeare, Shakespearean England, as natural a term as if he were a monarch. His writing, meanwhile, is performed onstage as if he were a contemporary artist. The phrase, then, "for all time," from Jonson's epitaph to Shakespeare in the First Folio has come to have a greater than usual significance for what is after all a rhetorical cliché. *For all time* is a mantra of Shakespeare studies, repeated to schoolchildren every class, used as a motto by theater companies or as the title of a new Shakespeare biography almost every year. It is accorded the veneration of a prophecy.

Shakespeare's timelessness is a corollary of his universality. The two propositions coalesce in Harold Bloom: Shakespeare "has become the universal canon . . . Every other great writer may fall away . . . Shakespeare will abide."[9] Up to the 1950s such a statement was fairly standard in the literary schools; Shakespeare was read, performed, and taught as the embodiment of human value in artistic form; "all humanity is in him" (in Coleridge's words). By 1999, when Bloom wrote *Shakespeare and the Invention of the Human*, however, it was part of a defensive counterblast. Bloom aggressively reasserted "the Western Canon" against what he called "the current debasement of our teaching institutions," the "anti-élitist swamp of Cultural Studies" (p.17). Shakespeare is the last bastion against Batman and Madonna.[10] In the other direction, meanwhile, Shakespeare's "universality" has come under suspicion as a covert form of Eurocentrism and cultural colonialism. This argument claims that universalism has only ever been partial in both senses, that it has been a way of prioritizing Western values and forcing them onto the rest of the world. And, in an interesting turn on Shakespeare's timelessness, it claims that this timelessness is itself historical: Shakespeare only began to be a universal author in the eighteenth century, and he only fulfilled his role as the British Empire held sway in the nineteenth century and beyond. Shakespeare's humanity is a construction, and his existence as a poet outside of time is a creation of a particular time in history.[11]

Whichever way we go on this question, it is clear that locating Shakespeare within historical time is not a matter of idle fancy or mere scholarship but a principle with deeply philosophical implications. For Bloom, the universalist argument about Shakespeare is predicated on removing Shakespeare's writing from any historical matrix. Atemporality is the precondition of Shakespeare the artist, or as Bloom calls him, the "archetype of the artist," a poet without limits who writes the "poem unlimited."[12] Atemporality consists in removing from Shakespeare any association with context. Two plays in particular epitomize this estrangement of Shakespeare from the past: *Hamlet* and *King Lear*. *King Lear* (I quote) is the play where "the flames of invention burn away all context and grant us the possibility of what could be called primal aesthetic value, free of history and ideology."[13] It is easy enough to identify within this statement the animus of an attack on the doctrines of New Historicism, which dominated Shakespearean studies in the 1980s and 1990s. Bloom dismisses Stephen Greenblatt as pursuing what he calls "French Shakespeare" (the Shakespeare of literary theory), a trend he aligns with a general "School of Resentment," which prefers context over text. There is, in addition, a second and more specific decontextualization on which Bloom insists, one he applies especially to *Hamlet*. This is particularly relevant to the theme of the pastness of religion. It is the idea of secularization. Central to *Hamlet*'s claim to universality is the view that it is a play without religion. Indeed it is this quality that enables Shakespeare, above all writers, "to compete with the world's scriptures." *Hamlet*, Bloom asserts, is "a secular scripture."[14]

King Lear, as much as *Hamlet*, is the paradigm of Shakespearean secularism. The text of the play is self-consciously pagan in setting. Lear in the first scene of the play refers to "the misteries of *Heccat*" and swears by the name of Apollo; Kent replies:

Now by Apollo, King
Thou swear'st thy Gods in vaine. (act 1, scene 1, F173–04)

With pedantic rigor, the gods are referred to in the plural throughout the play. The world of the play is polytheistic and thus removed from the God of Judaism and Christianity. There is just one ambiguous instance in act 5, in the all too brief reconciliation between Lear and Cordelia, wherein he refers to the two of them as "Gods spies."[15] But of course there was no apostrophe for the genitive in early seventeenth-century English, and it is at least possible that the gods here, too, are plural. What is the reason for this?

The immediate pretext is a historical fastidiousness. The historical reign of Lear, to which the play alludes, is part of the mythical origins of Britain, a world well before the Christian era, a world of romance.[16] Lear appears in Geoffrey of Monmouth as the son of Blaiddyd or Bladud, a Celtic king tenth in line from Brutus, in turn the descendant of the Trojan Aeneas.[17] Geoffrey specifically mentions in the practice of these kings a cult of the worship of Minerva.[18] Other sources could be a little more vague or confused about the religious culture of these very ancient Britons. The other "Lear" play, the chronicle history play (perhaps written in the early 1590s and printed in 1605) that Shakespeare is usually believed to have borrowed from in composing his own play, sometimes uses Greek mythology as a frame of reference, comparing Leir and his daughters to Priam and his children, and glancing at the tales of Hero and Leander and Dido and Aeneas.[19] But this play also had access to the chronologies that cross-referred ancient British history with the events of the Old Testament. In an interesting case of solecism, which nonetheless attempts deliberately to avoid anachronism, Leir is made to say:

> The blessing, which the God of *Abraham* gaue
> Vnto the trybe of *Iuda*, light on thee.[20]

This writer places mythical Britain in a carefully Old Testament and pre-Christian world. It represents a universe in parallel both to Mycenaean Greeks and Judaism before the age of kings. But it has no consistent religion. Characters refer to the "king of Heaven" and sometimes simply to "God" without making it clear which God it is they believe in or why. At one point Ragan says Cordella is fit to be a "parson's wife," whereas her sister Gonorill replies, "She is far too stately for the Church" (sig. B3v).

Shakespeare's exactness in comparison is striking. His characters swear very precisely only by the pagan gods. They also develop a very specific form of argument about the pagan gods in relation to concepts of divine order and justice. This culminates in the famous moment on the heath when Gloucester, following his blinding, comes face-to-face with his son Edgar, whom he has banished, and fails to recognize him. In the depth of his suffering, he cries out:

> As Flies to wanton Boyes, are we to th' Gods,
> They kill vs for their sport.[21]

While the critical tradition has argued back and forth about the precise significance of these words—they are clearly ironic, in that Gloucester at this very moment because of his blindness fails to see how providence is bringing him back into contact with his abandoned son—one thing that has caused more or less uniform consensus is that Shakespeare through these lines consciously excises from the play any line of trajectory with Christian theodicy. In this, the claim has often gone, Shakespeare is being like the Greeks. This is a philosophical realm of tragedy carefully removed from the arguments over divine justice in post-Reformation England. This is a world beyond or above God. It pays no attention to the easy consolations of religion, particularly the Christian religion of love, and places us instead in the world of existential human suffering. This is not the only reading of *King Lear*, but it is the reading of the most influential of early twentieth-century commentaries on the play, that of A. C. Bradley (brother of the idealist philosopher F. H. Bradley), in *Shakespearean Tragedy*.[22]

Religion, I am arguing, is at the center of the problem of Shakespeare's pastness. Yet *a priori* it appears to have this function in precisely the opposite sense to that proposed by the idea of religious "pastness." Religion is the excluded middle of Shakespeare studies. Indeed, the religion of Shakespeare is a shibboleth, something to be abjured even if we could find it. It is defined by its absence, its nonbeing. Put at its simplest, Shakespeare leaves behind him no writing in any remotely devotional genre. More than this, he leaves behind no record of any religious affiliation, no testimony, no *auto da fé*. He is the poet without confession, without denomination. And this accords with the general rule of Shakespearean criticism since the Romantics; namely, that Shakespeare is the poet of impersonality, or as Keats defined it, "negative capability." Apart from the *Sonnets* he is the poet with no first person voice, and the *Sonnets* themselves leave a voice so ambiguous as to be impenetrable. Shakespeare leaves no trace of himself: Instead he has transferred all his energy into the characters of his stage. In himself he has no personhood; instead he is the great impersonator.

In this sense, to discover the religion of Shakespeare would be to break the fundamental taboo of his identity. "Shakespeare seems too wise to believe anything" political or religious, Bloom says, adding, "I am baffled when critics argue as to whether Shakespeare was Protestant or Catholic, since the plays are neither."[23] The mystery of Shakespeare the person is assisted by the vagaries of the documentary evidence. The life records of Shakespeare are notoriously thin and ambiguous. There is only one surviving letter, about someone else's debt; one surviving court case, about someone else's daughter's marriage; and one private document, the last will and testament, with its obscure reference to a second best bed.

Despite this paucity of documentation, the question "What was Shakespeare's religion?"—once a matter of indifference—has in the last few years become the most pressing issue in Shakespeare studies. Part of this impetus has been documentary. The rumor that Shakespeare "died a papist" goes back to 1701.[24] In 1790 a considerable stir was caused by the report of the finding (originally in 1757) of a "Spiritual Testament" signed by Shakespeare's father, John, in the rafters of an old Stratford house. These tales have often been treated in the past as either apocryphal or else forgeries. They had their ups and downs in the way that all the paraphernalia of Shakespeare do. In the 1990s they received new credence. A pattern has been drawn between the possible Catholic affiliations of Shakespeare's father, of parts of the family of Shakespeare's mother, and of some of the teachers in Shakespeare's school. Further excitement has been aroused on the trail of one William Shakeshafte, who lived for a time in Lancashire, may have been a player, may have been a Catholic, and may have been Shakespeare.[25]

What I am interested in here is not the authenticity or otherwise of this documentary trail. I am interested instead in the way this trail has been put to use in the services of a particular kind of epistemology of religion and a particular kind of phenomenology of religious identity. We can argue back and forth about the archive. Patrick Collinson, doyen among historians of Elizabethan religion, summarizes it this way: Shakespeare's father "was probably a Catholic of the old stamp." His son-in-law, John Hall, by contrast, "was an impeccable Jacobean Protestant." "As for Shakespeare himself," Collinson concludes, "we cannot say."[26] But even if we could, what would this tell us? In recent times, the documents about Shakespeare have been used to endorse readings of Shakespeare's plays as informed by Catholic sympathies. The view of religion invested in this seems to me particularly crude and monolithic. It is also hopelessly biased toward that linear view of time and belief that a complex idea of "pastness" attempts to dismantle. A confessional Shakespeare is fixed within a particular verifiable time and therefore meaning, a closed identity.

I propose a rather different approach to Shakespeare's religion. It seems to me that this question has the capacity to open up the subject of Shakespeare's past and of his future in novel and imaginative ways. It also opens up the question again of Shakespeare's timelessness. We are confronted here, first of all, by the impossibility of Shakespeare's own past. The life of Shakespeare is a self-consuming artifact, a fantasy brought to life in exact disproportion to the disappointment of the archive. It is hard to think of any writer of stature for whom the biographical record is so thin; we know far more about medieval predecessors such as Geoffrey Chaucer; we even know more about Sophocles. Shakespeare's life disappears before us, but the very absence brings with it a longing for more. Myself I find this longing, or anxiety (we might call it a mourning), as interesting as any fact. But the academy and the public alike wishes more to close up the wound by filling in the gaps and producing a plausible semi-life or half-life. In this age of reality television and of celebrity it is no longer sufficient for Shakespeare to have no personality. This is what is happening in our own decade with Shakespeare's religion. But what if we turn the problem round? What if we look not for a linear narrative of reconstruction but for an epistemology of the gaps in between?

The first point of observation here would be that Shakespeare's religion can only be constructed (it seems) by reference to a continuous regression. His religion is bound up with the religion of his father. Indeed, more precisely, the so-called facts of Shakespeare's Catholicism are really the facts of John's life, not William's. There is clearly a problem here: Martin Luther's father was also, we remember, a Catholic. As a general rule, to know a person's religion we look to how they bring up their children rather than what their father did. Shakespeare's children were baptized in the reformed church of Elizabethan England: Does that make their father a Protestant? Not necessarily. William does not appear among the records of communicants in the parish of Southwark, where he lived in the 1590s. But then, he does not appear among the records of recusants, either. The name "John Shakespeare" does appear in a list of those failing to take Communion in Stratford-upon-Avon in 1592. But according to the commissioners this was "for feare of processe for Debtte," not for religion. In any case, as the more careful commentators point out, there were four different John Shakespeares living in the area in the 1590s.[27]

In a more general sense, I think we can see that Shakespeare's pastness is bound up with the pastness of England's religion. In this sense it is not surprising that it is the religion of the old faith, the lost Catholicism of pre-Reformation England, which has come to appear Shakespeare's signature belief. Even if the documents suggested completely otherwise, we somehow need Shakespeare to be a Catholic. Shakespeare's faith is repeatedly imagined as the recuperation of a lost religious identity—the pre-Reformation religion of his fathers and forebears.

One reason for this lies in the origins of Shakespeare's life. I do not mean by this the life he lived, but the life that was brought into life by our

need for him—the life of biography. Nobody dreamed of writing a life
of Shakespeare until too late. Thomas Fuller included Shakespeare in his
History of the Worthies of England. This was published in 1662, by which
time Fuller was himself dead; in a finely balanced epitaph on his tomb in
Cranford it is said of the great church historian that his attempt to give immortality to others in the *Worthies* had made him immortal, too. Like everything in that work, Fuller's account of Shakespeare is tinged by Fuller's
sense of the evanescence of time:

> He was an eminent instance of the truth of that Rule, *Poeta non fit sed
> nascitur*, one is not *made* but *born* a Poet. Indeed his Learning was very
> little, so that as *Cornish diamonds* are not polished by any Lapidary, but
> are pointed and smoothed even as they are taken out of the Earth, so
> *nature* itself was all the *art* which was used upon him.[28]

Shakespeare was born outside of natural time; he does not have an ordinary
context in history. Yet he also appears already to be from before his own
time. Fuller's whole account of Warwickshire, like much of his book, is
tinged with a memorial to an unreachable past before the Reformation. A
typical passage is his description of the current state of the castles of Kenilworth and Warwick:

> Some Castles have been Demolished for security, which I behold de-
> stroyed, *se defendendo, without offence*. Others Demolished in the heat of
> the Wars, which I look upon as *Castle-slaughter*. But I cannot excuse the
> Destruction of this Castle, from *Wilful-murder*, being done in *cold blood*,
> since the end of the Wars.
>
> I am not stock'd enough with Charity to pity the Ruiners thereof,
> if the materialls of this castle answered not their expectation, who
> destroyed it.
>
> Pass we now from the *Preterperfect* to the *Present Tense*, I mean, from
> what was *once*, to what *now* is most magnificent, the *Castle* of *Warwick*.[29]

Kenilworth had become a ruin in his own lifetime, "slighted" in 1650 by
Cromwell's soldiers. The past is disappearing from in front of us, from the
present to the preterperfect.

To understand this we have to remember the time in which Fuller lived.
He is a peculiarly ambiguous soul of the vexed period of the English civil
wars. Caught between King and Parliament he turned to writing history
because he had become exiled from his own present, rather as Kenilworth
Castle had been, the great edifice pulled down by the Roundheads and its

mere returned from water to land. Fuller was an internal exile, an exile of the mind. His two great works reflect this: *The Church History of Britain* (1655), the first comprehensive English protestant account of Christianity in the islands from the earliest times; and the *Worthies*, the first English biographical dictionary. Each is caught by a sense that the history he is attempting to record is not an easy single line but is characterized instead by a sense of the ruptures of time, of moments broken off from each other. Christian history in particular is trying to do two irreconcilable things: to present a unified single tradition, and to respect the differences of different Christian pasts and cultures. Protestantism especially is permanently marked by this sense of a broken tradition: It is founded on a sense of rupture from the past even as it attempts to reclaim a connection across the gulf of time with the age of the primitive church, the church of the gospels, or of Christ himself. No rupture is greater for Fuller than the Reformation. All of his county histories contain separate entries for "Since the Reformation," dividing time between the recorded and the mythologized. And yet the Reformation is also responsible for bringing the central structures of his own life into being.

Shakespeare's biography is a quintessential product of the Restoration. It is haunted by the sense of time past, perhaps of an irrecoverable past. Next after Fuller came the effort of John Aubrey, in his so-called *Brief Lives*. Aubrey jotted these down in notebooks; he found it almost impossible to complete any writing of his own, indeed his most substantial work consisted of *Miscellanies, viz. I. Day-Fatality. II. Local-Fatality . . . XXI. Second-sighted persons. Collected by J. Aubrey, Esq.* (1696). Born in 1625, in his forty-sixth year he descended into financial ruin, attributing misfortune to a complex horoscope derived from the exact hour of his nativity. Part of his motivation for recording the lives of others, in fact, seems to have been to trace the chances and mischances of a life from birth onwards: He set about collecting the hour of birth of previous individuals, collected from books and from the memories of friends. Whether his friends were always reliable was a moot point: Anthony Wood told him he could not recall any longer the year of his birth, but thought it might be 1647; elsewhere, Wood was the eyewitness source for the story of King Charles's entry into Christ Church, Oxford, in 1636.[30]

Aubrey's "lives," for which his name is now best known, were indeed posthumous, for Aubrey left behind only fragments and drafts. He desired to preserve the record of a world that he now perceived to be irretrievably lost, the England of the Tudors and Stuarts before the Civil War and the

Puritan Commonwealth of Oliver Cromwell, that great modernizer. His eight hundred words on Shakespeare are wonderfully nostalgic and romantic and haunted by the image of loss:

> The Humour of the Constable in Midsomernight's Dreame, he happened to take at Grendon, in Bucks (I thinke it was Midsomer night that he happened to lye there) which is the roade from London to Stratford, and there was living that Constable about 1642, when I first came to Oxon.[31]

Shakespeare's plays appear as the result of an accident of memory, random thoughts ("he happened to lye there") drawn from his journeys through the countryside. Their recovery depends on an even more ephemeral process, as Aubrey himself tracks down the small number of survivors who themselves can still preserve some living trace of the original author. We are in the world here of what sociologists call "communicable memory": what Aubrey can recall in the late seventeenth century of what a constable could recall in 1642 (the year, significantly, of the outbreak of the Civil War) of what Shakespeare may have seen two generations before that.

However, in this sense of loss I think that Fuller and Aubrey were also recognizing something present in Shakespeare himself. Shakespeare's religion, too, is residual and memorial: It is a religion of the past. Let us consider here again *Hamlet*. The play, everybody recognizes, is caught between religious worlds. Perhaps this is best expressed by Greenblatt's observation, "a young man from Wittenberg, with a distinctly Protestant temperament, [is] haunted by a distinctly Catholic ghost."[32] I think, though, that Greenblatt is overly keen in this statement to tie Shakespeare himself down to the specificity of a particular confessional crisis. At the same time Greenblatt's complexity is preferable to the monomaniac secularity of Bloom. It is Bloom who is guilty of failing to read properly in not noticing the profound relationship of the play to the Reformation. But this relationship is oblique and even duplicitous rather than either nostalgic or doctrinal. *Hamlet*, the play, is haunted by many things, but one of these things is the religion of not only his father but of all England's fathers. *Hamlet* is haunted by a sense that it is no longer living in its own time — that its own time is already lost.

I return then finally to *King Lear*. The play plunges its audience and its readers into a pagan world. But this is not, as Bradley has it, because the play is indifferent to religion. Something much more remarkable is taking place. Shakespeare has created a heterocosmic religion, a religion of fiction. He is trying to understand how a distinctive culture, separated from us by space and time, thinks and believes. Above all, he tries to imagine how this religion constructs for this culture its sense of how justice and suffering are to be reconciled:

> Let the great Goddes
> That keepe this dreadfull pudder o're our heads,
> Finde out their enemies now. Tremble thou Wretch,
> That hast within thee vndivulged Crimes
> Vnwhipt of Iustice.[33]
>
> (*King Lear*, act 3, scene 2, F1702–07)

In this, indeed, I think the play is terribly Greek; again, not by eschewing religion but by being tormented by it. Have the gods abandoned us, or do they still love us? This is hardly an irrelevant question in the aftermath of the Reformation. The great sixteenth-century polemics of freedom and destiny resonate strongly. But they are also kept at arm's length. The play keeps present quarrels at bay by imagining instead a quarrel in a parallel universe displaced in time. It imagines for its characters a religious language just different enough from that of its audience to keep it in limbo, to keep it in fractured suspense.

It does this by an act of historical imagination. In this it shares something with those efforts of that new breed of men who called themselves antiquarians: people like John Leland or John Stow earlier in the century, or William Camden, Shakespeare's exact contemporary, who rummaged around Hadrian's Wall looking for the remnants of the cult of Minerva or of Mithras:

> This Prince reformed many things thorowout the Island, and was the
> first that built a wall between the barbarous Britans and the Romans
> fourescore miles in length, laying the foundation therof within the
> ground of huge piles or stakes, and fastning them together in manner of
> a strong hedge or mound.[34]

It was a similar spirit that later inhabited Fuller and Aubrey, or Sir Thomas Browne in his lugubrious work of morbid anthropology, *Urn Buriall*:

> When the Funeral Pyre was out, and the last Valediction over, men
> took a lasting Adieu of their interred Friends, little expecting the
> curiosity of future Ages should comment upon their Ashes, and having
> no old experience of the duration of their Reliques, held no opinion of
> such after-considerations.

But who knows the fate of his Bones, or how often he is to be
buried? Who hath the Oracle of his Ashes, or whether they are to be
scattered?[35]

The Reformation brought about a historicizing of the past, as Margaret
Aston has observed in her account of the invention of the idea of the ruin
after the dissolution of the monasteries.[36] This provoked a new interest
in the anthropology of death, in the rituals of ancient non-Christian so-
cieties that could be observed in archaeological sites. But it also brought
an anxiety about the past, about its irretrievability and alienation from
the contemporary moment. At the same moment, the literature of pre-
Reformation England—and in time, the literature of the Reformation up
to Shakespeare and perhaps a little beyond—was opened up to a kind of
double reading, a simultaneous vision of the present and the past, or of the
presence of the past, or of the pastness of the present.

The struggle of these writers to find some proper perspective in their
sense of the past, to become what we consider proper historians, by which
we mostly mean linear historians, has often been observed. What interests
me is how much they are also caught up in a collision between different
visions of the past, and perhaps the most important reason for this is that
they are divided even from the recent past by a sense of inevitable discon-
tinuity, in the divine interregnum of the English Reformation. Some of
these early antiquaries have been discovered to be crypto-Catholics, rather
like Shakespeare is said to be; but others are keen Protestants.

Rather than fit Shakespeare into some confessional camp, however, I
wish to see him as caught in the time loop of the Reformation, which looks
a long way back and a long way forward at the same time. From the time
of William Tyndale or Thomas More to the time of the Earl of Clarendon
or John Bunyan, Englishmen struggled to tell whether they were walking
again in the time of Christ or marching toward the new millennium. It is
this sense of a double time that I find so strongly in *King Lear*, a play of antiquarian immediacy and futuristic historicity. In it we are presented with
how Shakespeare imagined the past, how we imagine Shakespeare's past,
and how we reconstruct the past through religion, in a series of powerful
paradoxes. In this it is a play very much of its time. Yet it also speaks across
time to our own posthistoric age, perhaps nowhere more so than in the
Fool's weird prophecy, which concludes Lear's catastrophe on the heath:

When Vsurers tell their Gold i'th' Field,
And Baudes, and whores, do Churches build,
Then shal the Realme of Albion, come to great confusion:

Then comes the time, who liues to see't,
That going shalbe vs'd with feet.
This prophecie Merlin shall make, for I liue before his time.

(act 3, scene 2, F1745–50)

What time does this speech take place in? It cannot be the time of the legendary Lear, the son of Bladud. Churches are unknown in his time. Shakespeare creates here a deliberate error of time, indulging in the romantic indistinctness and chorological and chronological vagueness that pervades the chronicle *Leir*, but which is banished with exemplary carefulness in *King Lear*. Of course, the error is allowed within the fiction, as it appears in the form of a prophecy. The audience enjoys the joke. But it also senses something uncanny. The Fool, like the audience in the Globe, or like us, lives before his time and after. In that wildly proleptic anachronism, as the Fool steps out of his own remote history and comes out into Jacobean London as a contemporary, he also escapes beyond Shakespeare's grave and into our present.

We are confronted here by the impossibility of Shakespeare's own past, by Shakespeare's sense of the past and *his* sense of its irrecoverableness. For his religion can only be constructed (it seems) by an asymptotic reconstruction: toward the religion of his fathers and forebears, and more generally, toward an impossible origin of the religion of England's past. Shakespeare's religion is the unrealized and imagined recuperation of a lost religious identity. The irreducible fact of religion in Shakespeare's time is that it is constantly on the point of oblivion. As one confessional identity replaces another it buries a host of former practices, which had previously been taken for granted. Shakespeare's religion is thus residual and memorial, for him and for us: It is a religion of pastness.

CHAPTER 12

The Anger of Angels:
From Rubens to Virginia Woolf

Peter Cramer

I.

In the Ashmolean Museum of Art and Archaeology in Oxford is a drawing of Rubens' entitled *Landscape with Mill Buildings*. The drawing is in pen and ink on gray "stone-coloured" paper.[1] The lines appear to have been made with the rapidity and the fluency of what is drawn from life, and even the nonchalance of the virtuoso capable of perceiving the scene as an organized whole and then without strain executing this whole through equal attention to the parts that make it up. The parts correspond to one another to the point where the beholder is inclined to believe in their mutual participation. In some areas, the lines have been heightened by white paint, almost giving the sense of snow collected in small drifts against the fences in the field in the foreground of the mill house to the left. The trees in the center, on a level behind that of the house but to the right as the viewer sees it, are also heightened with white, and the trees on the right of the drawing are slightly heightened, where the pen strokes become more agitated and carry urgently toward the right, as if seeking a space beyond the frame. At the center, the trees are more balanced, less mobile. The

Figure 4. Rubens, *Landscape with Mill Buildings* (Ashmolean Museum of Art and Archaeology)

mill house, its wheel visible, is to the left of the drawing, with a steep gable toward the beholder: a triangle with a flat base whose two ascending lines bow inward at the middle of their span, and toward each other, no doubt under pressure of time and repeated bouts of weather. The house is in equilibrium with the trees of the center and right of the composition. House and trees: one organized, solid, self-sufficient, huddled by time, the other spare, leaved but wintry, slender, mobile in the wind, leaning up and out form two corresponding masses. Beyond, between mill and trees, fields rise a little to form a low hill. The hill is slight, but high enough to communicate enclosure. With its trees and folds the mill is in self-equilibrium.

Yet there is a suggestion of Wölfflin's *atektonisch*, the absence of boundary, or openness, which he takes to be one of the defining characteristics of baroque, and which in the art of the seventeenth century is (so often) accompanied by the painter's search for an ordering of reality by depth and mass rather than through composition on the painted surface. The sixteenth century, the era of the classical, had stressed the logic of regular, organized forms, of the dominance of verticals and horizontals around a central axis and in clear relation to the frame or edge.

Dem 16. Jahrhundert war es natürlich, sich in der Bildfüllung nach der gegebenen Fläche zu richten. Ohne dass damit ein bestimmter Ausdruck erreicht

*werden soll, ordnet sich der Inhalt innerhalb des Rahmens derart, dass der
eine für den anderen da zu sein scheint. Randlinien und Eckwinkel werden
als verbindlich empfunden und klingen nach in der Komposition. Im 17.
Jahrhundert hat sich die Füllung den Rahmen entfremdet. Man tut alles, um
den Eindruck zu vermeiden, dass diese Komposition gerade für diese Fläche
erfunden worden sei. Trotzdem eine versteckte Kongruenz natürlich fort und
fort wirksam ist, soll das Ganze mehr als ein zufälliger Ausschnitt aus der
sichtbaren Welt erscheinen.*[2]

The distinction between the classical preoccupation with composition
(reaching back to Alberti's *composizione* and *circonscrizione* in *Della Pittura*
2:30–45) and the baroque tendency to allow the shapes of nature their
own insistence, with an effect that is often mysterious, even vague, because
originating in the boundless density of the object itself is modestly played
out in this drawing of the mill house. It is modestly played out, but all the
more eloquently for being caught on the wing by this virtuoso pen. For
the drawing from life has the peculiar eloquence of a self-absorption fused
with unbridled attention to the object. It is like a primordial language re-
discovered after the loss of innocence, or the joy of disenchanted age as it
recalls the joy of the child:

> That nature yet remembers
> What was so fugitive!

The naïve vision survives the blunting, disconsolate effect of mediation.
Rubens, in the freedom of his Silenus painting in the Alte Pinakothek in
Munich, or in the still greater freedom of his drawings, is rediscovering a
lost simplicity, an original, primitive, untroubled union of vision and nature that had been lost with the distancing involved in the Quattrocento:
the discipline of the classical. It is as if the energy given by distancing, by
reflection, is pressed into service by immediacy of vision, strengthening it
rather than muting it.

For the *method* of single-point perspective tends to distinguish the surface of the painting from the object it represents. Method introduces estrangement: It interposes a fixed layer of principles that can be repeated for
every occasion, every object, and every *istoria*, between the eye and what it
looks on.[3] Baroque, Rubens in particular, looks like a will to break through
this and back to the rudimentary force with which once the seen object
struck at the eye and was struck by it. Rubens often strove backward in
this way in his oil sketches, of which a remarkable example is the sketch of
The Betrothal of St. Catherine in the Städel Museum in Frankfurt am Main

(c.1628), one of a number of studies made for an altarpiece in the Augustinian Church in Antwerp (now in the Musées Royaux des Beaux-Arts). Here the freedom of execution rises to a pitch suggesting painterly drunkenness: The rapidity of the brushstrokes, the eddying movement they add up to, enlist the eye with such intensity that the motion of the devout protagonists, a kind of devotional surge that binds St. Catherine and her companion saints into one euphoric merry-go-round, is of a piece with the guessed, easily guessed, urgency of the paint's application to the oak board beneath. The energy of an upward movement is lost to a blurred, unchecked wheeling, where upper and lower seem no more than momentary creatures of fluid gesture, the whole effect helped by a reminiscence of "assumption" (in the nearby Church of Our Lady there is an Assumption of the Virgin, about 1625, which is analogous in movement), of a motion upward to heaven, which is equally the downward pull of Mary's leaning down to Catherine to place the ring of betrothal on her finger. ("Unless someone helps us, we do not know whether we are going up or down," said Empson once.) In *The Fall of the Damned* in Munich, a further extreme is reached where the paint seems not to describe but to shape and knead flesh into being—a flesh that, as Svetlana Alpers observes, disconcerts, and therefore engages, because it uses the *copia* of female flesh, as Rubens would have seen it, to paint the body whether male or female. He disconcerts by transgressing boundaries, by a disregard for difference. This is what Alpers calls Rubens's drunkenness, and she argues that his attachment to Silenus, the companion of Dionysus and the satyrs in Virgil, of which the painting in Berlin of the drunken, orgiastic Silenus figure is the most accomplished example, is not merely the depiction of an interesting theme but an embodiment—*the* embodiment—of his central drive as a painter.[4] One might say that the beginning of the painter's revelry, what Bellori called Rubens's "*furia del pennello*," is in the suppression of difference, which is at the root of drawing from observation: that initial loss of difference between the eye and the thing seen, and the ensuing trace of this immediacy on a surface.

Yet here something jars. For the characteristic of drawing from observation is not obviously the anarchy of what is born of Silenus. The message of Silenus is that inspiration is associated not only with the tearing down of boundaries—old age and sexual vigor, wisdom and intoxication, black and white, master and slave, maternity and eroticism, and so on—but with the dark rapture of moral chaos that all this implies, a kind of heart of darkness or something in the field of force of Hans Castorp's ghastly waking dream, as he was engulfed by snow on the height of the mountain, of child murder at the hub of all that is humanly civilized (Thomas Mann, *Magic Mountain*). Drawing from life has to do, rather, with historicity. It is remarkable, perhaps most of all in the particular version of it which is the portrait, for the conviction with which an unrepeatable moment is caught. The Chinese called this transference of life *ch'i*: breath.

> This sort of portraiture, by which not only a sitter's features but something beyond [them] is caught by the graphic medium, puts portrait drawing in the first rank as the quintessence of drawing from observation. As for example Dürer's portrait of his mother (*Barbara Dürer*, 1514, Berlin, Kupferstichkabinett) or the double portrait-sheet in silverpoint of *Paul Topler and Martin Pfinzing* (1520, Berlin-Dahlem). The sitters' identities appear to be unquestionable. Such a trace of life couldn't possibly have been recorded from memory. It must have been seized at once, as fruit is from a tree. Instantaneous studies such as the reed drawing by Rembrandt, supposedly of *Saskia III* (c.1640, Paris, Musée du Petit Palais) or *Isabella Helena* by Rubens (c.1636, Paris, Musée du Louvre) are examples of such drawings in which truth picked in a few instants holds those instants timelessly.[5]

Breath. The breath of the sitter breathes in the trace of the drawing. In his charcoal-and-ink drawing of Lazarus (if it is Lazarus) stirring from the dead (1475–85, London, British Museum) Mantegna brings off a re-enactment of the event itself: The dead man, still not reconciled to his return, but manifestly done from life, has managed to raise himself up on one elbow. Breath returns as the pen makes its marks. Beneath the figure lies the flat slab of marble that has been his grave. The dead and death are present in the marble, in the reference to ancient sculptures such as the *Dying Gaul*. Mantegna has accomplished the oxymoron of drawing the ancient (and dead) from life—no doubt using a model in the studio. The drawing is the linear draftsmanship (Alberti's *circonscrizione*) that carries through Mantegna's taste for archaeological scrutiny, and, as a glance at the head, which seems tempted by a relapse into sleep, will show, it is also the immediacy of "instantaneous study": It is both at once, both scrutiny and absorption. One could say: Historicity as pastness is fused with *historia* as observation; erudition with reflex.

Rubens, an admirer of Mantegna, whose work he would have seen during his stay in Mantua at the court of Vincenzo Gonzaga, draws from life with equal (though less exacting, less archaeological) aplomb; with equal attention to the instant, to the singular, in this sense of historicity as immediate observation. But the baroque, with its less-than-clarity, its tendency to drunken undifferentiation—and in particular the oil sketches of Rubens—pose the question of what relation the virtuoso collapse of difference, this rapt kinetic blur, this near identity of the gesture of the brush and the movement depicted, has with the exactitude of, say, Mantegna's Lazarus. Both have "breath." Both are a refusal of stable forms as organizing principle. Wölfflin would say one was "painterly," the other "drawing" (*malerisch/zeichnerisch*) and would make these the first terms of his distinction between baroque and classical. But the thrust of what I want to say is this: The confusion of the baroque, the stir, the boundlessness within a haphazardly chosen space, the virtuosity, the blurring, the *Offenheit*, the infinite of folds, is a Silenus-sprung continuity, fluency, loquacity, *Rausch*, drunkenness, *copia*, an unbrokenness that has in it, nonetheless, the manifold, the multiple singular things that make it up, the succession of isolated one-offs—the unrepeatability of this object at this moment; the unrepeatability of the *marks* on paper (of each mark) or, ultimately, the unrepeatability of texture or, for example, of the broken funerary script of Cy Twombly's *Nini's Painting* (1971, Udo and Anette Brandhorst Collection). Each mark is the mark made at creation; an event spilled from the creator's hand. The *ex nihilo* of the mark on paper. The *ex nihilo* of event. The historicity of drawing. The drunken coherence, self-absorption, of baroque and the absorbed observation of drawing from life may not be reducible to one another; but their dialogue is a scintillating affair. One can see the temptation of trying to get *both* the rush of coming into being *and* the singularity of each episode in being.

In the Ashmolean drawing the openness that Wölfflin felt to be a defining characteristic of baroque is in the positive yearning in the branches to the right toward spaces beyond the frame, so that, from our view, the drawing has a strong left to right movement, as if the walled stability of the mill unfolds, and would go on unfolding, in the reiteration of the trees. It is difficult, after Michael Fried's study of absorption in Caravaggio, and in view of Rubens's borrowings from Caravaggio, not to speak of the absorption of Rubens's country scene. Absorption, the inwardness of a painting in Fried's vocabulary—taken from Diderot, who used it in antithesis to theatricality, involving address by the figures in a painting to the beholder—is an option for Rubens, not a method to which he has systematic recourse. Fried's entertaining suggestion is that the discovery of absorption, sometime in the 1590s, by Caravaggio, by withdrawing his paintings from the beholder and depicting action (martyrdom, cheating at cards, *The Supper at Emmaus*) turned in on itself without the bridge to the beholding consciousness provided by a "theatrical" figure who looks out from the scene of action and invites the gaze in to its story-line, is a response to—even a solution to—the sixteenth- and seventeenth-century anxiety over skepticism: less the intellectual skepticism of Descartes (for example) than the skepticism that stands between one human being and the next. The thinking (now Fried leans on Stanley Cavell) is that Shakespearian tragedy

> is the working out of a response to scepticism . . . that tragedy is an interpretation of what scepticism is an interpretation of; that, for example, Lear's "avoidance" of Cordelia [i.e. Lear's fatal self-destructive refusal to acknowledge her love for him] is an instance of the annihilation [of the world of others, ultimately of oneself] inherent in the sceptical problematic, that skepticism's "doubt" is motivated not by (not even where it is expressed as) a (misguided) intellectual scrupulousness but by a (displaced) denial, by a self-consuming disappointment that seeks world-consuming revenge.[6]

And the disappointment has its root in the failure of the world, and the human fellowship within it, to be anything more than finitude. To this it might be added, for the purposes of the portrait, no more fitting example could be sought from Shakespeare than *The Winter's Tale*, in which the refusal of Leontes, against all the evidence—and no doubt his own better self—to believe in anything other than his wife Hermione's infidelity, is apparently driven by a self-destructive will that casts her out and causes her death. The self-destruction—which converts from anger to self-lacerating and hopeless repentance in the King—is only healed by the "resurrection" of the dead, or given-up-for-dead, Queen, in the disturbing shape of a dead, and indeed absorbed, statue of her likeness, which, to the King's astonishment, in its marble pallor, begins to *breathe*. It is cardinal to Fried's understanding of absorption that it has force on the beholder not through a theatrical messenger, as it were, who exists *in* the picture but looks out *from* it; but through the recognition by the beholder's own inwardness of the analogous inwardness that must be there within the physical-sensual drama of absorption depicted. The case of Hermione in *The Winter's Tale* suggests something else than this like-mindedness, this echo of one inwardness in another. For Hermione's absorption is also her lifelessness. She is absorbed by death. She has been plucked away from the viewer— from the viewer who is the stricken King who destroyed her in order to destroy himself. What is suggested is thus a kind of self-sufficiency of the painted or sculpted image that comes from its failure to be the real thing it represents. Representation is the radical presence of loss, so radical it threatens resurrection as ensouled flesh. Conversely, it is a presence so literally or nearly literally repeated—a resurrection—that it gives to loss, death, its definitive shape: "What fine chisel / Could ever yet cut breath? Let no man mock me. / For I will kiss her" (5.3.77–9).

Rubens, as to him, adopts absorption, but the version of it he exploits in his drawing of the mill house (and which can be picked up in other landscape studies), is, in a sense, more radical again. Absorption now has to do not with the "mindedness" of actors in a scene and the corresponding mindfulness of the museum goer, but with the aloofness of creation; and whatever touches earnestly on creation must also have to do with the nothing from which creation came—and which it has been unable to shake off: the palpable silence of the painting or of the drawing.

The mill house could not be more silent. We could be forgiven for thinking of a home. It is a winter's day, dusk perhaps. The gray of the paper puts us in mind of dusk—but then apparently no suspicion of the human. Or again: This is a mill. It must be worked. Two figures appear, cursorily sketched, near the base, a little to the viewer's left, perhaps working a field. But they don't belong. They are an afterthought—even by another hand? They don't occupy the same space as mill and fields. They act to point up the uninhabitedness of the first days of creation. "Evening came and morning came: the first day." Or of the sea. The abstraction of the sea, the objecthood it rebukes us with through this abstractness. A farm or a mill scene, but the heartlessness of the sea. Yet one might encounter a not very different forsakenness in the pallor of a portrait head.

The flicks of the pen in Rubens's sketch of the mill house, registering the trees in the middle space, especially to the upper left of this space, seem to say: "And so on . . ."; not so much in view of a continuation beyond the frame now, but a continuation within this area of drawing. As if to say, in the scarcity of winter a possible density, some other, but not forgotten, season of plenty. Again, there is a recollection of Twombly. In the early 1950s, working as a cryptographer during military service, he would draw in a completely dark room, at night, in the interests of cutting back all the habitual, learned, movements of his hand—all the method. He called it "de-skilling." Free of method, each stroke or mark becomes an absolute beginning. Each mark is a new sound, a note emerging from and falling back into silence, a birth and death. ("[B]irth astride of a grave," says Beckett.) But the marks are, equally, a record of original wilderness. They are marks of something, perhaps of trees. Or they may be the wilderness given by marks on paper that are only themselves. There is a kind of grief in marks which in themselves make for density or scarcity themselves. They are unstable: *merely* virtuosic or skill-less. The Hellespont into which

Leander plunges—with no guidance that night from Hero's torch on the other shore (Twombly's *Hero and Leander*, parts 1–4, 1981–4, across one panel of which are scrawled the words of Keats: "He's gone. Up bubbles all his amorous breath.") Grief alternates with delight in beginning: Each mark is a birth, a seed. In the marks of the drawing, we catch Rubens off duty. He is not preparing a painting. He paints without care. Much the same nonchalance, more obviously comparable to drunkenness, is in play in Rubens's *Betrothal of St. Catherine*, or rather the oil sketch for this in the Städel Museum in Frankfurt am Main. The approach of the unprepared museum denizen to the painting is through grief: through disappointment in the paint, which is there for itself; in the fake substantiality of a turbid motion, which raises our hopes for a moment but then shows up as self-reference, the energy of a desire that cannot rest in an object. Later, we are relieved by the content. St. Catherine is betrothed to Christ. After grief comes feast. The very paint, as paint, is now restored as feast. A more thoroughgoing satisfaction, though, is to be had from the persistence of a negativity, of a kind that presses on us the void we glimpsed at the first approach, now striking us as a felt absence within the painting; not an absence located somewhere behind it, like a solution we cannot yet see, but in the painting, unmistakable and consummated. I will try to say something more of this bounteous, earthy negativity.

II.

The loquacity of Rubens has to do not only with the paint but with the object; the unrepeatability of this thing taken down at this moment. A vagueness, a blur, is kept in place together with precision of observation. In Rubens, or in Twombly or de Kooning, the paint, or in their drawings the Dionysiac line, have a life of their own because they bear the tension of these tendencies as they are thrust together in one sequence of gestures.

Again, the transience of what is observed touches on nonbeing, which is, however, integral to the intensity of presence in the finished product. Transience and eternity flit across the experience of Baudelaire's "modern painter":

> *On peut aussi le comparer, lui, à un miroir aussi immense que cette foule; à un kaléidoscope doué de conscience, qui, à chacun de ses mouvements, représente la vie multiple et la grâce mouvante de tous les éléments de la vie. C'est un moi insatiable du non-moi, qui, à chaque instant, le rend et l'exprime en images plus vivantes que la vie elle-même, toujours instable et fugitive.*[7]

What is unstable and fugitive, the grue of Degas's who picks her tooth in contemptuous provocation, the crowd, the café, the racecourse, the unreliable dodging and turning of fashion, has also to do with the eternal. Taking the fugitive as his subject matter, rather than the permanence of the mythic or of the great historical or Biblical event, the painter's job is to "draw the poetic from the historical . . . , the eternal from within the transitory." The instability is that of the crowd in Baudelaire's essay; and with the crowd, it tends to dissolution all the time.

Later, Virginia Woolf would find in dissolution not only her subject matter, but a way of getting what is most solid: the true-to-life. There is giddiness in her method not unrelated to the unreliability of the frame in baroque, which comes from the improbable discovery of a solid core, an ultimate coherence, within dissolution: a clarity of seeing got through gazing on the abyss. The domestic contours, the old-fashioned Englishness, which appear to be Virginia Woolf's subject, become thoroughly unsettling in this perspective. Snobbery provides a shimmering, humorous texture in the pages of Proust, which doesn't detract from the truth of Marcel's insight that the remote and aristocratic Mme de Guermantes shares with the servant Françoise the same command of an earthy, unstifled language: an idiom at once peasant and aristocratic that hits the mark. The snobbery, absurd as it is, gives the stability within which such innocent language can work. In Virginia Woolf is a greater violence. There is snobbery again—all the Bloomsbury snobbery—and the confinement of a Little England, the claustrophobia of Mrs. Dalloway's drawing room or of her friends, or the backwater of Pointz Hall and the village in *Between the Acts*, and of the English past it depicts in the pageant that closes the book. The snobbery and the social-historical claustrophobia are seldom humorous, as they are in the Guermantes household, though there is humor in Virginia Woolf, but make themselves felt as psychological burdens. They are symptoms of potential dissolution. They show society, the whole house of cards of class, on the brink of falling in; or they show characters poised for dispersal. The characters in these novels of Virginia Woolf in many cases carry the burden of closeness to biography, the closeness of a room that lacks air. Thus the closeness of Mr. and Mrs. Ramsay to Virginia Woolf's parents, Leslie and Julia Stephen. It is an atmosphere that is bound to unburden itself, to break as a storm breaks the sulking before it. Character, in the late novels at any rate, is dissolved, and with a dexterity resembling, perhaps borrowing from, the satirical stringency of Lytton Strachey—whose Cardinal Manning, for example, is the work of a few fierce strokes of the pen, each one of which lays waste as it goes about depicting. Manning's career, and "career" is the word, emerges as a fable of failed political ambition rescued by insincere conversion to Catholicism. A few quick strokes, but a breathtaking insight into the vacancy of a soul. The severity of insight leaves the biographical facts, and by extension across several biographies the historical tissue, anatomized into so much rubble. But when Virginia Woolf lays character bare with similar rapidity, the result is quite different. She conveys a wasteland that is somehow a felt enrichment, as if a sudden errancy into nonbeing brings us face-to-face with a more closely woven, more sensually insistent, more dense and sumptuous cloth. Character—the particular character of Neville in *The Waves*, for example, which is disarmingly put before us with the ruthlessness of a last judgment; and equally the whole business of character, the joining of this willed self with these toings-and-froings in time, to form some visibly coherent shape—is in rags. It has been torn. But the tearing, the raggedness—the rubble of historicity—has its own, seamless shape, as if "woven from the top throughout" (John 19:23). The cloth might veil the abyss; the tears in it might give glimpses through to the abyss. There are a number of possibilities. But here the dissolution of character brings about a suspension in which a certain coherence enduring in time is held in the same focus as disintegration. The accomplishment is in the end without negation; yet it is far fiercer than Lytton Strachey's negativity. We will see later more clearly how *To the Lighthouse* holds together a certain composition, an arrangement of figures and voices and scenes, a formal surface effect, with a dispersal that has to do with historicity.

The historicity of the torn body in Virginia Woolf's conception is broached through voices: the plural voices of dialogue where voices do not quite meet one another. This is where we get an inkling that things will fall apart, or already have.

> "Well, we must wait for the future to show," said Mr. Bankes, coming in from the terrace.
>
> "It's almost too dark to see," said Andrew, coming up from the beach.
>
> "One can hardly tell which is the sea and which is the land," said Prue.[8]

At times, in *To the Lighthouse* or *Between the Acts*, this last "a novel about language at a time of stress," written in 1940–41, the voices are in conflict. Between the colliding and awkward voices in *Between the Acts*, and the voices "on her own air-waves," there is an echo, as Hermione Lee explains:

Roger Fry's—Freud's—Hitler's—the BBC's—scraps of poetry—all interrupting one another. One of the voices which added significantly to this war-time chorus of disharmony was that of Coleridge, whose letters and poems she was reading through the summer of 1940. His voice (and that of other Romantic poets, Keats and Shelley) was, to her, an enchanting alternative to all the rest, "delicate and pure and musical and uncorrupt": "How lightly and firmly they put down their feet, and how they sing; and how they compact; and fuse, and deepen."[9]

And she tells the story in her diary of how a little girl who had been listening to Coleridge talking on and on "was overcome by the magic of the incantation, burst into tears when the voice ceased and left her alone in a silent world."[10] Hermione Lee likens the crumpling of the little girl to the emotion of Virginia Woolf when her father died. Perhaps it is still nearer to her memory of her mother, as it is portrayed in Mrs. Ramsay, the mother in *To the Lighthouse*, whose remote beauty, as in a *sacra conversazione*, is in equal measure the focus of chattering children (not to mention of the many voices of the visitors staying in the holiday house by the sea in western Scotland) and aloof from these voices: self-sufficient, even cold in its distance from them.

> Yet seem'd it winter still, and, you away
> As with your shadow I with these did play[11]

"with these": with the "lily's white," "the deep vermilion in the rose," the manifold "figures of delight." To Shakespeare's lover, spring is a reminder of the absence of the beloved, and so makes winter more present than ever. Yet spring it is, sweetness insists, and so the two seasons accompany one another: "with your shadow I with these did play." Shadow and the world of play are both true.

To Mr. Ramsay, Mrs. Ramsay sitting there in her reverie as he enters the room is a mystery he hopes to dispel by calling her mood one of pessimism. Yet, sitting with one another in the evening after dinner, after a day when he has too abruptly disappointed his small son, James, whose one wish is to sail to the lighthouse the next day, but whom his dismissive father tells weather will not permit, Mr. Ramsay is overcome by his wife's beauty. In its heartlessness, it gathers everything, down to the smallest crumb.

> A heartless woman he called her; she never told him that she loved him. But it was not so. It was not so. It was only that she never could say what she felt. Was there no crumb on his coat? Nothing she could do for him?[12]

The voices of children and guests have died down. This is the slack of evening, in which the day's ups and downs are quietly resumed, though not resolved; resumed in the stability of the lighthouse outside the window. These two voices remain, over against one another, opposed voices, if reduced by caricature, and in light of caricature no doubt the voices of reason and affect, of philosophic clarity and feminine apperception; but in their utterance, their idiom, in the life of affect they draw to the surface, more composite, more inclined to overlap, each having in it elements of the other, and so, carried forward by proximity, leaning toward each other.

> But through the crepuscular walls of their intimacy, for they were
> drawing together, involuntarily, coming side by side, quite close, she
> could feel his mind like a raised hand shadowing her mind . . .[13]

They lean together like two musical lines, or two stories running alongside one another, sometimes jarring, sometimes in sympathy, always with the implication that they might be or become one voice: Mr. Ramsay with his irritability, born of the mental discipline of the professional thinker who lacks the suppleness of mind to see why others, less "book-learned," do not cleave as he does to method and reason and knowledge of the facts, an asperity compounded by the ambition for public recognition which sits so ill with family life, where, however, it is translated quickly into a childlike wish to be loved; and Mrs. Ramsay, the Madonna of *sacra conversazione*, apparently all motherly sympathy, but whose sad past, only referred to indirectly, already suggests the sightless eyes of one who sees all. "How satisfying! How restful! All the odds and ends of the day stuck to this magnet; her mind felt swept, felt clean."[14] Later, Mrs. Ramsay seems to Lily Briscoe, the painter who is a guest of the Ramsays in Scotland, "ghost, air, nothingness, a thing you could play with."[15] The voices, reduced to two, accompany one another—as a pianist accompanies voice; play over, against, along with one another, till, in their difference, they are one strain. This can happen because no voice—no character, no musical line, no text for that matter—is staunch: each spills over into the other voice or voices. Giordano Bruno explained the mutual participation of one thing in another by the metamorphosis of gods, one into the other, or by the riddle of judgment put before Paris: Beauty is in Venus, Wisdom in Minerva, and Majesty in Juno. Each is predominantly in one of them, but the three of them share in all three virtues. Venus is also wise and majestic; Minerva beautiful and majestic; and Juno wise and beautiful. Paris should have given the apple to all three, or rather to the divine power in which their virtues coincide. Here in this intimation of one in two, or three, or many, is the proof of the unknown god. The truth of oneness is not somewhere outside number. It is in the intervals between the many. [16]

Ich bin die Ruhe zwischen zweien Tönen,
die sich nur schlecht aneinander gewöhnen,
denn der Ton Tod will sich erhöhn—
Aber in dunklen Intervall versöhnen
sich beide zitternd.
                              Und das Lied bleibt schön. [17]

Here, in the interval, Mrs. Ramsay smiles: "And as she looked at him she began to smile, for though she had not said a word, he knew, of course he knew, that she loved him."[18] The notes are reconciled in the space between them. The voice of Coleridge talks on and on. But something is amiss in Mrs. Ramsay's smile: something never spoken, but plain enough. The depth, the absence of her reverie before the smile are telling us she is a ghost already. She has already died. And when she reappears, after the event of death, in the middle and third sections of the book as a figure remembered from the past, she is no less alive than before. "Mrs. Ramsay's things. Poor lady. She would never want *them* again."[19] Yet only now she has gone can Lily Briscoe make her presence felt in a painting. There is more to be reconciled in the smile than voices.

The voice of Coleridge, almost disembodied, "humming, magical, inspired, rich, various,"[20] is many voiced. If *Between the Acts* is the effect of a calculable, identifiable number of voices in collision, *To the Lighthouse* collapses number (the voices of the children, Bankes, Lily Briscoe, Carmichael, Mr. and Mrs. Ramsay, and so on, then the duet of Mrs. McNab and Mrs. Bast, who gossip and clean the neglected house by the sea in preparation for the family's return after the Great War) into an endless *scattering*: a dissolution of many into all. In the autumn of 1940 (well after *To the Lighthouse* was published) Hitler put off his plan for invading and bombed London every night from the seventh of September till the second of November. On Sunday the eighth of September, there was a raid over Mecklenburg Square, where Leonard and Virginia Woolf had a house. On Tuesday the tenth they went up from Rodmell in Sussex to see the damage. Number eleven

was a great pile of bricks (writes V. W. in her diary). Underneath all the people who had gone down to their shelter. Scraps of cloth hanging to the bare walls at the side still standing. A looking glass I think swinging. Like a tooth knocked out—a clean cut.

Then, driving to Holborn:

> A vast gap at the top of Chancery Lane. Smoking still. Some great shop
> entirely destroyed: the hotel opposite like a shell. In a wine shop there
> were no windows left. People standing at tables—I think drink being
> served. Heaps of blue green grass in the road at Chancery Lane. Men
> breaking off fragments left in the flames. Glass falling. Then into Lin-
> colns Inn. To the N.S. office: windows broken, but house untouched.
> We went over it. Deserted. Wet passages. Glass on stairs. Doors locked.
> So back to the car. A great block of traffic. The cinema behind Mme
> Tussaud's torn open: the stage visible; some decoration swinging. All
> the R. Park houses with broken windows, but undamaged. And then
> miles and miles of orderly ordinary streets . . .[21]

Thus: sketches of a *flâneuse*, seizing on the weightlessness of a bombed city.
Sketches from life. The fragment, though, is the proper form for desolation, for what has been called "absolute tragedy": "only the fragmentary,
whose completeness is expressly that of mutilation, of end-stopping, can
be immune to light."[22] Yet one hesitates. The dilapidated notes of this diary entry, like the broken pieces of glass, are positively light bearing, a series of hard reflective shards. Ruination and light play across one another.
Sketches, done from life.

The view expressed by Erich Auerbach of *To the Lighthouse* is that the
novel is in the first place a convergence of impressions, points of view,
voices, on the sad figure of Mrs. Ramsay, who, however, remains a mystery.[23] Her sad beauty, perceived from different angles, is never explained.
The beauty, as in baroque one might say, is central, almost as that of the
Virgin in Rubens's *Betrothal of St. Catherine*, but also vague. She is vague
in the eyes of others: Bankes, Mr. Ramsay, Lily Briscoe; and the painter
Lily can only express the solidity of her, the coherence of her in paint, as a
memory after Mrs. Ramsay has died. And she is vague in herself when we
overhear her reverie. She enters the room where her husband is reading.
She is looking for something, but doesn't remember what it is.

> And dismissing all this, as one passes in diving now a weed, now a
> straw, now a bubble, she felt again, sinking deeper, as she had felt in
> the hall when the others were talking, There is something I want—
> something I have come to get, and she fell deeper and deeper without
> knowing quite what it was, with her eyes closed. And she waited a little,
> knitting, wondering, and slowly those words they had said at dinner,
> "the China rose is all abloom and buzzing with the honey bee," began
> washing from side to side of her mind rhythmically, and as they washed,

words, like little shaded lights, one red, one blue, one yellow, lit up in
the dark of her mind and seemed leaving their perches up there to fly
across and across, or to cry out and to be echoed; so she turned and felt
on the table beside her for a book.

> And all the lives we ever lived
> And all the lives to be
> Are full of trees and changing leaves,

> She murmured, sticking her needles into the stocking. And she
> opened the book and began reading here and there at random, and as
> she did so she felt that she was climbing backwards, upwards, shoving
> her way up under petals that curved over her, so that she only knew this
> is white, or this is red.[24]

To go deeper is at once to run adrift on dispersal and to find coherence.

> she read, and so reading she was ascending, she felt, on to the top, on to
> the summit. How satisfying! How restful! All the odds and ends of the
> day stuck to this magnet; her mind felt swept, felt clean.[25]

Going back to it, Auerbach stresses something else, this time not the converging impressions, but the randomness of odds and ends whose foregrounding he considers the defining characteristic of modernism. A synthesis of diverse perceptions, a stage of which might be the uniting of the
inner voices of Mr. and Mrs. Ramsay, falls away into the pure objectivity
of uncommented encounter with the random which makes up the world.
The fragment prevails. Instead of being the *occasion* of reflection (as Auerbach began by thinking), the fragments that drift in the memory, in a state
of mind close to dream, are the very stuff of reflection. They make up
reflection. Odds and ends are of the essence, as much depth as surface.
And instead of convergence on the enigma Mrs. Ramsay, there is the sat-
isfactory but terrible dispersal, not of several voices and views juxtaposed,
but of an apparently endless many gathered into one disembodied voice
belonging to no one character—not even to Mrs. Ramsay herself, not even
to the "little airs" that playfully but inexorably unstitch the house as the
Great War runs its distant course in "Time Passes," the second section
of the novel. It is the part of the book V. W. thought experimental and
risky. It recounts an absolute vision of what there is in the world, untamed
by plot, only dimly shaped by chronology and innocent of any sense of
cause and effect. From voices we have passed to the voice of voices, to an
ultimate dispersal. How ultimate, how deep-rooted, can be seconded from
the sixth part of "Time Passes." World war prevents the family from re-

turning on holiday to the house in Scotland. Malicious airs, iterating and reiterating, undo the fabric of the house over a duration of time of which the vagueness is built up from the accumulated precisions of observed fragments:

> Flies wove a web in the sunny rooms; weeds that had grown close to the
> glass in the night tapped methodically at the window pane. When dark-
> ness fell, the stroke of the Lighthouse, which had laid itself with such
> authority upon the carpet in the darkness, tracing its pattern, came now
> in the softer light of spring mixed with moonlight gently as if it laid
> its caress and lingered stealthily and looked and came lovingly again.
> But in the very lull of this loving caress, as the long stroke leant upon
> the bed, the rock was rent asunder; another fold of the shawl loosened;
> there it hung, and swayed.[26]

The exactness of observation at work in the light beam through the win-dow at night—itself a painterly image—is blurred by the lull and by the unexpected sublimity of a rock splitting. The geologically sublime, the "long duration" that outlasts the before and after of human historical time, befalls the silence of a shawl loosening from its hanging in an abandoned child's room. Both are fragments, severed from continuity of experience; from the evolution of character, for instance, or from plot. Both bear light, the light of the lighthouse beam, the light of attention to the chiaroscuro of what is beheld. Both are tragic, because both point to, accompany, are uttered in the same voice which records with the distance given by brack-ets, the riven terrain of war.

> [A shell exploded. Twenty or thirty young men were blown up in
> France, among them Andrew Ramsay, whose death, mercifully, was
> instantaneous.][27]

It remains the same voice, but passing from fragment to fragment, from shawl to rock and then across the different theatre closed within brackets, to the quasi-cinematographic reportage of trench warfare in France; from the nonevent, the uneventfulness, of the shawl, to the seismic break of the rock to the magnitude of event in war. The effect of this manner of indis-criminate juxtaposition is to make us unsure whether we are in the midst of *copia* or dearth. We have been uncertain of the same thing before, in the dinner scene of part 1:

> But which was it to be? They had all the trays of her jewel-case open.
> The gold necklace, which was Italian, or the opal necklace, which Uncle
> James had brought her from India; or should she wear her amethysts?[28]

We are made to hesitate between dearth and plenty, between fragments littering a surface but distinct and fragments heaped up and blurred together by shared brightness; between the immediacies, one might say, of drawing and painting. We hesitate because of some shadow of irony in the telling. We suspect it might be Mrs. Ramsay's own irony about her jewels. What could they possibly matter? And yet the voice is not quite hers. It comes from all of the children, too, as they gather round her and help make the choice; and so the irony merges with their competing delight.

In this middle section of the novel, the doubt over whose voice, the hesitation over dearth and plenty, is strung out from death to life. We are brought to a state of reading where objects strewn, their singularity stressed by decay, and the richness of objects, are complicit as they rise from the page at us, in a manner which approximates to visual directness, even to vision. The fragment is not immune to light, but at the intersection of light and dark. And this is why the prose of "Time Passes" pulls off the improbable feat of making life from "a heap of broken images," though not through the discovery of the reticent, tempered confessional lilt of Eliot's *Waste Land* but rather by a struggle of elements that do not fit together. Mrs. Ramsay in all this is less the place on which converge the multiple perceptions (the vanishing point as it were) but the tendency, almost a sort of force, by which the world—and time most palpably—breathes in and out: gathers and opens, like the breath of an accordion out of which music of a sad gaiety tumbles. Or a *Madonna della Misericordia* perhaps, folding into her outspread coat the multitude of sinful humanity, unsettling as she is in the distraction with which she includes all that eddies round her. The hesitancy lodges most consistently of all in Lily Briscoe, unable to finish her painting of Mrs. Ramsay till the very end of the story, when the last brushstroke, the last application of color to the "wedge of darkness" that is Mrs. Ramsay, comes effortlessly at last, as if to say: The only real certainty is in the core of doubt. One might compare it to the marks dashed off by Rubens to suggest the "and so on . . . " of the trees: They express a "might be," which contains hesitancy and confidence in one hooped motion of the pen.

On a page of her notebooks, Simone Weil confesses:

> *Il y faut un apprentissage. Le je est aussi grand que le monde; tous les sons se rencontrent dans l'oreille, etc. . . .*

Then a few lines later:

> *J'ai beau mourir, l'univers continue. Cela ne me console pas si je suis autre que l'univers. Mais si l'univers est à mon âme comme un autre corps, ma mort*

cesse d'avoir pour moi plus d'importance que celle d'un inconnu. De même mes souffrances.

Que l'univers soit pour moi, par rapport à mon corps, ce qu'est le bâton d'un aveugle, pour l'aveugle, par rapport à sa main. Il n'a réellement plus sa sensibilité dans sa main, mais au bout du bâton.[29]

To such rigors the world of Mrs. Ramsay is, in the end, foreign. Her ghost-liness, her nothingness, is an extension, to the point of emptying out, of body to world. So far, there is common ground. The voices that converge on Mrs. Ramsay scatter again to the four corners to be resumed in one Babel-like yet continuing voice, the voice of the sea. But the sea is a mirror that breaks:

> Also the sea tosses itself and breaks itself, and should any sleeper fancy-ing that he might find on the beach an answer to his doubts, a sharer of his solitude, throw off his bedclothes and go down by himself to walk on the sand, no image with semblance of serving and divine prompti-tude comes readily to hand bringing the night to order and making the world reflect the compass of the soul.[30]

The sea as mirror reflecting the soul, mirror and soul acting to frame what will otherwise flow over, now breaks. The shards of things exposed by de-cay do not resolve into an image.

> Impatient, despairing yet loth to go (for beauty offers her lures, has her consolations), to pace the beach was impossible; contemplation was unendurable; the mirror was broken.[31]

The blind man's stick, with its consoling effect of equalizing the exterior world and calming the inward one, doesn't withstand this. The stick is too philosophic, even too aesthetic, an answer. Too brittle. For a world of things so strewn—the horn of plenty from shawl to rock to war—cannot be tamed of its desolation by the absence that is beauty: by the mirroring of the aesthetic. For Kierkegaard, the blind man's stick was in irony; but he thought the truth must be nearer to humor, which turned the irony on the ironist and forced him to begin again from scratch through faith. The solitary walker on the beach must begin again from scratch, though in V. W. it is not clear he can refer to faith. What is left is not an equivalence of great and small event—shawl, rock, war—but an accompaniment of deep reverie and random event. Accompaniment, though, is often more like struggle. The elements that strive with one another are not motes of dust dancing in a shaft of light. They are figures in an animist passion: the rock rent asunder, the shawl loosened.

> Now some glass tinkled in the cupboard as if a giant voice had shrieked
> so loud in its agony that tumblers stood inside a cupboard vibrated
> too.[32]

Auerbach suggests that the attention to the random thing and event is the
taking up into the novel of a modern historicity. The historical understanding has reacted to an increase in contact between peoples, ways of
life, languages, customs, which suddenly, having to live cheek by jowl, become aware of one another, and of the heterogeneity of human society and
its transformation through time.[33] The sensibility that develops in these
circumstances turns to the common ground of the random occurrence,
for if we are to live cheek by jowl, we must find the common ground, and
away from the rarer climate of sequences of events that make up plausible,
explanatory narratives, or of theories of cause and effect of the kind that
thrived in the nineteenth century, or of history as the exercise of judgment
of a kind analogous to moral judgment, or of history as the reenactment
of the motivation at work in past minds, and so on. Nor is it only the novel
(Joyce, Proust in parts) which has held up for scrutiny the random event
of past and present. The historians themselves have renounced the history given in these older explanatory versions. Michel Foucault argued eloquently for the abandonment of the "Work": the oeuvre or sum of books
and other items of research and thought written by an author over a life
time.[34] The "Work" is to be replaced by the "Archive." (I once asked for the
"works" of a seventeenth-century mystic in the Duke Humfrey Library in
the Bodleian and was shown by the most patient of librarians the several
cupboards in which his remains lay, all of them bound with other material
and kept in bundles in cardboard boxes.) Arnaldo Momigliano rubs shoulders with Foucault's "archaeology" when he points to the philosophical
history that results from the work of the antiquarians of the seventeenth
and eighteenth centuries, those remarkable collectors of the occasional
who were interested in the past but not in history (as Momigliano puts it)
and who were compelled by the riches of what they had collected in their
cabinets and libraries to make classifications which cut across chronology
and adopted timeless categories, but with a view to preserving the integrity
of the objects they had found: to leave things as they are (were).[35] Richard
Cobb is most radical of all, living out the archive, immersing himself in
the Archives in Paris and the provinces to such a degree that his study
of the revolutionary armies reads (at least in some of its passages) as if
one had strayed into an eighteenth-century crowd, among the garrulous
menu peuple, a world that could never be mistaken for the Assemblée, with

its rhetorical periods, whose political big screen is not up Cobb's street. Cobb's refusal of any theory ("archaeology" or whatever it might be) only makes the return to the random episode, to history as an endless series of *novelle*, more thorough than ever.[36]

What Auerbach also notices is the discovery among the debris of the quotidian of strange and brilliant echoes. Echoes, but also, one might add, of suggestive agonies of sense. For the gathering of shawl falling and rock rent and war dead, exploits difference to the point of agon. There is a materialism in the pages of V. W. Her infinite is the infinite of the interval. It is within the stuff of creation. Yet it seems natural enough, in trying to follow the intensity of these conjunctions, to borrow from the mystical writers, whose tendency, when it comes to it, is also perhaps back to the felt world. One might even take a detour back to pseudo-Dionysus, and the problem he faced of what he calls "unlike likeness" early on in *The Celestial Hierarchy* (2.4). Better, he says, to be disturbed by an inept likeness in talking about the divine, by a grossly material simile, into an upward flight toward the utopia of pure spirit where likeness gives way to identity; better this than to be duped by the sham plausibility of a higher, more fitting and comely likeness, into believing we have arrived already at the object of our desire. Better unlike likeness than like likeness; the worm of God than the God who is light. The grounds of this is the existence ("as I see it," says Dionysus) of a hierarchy that encompasses all created things. Everything belongs to the heavenly hierarchy, from worm to angel, material to immaterial, and so the conspiring, in this game of desiring beyond one's station, this grand system of metaphysical snobbery, of low with high, of beasts and stones with the things in heaven, is always legitimate. Hierarchy is both discipline and playground: It canonizes the absurd, the improbable, the upside down. In this, it is one of the sources of the theology of laughter in Rabelais, of the god of innocent burlesque that accompanies the translation of the texts of religion (the Bible but not only the Bible) into the vernaculars, but which also has a long medieval history in carnival. In mysticism, unlike likeness is the place where the breach is made in language, through a deliberate policy of provoking its breakdown through asking it to speak of the unspeakable. As if through the oculus at the summit of a painted cupola, the unspeakable is drawn in among frustrated, straining words. An example Dionysus gives is the anger of angels. The impulse is upward: flight from the literal to a supposed region beyond horizons, of a higher coherence where angels and anger no longer cancel one another out. Dionysus even supplies a possible sense.

Anger is born, in fact, among irrational beings, of a passionate impulse, and the emotion of anger is sullied, in them, by all kinds of irrational content. But among intelligent beings [the angels], the impulse to anger is to be seen differently. It means, I think, a kind of virility in reasoning; the unbending way they hold themselves in the condition they have of being shaped by God and unchanging.[37]

A characteristically high-wire analysis by Michel de Certeau of the "dialect of love" ("*amor habet suam dialectam*," says Diego de Jésus in his commentary on St. John of the Cross) shows how the strain in such language, and the flight from it, is not only the result of dearth. True, words can be suggestive because they are weak. Anger is too mired, impulsive, unreliable, spasmodic to be used for the steady life of angels, and so our first response is to abandon anger for the steadiness of angels. But a phrase like "the anger of angels" or, in Diego de Jésus's example from St. John of the Cross, "cruel rest" is also an exploitation of the excess there can be in language. The oxymoron binds two meanings in a way that troubles and arrests and delights us much more than if they were simply in opposition. Two fields of sense, of association, are awkwardly yoked, but somehow with authority. They are not easily dismissed as nonsense—or not by everyone. Perhaps there is such a state as "cruel resting." Perhaps the beat of the angels' wings has anger in it, and perhaps we learn something about anger from thinking of angels who are angry; or about some kinds of anger. Or perhaps we fall back from our efforts with angel anger to the two richnesses of anger and angels. Yet once put side by side they cannot be kept apart. They are two color fields, taken in together by the eye. The incommensurability of the terms is painful, but through excess, not want, of sense. It sings as color fields sing in Matisse's *Jazz*. The awkwardness is not the tragedy of a contradiction of terms in the same domain (good versus bad; gods of the hearth, gods of the city and so on), but the proximity of a paradise affirmed.

Proche de l'antiphrase et du paradoxe, l'oxymoron "viole le code" d'une façon particulière. Certes la contradiction qu'il pose n'est pas "tragiquement proclamée" comme dans l'anthithèse, mais "paradisiaquement assumée"; elle a valeur de plénitude, alors que, dans l'antithèse, elle est tension insurmontable. Mais d'une part, les opposés qui sont rapprochés relèvent chacun d'échelles ou de mesures différentes. À ce titre, ce ne sont pas vraiment des contraires, dont Aristote dit justement qu'ils sont du même genre . . . Les termes combinés par l'oxymoron appartiennent chacun à des ordres hétérogènes: la "cruauté" n'est

pas comparable à la "paix," pas plus qu'il n'y a commensurabilité entre les ter-
mes rapprochés par Jean de la Croix dans "brûlure suave" ("cauterio soave")
ou "musique silencieuse" ("mùsica callada").[38]

De Certeau—in a historical commentary on European mysticism in the
sixteenth and seventeenth centuries which often internalizes, by its scintillating juxtaposition of historical domains normally alien to one another
(the "enfant sauvage" and the mystic for example), the use of oxymoron by
the likes of Diego de Jésus, John of the Cross, Ruysbroeck, and others—
goes on to stress two things. The first is that "cruel rest" maims the operation of sign so badly that the sign can no longer get to a referent, to what
it is a sign of. "Cruel rest," and one might add "the anger of angels" (or the
shawl that roars), are not signs *of* anything. They introduce an opacity of
sense, which in turn emphasizes the opacity of the sign itself, of anger and
angels or cruelty and peace. The same opacity is characteristic of biblical
language. The effect is confirmed by the authority of the whole of which
these opaque signs are a part: the Bible or, in Dionysus, the hierarchy. De
Certeau compares this extraordinary plausibility of the absurd to the way
the details depicted in the engraving of a city leap out at us in their particularity because they are contained in the bird's-eye view.[39] Once we know
we are seeing a whole, the assumption is made that the multiple schisms of
sense add up to something. One might speculate on the role of the classical
novel, and the very notion of the classical as whole and parts logically distributed, in the makeup of V. W.'s novels. The mirror that breaks in "Time
Passes," the formless swell of the sea, is the coming apart of the classical. It
is a self-exile from the classical, a radicalizing of the opaque, of which the
classical had long suffered a presentiment.[40]

Here would be the place to say something about Virginia Woolf and ill-
ness. De Certeau hesitates over whether the mystic's oxymoron is a "powerlessness" (*"impuissance"*) or a quickening. The oxymoron is the "fall of
the sign" and in this it has weakened the usual discourse; but it also places
the attention back onto the body in its opacity, an opacity often figured
in the body under travail: wounded, fainting, afflicted with headaches,
dizzy; the body speaking the language of unlikeness, the body that cannot
be read because of a permanent obscurity in its connection with spirit. Is
this merely weakness again? Or is it the body *"mû et altéré,"* the metamor-
phic body, whose shifts and turns are "the unreadable lexicon of an un-
nameable speaker"? The excess of the oxymoron is a corporal excess.[41]

III.

Something can come only from nothing. But the aftermath of this opaque paradise is a withdrawal from the excitement into a world of less intensity. In the third and last part of *To the Lighthouse*, the expedition by sailing boat to the lighthouse is finally made, after the death of Mrs. Ramsay, after the death of Andrew in the war, of Prue in childbirth, amid the impatience of Mr. Ramsay, the resentment of James at his father, the fondness that Cam realizes she has for him as she splashes her hand in the slow-moving water, all the unreckonable loss and gain of family life, tragedy dispersed among trinkets, jealousies guessed at, frayed tempers, and the lurching motion of moods, all of it done through the prism of character. The resentment and the fondness are not only beautiful examples of the continuity and development of character—they are no longer the same resentment and fondness as in the first part of the novel—but they unfold like silent unobtrusive resurrections after the implacable waste glimpsed in "Time Passes." There is still the same sense that the tragic or deep is *accompanied by* the historicity of ordinary existence. Mr. Ramsay's impatience is the surface movement of an absolute loss. There is in V. W. a thirst to get back to the haven of character, in tension with the knowledge that character is not in the end an adequate recourse.

The fall of sign back into body is also the opacity of paint. But if the wish to sail to the lighthouse (part 1) and the death and life of the sea (part 2) are from the painter's hand—if they are *pictura* somehow overcoming *poeisis* in the old rivalry—then in this third part, when the expedition to the lighthouse makes good at long last, the requital of James's wish, of anyone's wish, is as much resignation to loss as it is requital. And this is done with due grief. Mrs. Ramsay has gone, so has Andrew. But it is done with comedy, too: the comedy of Mr. Ramsay's irritation over the sandwiches not yet ready or of his near-obsessive ecstasy over what makes a good pair of boots. Perhaps his philosophical literalism is comedy, too, set with Lily's painterly blurring almost as anger might be put with angels:

> But what a face, she thought, immediately finding the sympathy which she had not been asked to give troubling her for expression. What had made it like that? Thinking, night after night, she supposed—about the reality of kitchen tables, she added, remembering the symbol which in her vagueness as to what Mr. Ramsay did think about Andrew had given her. (He had been killed by the splinter of a shell instantly, she bethought her.) The kitchen table was something visionary, austere,

something bare, hard, not ornamental. There was no colour to it; it was
all edges and angles; and it was uncompromisingly plain. But Mr. Ramsay kept always his eyes fixed upon it, never allowed himself to be
distracted or deluded, until his face became worn too and ascetic and
partook of this unornamental beauty which so deeply impressed her.[42]

The want that is desire and the want that is grief run together in the hard
edges of the kitchen table. The near nothing of the table might flare up
into color, especially if Mrs. Ramsay comes into view. Then vision in
black-and-white, a photographic still, leaps into color:

> the empty drawing-room steps, the frill of the chair inside, the puppy
> tumbling on the terrace, the whole wave and whisper of the garden be-
> came like curves and arabesques flourishing round a centre of complete
> emptiness.[43]

Such is Lily's painting, its center "a wedge of black." In an essay on going
to Spain, V. W. reflects on the tide of beauty painted by the painters and
how to climb out of it with words:

> Blessed are painters with their brushes, paints, and canvases. But words
> are flimsy things. They turn tail at the first approach of visual beauty.
> They let one down in the most literal sense into a chaotic, an alarming
> chasm filled—for the eye pours it all in—with white towns, with mules
> in single file, with solitary farms, with enormous churches, with vast
> fields crumbling at evening into pallor, with fruit-trees blazing askew
> like blown matches, and trees burning with oranges, and clouds and
> storms. Beauty seemed to have closed overhead and one washes this
> way and that in her waters. It is always on the shoulders of a human be-
> ing that one climbs out; a profile in the corridor; a lady in deep mourn-
> ing who steps into a motor-car and drives across an arid plain—where
> and why?[44]

For most of her book, V. W. has painted in words. But the lady in mourning, the profile in the corridor, snatched moments that clarify and therefore save from the turbulence, perhaps the indolence, of beauty have the
precision of certain drawings. But the precision is not confined to drawing
itself. It is also that of words on the page, themselves a kind of drawing.[45]
Or it might be the retreat from painting into a kind of drawing that occurs
in film: Gelsomina imploring Zampanò after he has killed "Il Matto," the
high-wire man in Fellini's *La Strada*, where she, Gelsomina, is the modest,
monochrome echo of the Magdalene in Titian's *Noli me tangere*. Here, film
accompanies painting. The wretched circumstances of the child-clown

Gelsomina, bought for a few lire and used by the brutish strongman Zam-panò, illuminate the elegant Magdalene by the violent contrast between the figures, but the hopeless child borrows from her ancestress too. "Il Matto, il Matto," she whimpers with her hands clasped. But she is magnificent, still—an obvious still separable from the film's forward motion—and she is something permanent, something sacred in fact. The head of the child-woman is an oval, a shape drawn by a draughtsman trained to attend to line; the posture is from the world of painting. The echo of the Magdalene in the child-clown leaves a space; and the space seems a thing of very great importance. For we do not quite know what it is. *"Ich bin die Ruhe zwischen zweien Tönen."* The relation of child-clown and the Magdalene, between drawing and painting, between anger and angel, the relation of unlike-ness that nonetheless arrests us, is a space where there might be ultimate sense. The juxtapositions of art *might be* vestiges of the relation at work in creation itself, *for all we know.* The space is therefore the location of both doubt and festivity. It is delight, miracle. V. W. chooses to end her novel on a sober note which sounds as if it might issue soon in doubt:

> With a sudden intensity, as if she saw it clear for a second, she drew a little line there, in the centre. It was done; it was finished. Yes, she thought, laying down her brush in extreme fatigue, I have had my vision.[46]

Lily has completed her painting.

With all this, I have only managed to pose the question I had begun by wanting to answer: whether *historia,* history in the sense of the procession of events and of uneventfulness (in other words events that are not grand), in the old way of looking at it the tissue of what happened before it was leavened by allegory, might be a retreat, into black-and-white as it were, a vision (like the kitchen table), but a vision in retreat from those wilder forms whose juxtaposition is a vestige of the improbable event of creation. Retreat, not abandonment. Or again, and bearing in mind Lily's completed painting, perhaps in the midst of the retreat is the very confirmation of ecstasy.

NOTES

INTRODUCTION: ON RELIGION AND PASTNESS
Burcht Pranger

1. With the exception of Charles Hallisey's article "The Care of the Past: the Place of Pastness in Transgenerational Projects," which deals with Buddhism. Hallisey's article has been incorporated in view of its closeness to the volume's major theme. It is also in line with the "critical" definition of religion discussed in the introduction and the reference by a number of contributors to a broader and more comprehensive concept of "Christian" religion as put forward by thinkers such as Johannes Scottus Eriugena, Thoreau, Emerson, and Stanley Cavell.

2. My exposition of Augustine's view on temporality in this introduction is based on my *Eternity's Ennui: Temporality, Perseverance and Voice in Augustine and Western Literature* (Leiden: Brill, 2010).

3. *Conf.*, 11.17.14.

4. Ibid., 11.26.20.

5. *Conf.*, 8.12.29.

6. Baltimore, MD: Johns Hopkins University Press, 1999.

7. Michael Fried, *Absorption and Theatricality. Painting and Beholder in the Age of Diderot* (Berkeley: University of California Press, 1980), 173; "Art and Objecthood," in Michael Fried, *Art and Objecthood: Essays and Review* (Chicago: University of Chicago Press, 1998), 148–73.

8. *Conf.*, 8.10.23–26.

9. Ibid., 10.27.36.

1. THE VISION AT OSTIA: AUGUSTINE'S DESIRE TO BECOME A RED INDIAN
Burcht Pranger

I presented an earlier version of this article at the conference on which this volume is based: *Religion and Pastness*, Amsterdam, December 2008. Meanwhile, the bulk of what I am saying here has also gone into the making of my *Eternity's Ennui: Temporality, Perseverance and Voice in Augustine and Western Literature* (Leiden: Brill, 2010). I thank Koninklijke Brill Publishers for permission to reuse the material from the book for the present article.

1. Garry Wills, *Saint Augustine* (London: Penguin, 2005), 90. Wills translates *Confessions* as *Testimony*. "T, 11.20" is *Conf.*, 11.15.20. In this article I use Henry Chadwick's translation: *Saint Augustine: Confessions* (Oxford: Oxford University Press, 1991).

2. *Conf.*, 13.38.53; Chadwick, 304–5; "On your door can we knock" (Matthew 7:7–8).

3. *Conf.*, 9.10.24.

4. See, for instance *Ad Simplicianum* I, 2.19; *Patrologia Latina* 40:125: "That is the word, both fulfilling and abbreviating, that the Lord has wrought on earth. Through that fulfilment and abbreviation the robber was justified who, with all his members nailed to the cross, had the disposal of only two: with his heart he believed to justice, with his mouth he confessed to salvation, and, instantly, he was rewarded to hear: "Today, you will be with me in paradise" (Luke 23:43). His good works would have followed him if after this grace was given to him he had lived among men for a longer time. Yet those works had certainly not preceded [his confession] as if the robber would have merited that very grace. Out of his life of robbery he was nailed on the cross, out of the cross he was transferred to paradise" [my translation].

5. *Conf.*, 8.6.15; Chadwick, 143.

6. *Conf.*, 9.10.25; Chadwick, 172; the biblical quotes are from Matthew 25:21 and 1 Corinthians 15:51, respectively.

7. Hugh Kenner, *Samuel Beckett: A Critical Study* (London: Calder, 1962), 163.

8. *Conf.*, 9.10.21–6; Chadwick, 170–72.

9. *Wunsch, Indianer zu werden* in Franz Kafka, *Sämtliche Erzählungen* (Frankfurt am Main: Suhrkamp, 2008), 754.

10. Franz Kafka, "Desire to Be a Red Indian" in *Kafka: Metamorphosis and Other Stories*, ed. and trans. Michael Hofmann (London: Penguin, 2007), 28.

11. Heinrich Detering in *Frankfurter Allgemeine Zeitung*, August 7, 2008, 33.

12. Summary of the script: "In rural Texas, welder and hunter Llewelyn Moss discovers the remains of several drug runners who have all killed each other in an exchange gone violently wrong. Rather than report the discovery to the police, Moss decides to simply take the two million dollars present for himself. This puts the psychopathic killer, Anton Chigurh, on his trail as he dispassionately murders nearly every rival, bystander, and even employer in his pursuit of his quarry and the money. As Moss desperately attempts to keep one step ahead, the blood from this hunt begins to flow behind him with relentlessly growing intensity as Chigurh closes in. Meanwhile, the laconic

Sheriff Ed Tom Bell blithely oversees the investigation even as he struggles to face the sheer enormity of the crimes he is attempting to thwart." Written by Kenneth Chisholm (www.imdb.com/title/tt0477348/plotsummary).

13. Ever since Paul's discussion of them in Romans 9, Jacob and Esau are the prototypes of predestination. Augustine discusses Jacobs's perseverance and Esau's rejection at length in his *Ad Simplicianum*.

14. In his postscript to the Suhrkamp edition of the *Sämtliche Werke* (2008), Peter Hölfe makes an interesting observation about the element of perseverance pervading *The Desire to Become an Indian*. Writing about Kafka's order to burn his writings after his death and Max Brod's refusal to obey that order, Hölfe considers the possibility of reading this fragment as a metaphor of the desire to "write on" (*Figur des Fortschreibens*): "Already in one of Kafka's earliest texts, *The Desire to Become an Indian*, the metaphor of the 'writing on' can be found: the wild ride which takes place within one sentence, does not leave anything left of the initial situation of the Indian on his horse except the written paper. If one realises that for Kafka riding was a chiffre, which he uses time and again, of the process of writing, then the scene which, in *The Desire to Become an Indian*, is not so much described as, rather, actually materialises in the act of reading, is the writing on, the telling on, the tearing down of the narrative condition itself. Kafka applies this procedure with the highest degree of virtuosity in his *Sirenentext* [*Das Schweigen der Sirenen/The Silence of the Sirens*] where Ulysses as the only witness of his experience *forgets* the Sirens and, chained to his mast, slides away into a timeless future" (1424). With oblivion, the breakdown and perseverance of voice, and a timeless future we find ourselves squarely in Augustinian territory. Cf. Burcht Pranger, "Augustine and the Silence of the Sirens," *Journal of Religion* 91 (2011): 64–77.

15. See, for instance, Kurt Flasch, *Was Ist Zeit? Augustinus von Hippo. Das XI. Buch der Conf.* (Frankfurt am Main: Klostermann, 1993), 91: "Books 1 to 9 tell the story of how we should learn to forget the temporal and exclusively embrace the eternal. Books 9 to 13 show, in accordance with the overall structure of Scripture—that is, through the allegorical interpretation of Scripture—that Augustine's journey from time to eternity is the itinerary, preconceived by God, of *all* those endowed with grace."

16. Cf. Romans 9:16: "So then it is not of him that willeth, nor of him that *runneth*, but of God that sheweth mercy." Together with Jacob and Esau this is another running theme in *Ad Simplicianum* I.

17. See *Eternity's Ennui*, 219–42.

18. Cf. John Peter Kenney, *The Mysticism of Saint Augustine: Rereading the Confessions* (London: Routledge, 2005), 112: "In this light we would do well to notice Augustine's narrative framing of the vision at Ostia."

19. *Conf.*, 9.10.24; Chadwick, 171.
20. *Conf.*, 9.10.26.

2. MEMORY AND THE SUBLIME: WITTGENSTEIN
ON AUGUSTINE'S TROUBLE WITH TIME
James Wetzel

1. *Conf.*, 11.14.17. My source for Augustine's Latin is James J. O'Donnell, *Augustine: Confessions*, 3 vols. (Oxford: Clarendon Press, 1992). All translations of Augustine are my own.

2. *PI* §89, from *Philosophical Investigations*, 3rd Edition, Text and Translation, trans. G.E.M. Anscombe (Oxford: Blackwell, 2001). Excepting the minor emendation, translations of Wittgenstein are Anscombe's.

3. *PI* §89. Wittgenstein has been calling into question whether exactness admits to a single standard.

4. I will be using the D. F. Pears and B. F. McGuinness edition and translation of the *Tractatus Logico-Philosophicus* (London: Routledge, 1961). My reading of Wittgenstein's enigmatic masterpiece has been greatly enhanced by three works of commentary: Eli Friedlander, *Signs of Sense: Reading Wittgenstein's Tractatus* (Cambridge, MA: Harvard University Press, 2001); James Conant, "The Method of the Tractatus," in *From Frege to Wittgenstein: Perspectives on Early Analytic Philosophy*, ed. Erich H. Reck (Oxford: Oxford University Press, 2002); and Marie McGinn, *Elucidating the Tractatus: Wittgenstein's Early Philosophy of Logic and Language* (Oxford: Oxford University Press, 2006). My reading of Wittgenstein's other masterpiece—enigmatic in a wholly different way—owes most to Stanley Cavell, particularly his early essay, "The Availability of Wittgenstein's Later Philosophy" in *Must We Mean What We Say?* rev. ed. (Cambridge: Cambridge University Press, 2002) and his "Notes and Afterthoughts on the Opening of Wittgenstein's *Investigations*," in *Philosophical Passages* (Oxford: Blackwell, 1995).

5. *PI* §90.

6. *Conf.*, 11.20.26.

7. From Wittgenstein's notebooks. See the selection in *Ludwig Wittgenstein: Culture and Value*, ed. G. H. von Wright and Alois Pichler, trans. Peter Winch (Oxford: Blackwell Publishing, 1998), p. 41e (translation modified).

8. *PI* §116.

9. For a strikingly clear and engaging analysis along these lines, see chapter 9, "*Time and Creation*," of Gareth Matthews, *Augustine* (Oxford: Blackwell Publishers, 2005).

10. *Conf.*, 11.26.33.

11. *Conf.*, 11.27.36.

12. Cf. *Conf.*, 10.16.24, where Augustine discusses the apparent paradox of a remembered forgetfulness—a self-undoing act of memory.

13. *PI* § 1.

14. *PI* §32.

15. *Conf.*, 8.12.29; cf. *Conf.*, 8.1.2: *Adhuc tenaciter conligabar ex femina* ("Up to now I was knotted up tightly in woman").

16. Quoted in *Conf.*, 8.12.29.

17. *Conf.*, 11.29.39.

18. *PI* §109.

19. From part 3 of "The Dry Salvages" in *Four Quartets* (New York: Harcourt, 1971).

3. THE MAN WITHOUT MEMORY: PETER ABELARD AND TRUST IN HISTORY
Babette Hellemans

1. Such an anthropological description of the human condition suggests a touch of skepticism. However, this is a problematic aspect of "thinking" in the Middle Ages, since the period doesn't acknowledge skepticism in the classical philosophical sense. Nevertheless, as we will see in the work of Peter Abelard, by simply dismissing the presence of refuting arguments regarding knowledge of the world, we will not resolve this problem because "doubt" is one of the principles of his thinking. On the rediscovery of pre-Socratic traditions in the twelfth century, via Aristotle, and its encounters with the traditional Augustinian neo-Platonism see Christophe Grellard, "Comment peut-on se fier à l'expérience? Esquisse d'une typologie des réponses médiévales au problème sceptique," *Quaestio* 4 (2004): 113–35.

2. For a historical anthropology of medieval eschatology see Babette Hellemans, *La Bible Moralisée: une oeuvre à part entière. Temporalité, sémiotique et Création au XIIIe siècle* (Turnhout: Brepols, 2010).

3. For a critical assessment of Augustine's interpretation of Time, see Gerard J. P. O'Daly, "Augustine on the Measurement of Time: Some Comparisons with Aristotelian and Stoic Texts," in *Neoplatonism and Early Christian Thought*, ed. H. J. Blumenthal and R. A. Markus (London: Ashgate, 1981), 171–79. For an intrinsic analysis of Augustine's use of language of time, and performances of temporality in the *Confessions* see M. B. Pranger, *Eternity's Ennui. Temporality, Perseverance and Voice in Augustine and Western Literature* (Leiden: Brill, 2010).

4. He would develop this theory later in his life in *De Genesi ad Litteram* by refining the concepts into sense knowledge, imagination, and understanding. See Janet Coleman, *Ancient and Medieval Memories: Studies in the Reconstruction of the Past* (Cambridge: Cambridge University Press, 1992), 101–11.

5. See especially *De Trinitate*, 11.4.297, 11.9.353, 11.12.308.

6. This problem also partly explains why the monastic attitude to a theory of memory was characteristic in its disinterest in an individual past. If monastic memory existed, it was allegorical, recollecting images of things (*imagines rerum*) as parts of the entire cosmos. During the Middle Ages, the poetic theory of the mind's memories was paralleled with another tradition of logical inquiry of past's knowledge. Both traditions would "melt" into a new discourse on the nature and function of language as a structure.

7. Coleman, *Ancient and Medieval Memories*, xvi.

8. Ibid., 231.

9. I realize that somehow I might come close to Eileen Sweeney's article. Perhaps I put a stronger emphasis on a general critical-theoretical problem, however, in my suggestion to see the *Historia Calamitatum* as a paradigm for a much wider application in a theory of knowledge of past events connected to the mimetic process of putting these "past events" into drama. See Eileen Sweeney, "Abelard's Historia Calamitatum and Letters: Self as Search and Struggle," *Poetics Today* 28, no. 2 (2007): 303–36.

10. Coleman, *Ancient and Medieval Memories*, 273.

11. In following Boethius's interpretation of Aristotle (*De Interpretatione*), Abelard believed that the elementary particles of language, such as nouns and verbs, represent declarations of the mind's affectations, whether spoken or written.

12. Coleman, *Ancient and Medieval Memories*, 35.

13. This refers to Abelard's theory of intention; see my article "The Whole Abelard and the Availability of Language," in *How the West was Won: On the Problems of Canon and Literary Imagination, with a Special Emphasis on the Middle Ages*, Brill's Studies Intellectual History 188, ed. W. Otten, A. Vanderjagt, and H. de Vries (Leiden: Brill, 2010), 349–76.

14. Coleman, *Ancient and Medieval Memories*, 258.

15. Ibid., 260

16. Ibid., 258.

17. See Abelard's *Gloses on Porphyry* and *Super peri Hermeneias*.

18. Coleman, *Ancient and Medieval Memories*, 273.

19. See below for my example of ordinary language in the work of Stanley Cavell in Hellemans, "The Whole Abelard."

20. See Daniel Schacter, *Searching for Memory: The Brain, the Mind and the Past* (New York: Basic Books, 1996), 4–6.

21. See Sweeney, "Abelard's *Historia Calamitatum* and Letters," n. 9. See also Sverre Bagge, "The Autobiography of Abelard and Medieval Individualism," *Journal of Medieval History* 19 (1993): 327–50; Peter Dronke, "*Heloise's Problemata and Letters: Some Questions of Form and Content*," in *Petrus Abaelardus (1079–1142): Person, Werk, und Wirkung*, ed. Rudolf Thomas (Trier:

Paulinus, 1980) 53–73; the collected articles of Peter von Moos, *Abaelard und Heloise, Gesammelte Studien zum Mittelalter* (Münster: Lit Verlag, 2005); Carolyn Walker Bynum, "Did the Twelfth Century Discover the Individual?," in *Jesus as Mother: Studies in the Spirituality of the High Middle Ages* (Berkeley: University of California Press, 1982); the preface of Jan Ziolkowski, *The Letters of Peter Abelard: Beyond the Personal* (Washington, DC: Catholic University of America Press, 2008).

22. *Hist. Cal.*, 8.

23. Ibid., 10.

24. Ibid., 11.

25. I use the word "*skepsis*" in the Greek sense, that is, as an act of viewing and investigation.

26. While Bahktin coined the term "polyphonic" in his analysis of Dostoevsky's narrative I want to point out something different here than a (polyphonic) *poesis*. In my view, the temporal status of events in the paradigm of "pre-scholastic thought" can be compared to raindrops that change into crystalline complexities. As such, events come close to a connection between the existence of a mathematical logic and the question of being, embedded in language and discourse. I do not mean to suggest that the (past) event is tautological (the being is what it is, or was what it was) or mystical (the always changing approximations of a Presence). Instead, I want to acknowledge the richness and variety in truth procedures—as they occur in past, present, and future—with regard to a (deductive) fidelity. See for instance Alain Badiou on the theory of multiplicity, metastructure and the typology of being with regard to critical decisions in *L'être et l'événement* (Paris: Éditions du Seuil, 1988), 31–84.

27. *Hist. Cal.*, 43

28. The poem is a kind of *confessio*. This has also been suggested in the case of the *Historia*.

29. The term "composure" is common in oral history. See for instance *Narrative and Genre*, ed. Mary Chamberlain and Paul Thompson (London: Routledge, 1997).

30. While the text itself represents an *epistola* and the words "*Historia Calamitatum*" are Abelard's, it is not the official title of this work. *Historia Calamitatum* refers to a passage that is to be found at the end of the letter in which the author writes "This is the story of my misfortunes which have dogged me almost since I left my cradle" (*Hist. Cal.*, 42). Scholars always refer to these two words when discussing the text.

31. Within the limits of this article, it goes too far to examine more thoroughly the notion of the not-spoken (as not-meaning) in Abelard's writings, which will be developed in my forthcoming book. The term "silence of

Héloise" is from Peter von Moos, *Entre Histoire et Littérature. Communica-tion et Culture au Moyen Âge* (Florence: Edizioni del Galluzzo, 2005), 3–43. This chapter is a revised and much extended version of Peter von Moos's article "Le silence d'Héloise et les idéologies modernes," published in 1975.

32. "Abelard's idea about language, and his closely related thinking about human perception and cognition, bear on his ontology in two distinct ways. Abelard held that every thing which exists is a particular substance or a particular differentia or a particular accident. He also recognized, as he could hardly fail to do, that universals play a central role in language and in thinking"; see Marenbon, *The Philosophy of Abelard*, 138. For the connection between language, meaning, difference, and ontology, see esp. chaps. 5–8. See also Leen Spruit, *Species Intelligibilis: From Perception to Knowledge*, vol. 1 (Leiden: Brill, 1994), 113–14.

33. *Apologia against Bernard of Clairvaux*, trans. Jan Ziolkowski in *The Let-ters of Peter Abelard*, cf. n. 5; 116. For the edition: *Apologia contra Bernardum* in *Petri Abelardi Opera theological* I, CCCM 11, 359–68.

34. *Letters of Abelard*, 117–18.

35. For Bernard's letter accusing Abelard, cf. letter 190 in *Sancti Bernardi Opera* 8, ed. Jean Leclercq (Rome: Editiones Cistercienses, 1975), 39.

36. *Apologia against Bernard of Clairvaux*, trans. Ziolkowski, cf. n. 8; 120.

37. For the problem of "autobiography" and problems concerning the authenticity of a "personal" account, cf. Eileen Sweeney, "Abelard's Historia Calamitatum and Letters: Self as Search and Struggle," *Poetics Today* 28, no. 2 (2007): 303–50.

38. Cf. Hellemans, "The Whole Abelard," 365.

4. CREATION AND EPIPHANIC INCARNATION: REFLECTIONS ON THE FUTURE OF NATURAL THEOLOGY FROM AN ERIUGENIAN-EMERSONIAN PERSPECTIVE
Willemien Otten

1. For purposes of comprehensiveness and conceptual clarity, I in-clude in my definition of the humanities the study of religion, theology, and philosophy.

2. See for a recent overview of nature's "environmental" role Lawrence Buell, *The Future of Environmental Criticism: Environmental Crisis and Literary Imagination* (Oxford: Blackwell, 2005). See also his *Writing for an Endangered World: Literature, Culture, Environment in the US and Beyond* (Cambridge, MA: Harvard University Press, 2003).

3. Ecocriticism does still seem to be the dominant key in which theology and philosophy voice their criticism; see *Ecospirit: Religions and Philosophies*

for the Earthed, ed. L. Kearns and C. Keller (New York: Fordham University Press, 2007).

4. These issues are mentioned in Buell, *Future of Environmental Criticism,* 3–4, 12. For the remainder of this article it is relevant to point also to his *The Environmental Imagination: Thoreau, Nature Writing, and the Formation of American Culture* (Cambridge, MA: Harvard University Press, 1996).

5. See William of Conches, *Glosae super Platonem,* ed. E. Jeauneau, CCCM 203 (Turnhout: Brepols, 2006), 69–70. As I will explain more fully below, William's first level, which is also found here, is the *opus creatoris,* by which he indicates God's creation of the elements, the Virgin birth—both of which are mentioned below, too—as well as the resurrection of the dead mentioned in *Dragmaticon,* I.7.2, ed. I. Ronca, CCCM 152, 30.

6. See Bruno Latour, *Politics of Nature: How to Bring the Sciences into Democracy* (Cambridge: Harvard University Press, 2004), 4–5.

7. See Buell, *Future of Environmental Criticism,* 20–21.

8. Charles Taylor, *A Secular Age* (Cambridge MA: The Belknap Press of Harvard University, 2007).

9. See Taylor, *A Secular Age,* 539–93.

10. See Taylor, *A Secular Age,* 37–41, 262. The "buffered" self or identity, which Taylor places in opposition to the "porous self" of the enchanted world, describes the ability of the modern self to be disengaged from God and cosmos and create its own autonomous order and dignity.

11. Taylor associates exclusive humanism with what he calls "secularity 3" (2–3), namely the switch from a society in which belief in God was standard to one in which it is one option among many; i.e., the coming of a secular age in which for many the major default option is unbelief. As he states on p. 19: "My claim will rather be something of this nature: secularity came to be along with the possibility of exclusive humanism, which thus for the first time widened the range of possible options, ending the era of 'naive' religious faith."

12. At *A Secular Age,* 613, Taylor defines "excarnation" as the transfer of our religious life out of bodily forms of ritual, worship, practice, so that it more and more comes to reside "in the head." On p. 614 he calls another facet of excarnation "what disengaged reason demands of desire."

13. Latour distinguishes "Naturpolitik" (modeled on "Realpolitik" as a term of compromise) from the hard theoretical work done by political ecology.

14. Of course Taylor has a very complex notion of secularization, which emphatically avoids the subtraction narrative, meaning that religion has been replaced by other means. Nonetheless it is secularization, in combination with technological advancement and disengaged reason, which remains at

fault for him, which I am not at this point ready to concede. For a different view (for which as a medievalist I see some plausibility) that finds the roots for the objectification and human manipulation of nature much earlier, namely in Western scholasticism, see Lynn White, "The historical roots of our ecological crisis [with discussion of St. Francis; repr. 1967]," in *Ecology and Religion in History* (New York: Harper and Row, 1974).

15. For my analysis of William's contribution I rely on W. Otten, *From Paradise to Paradigm. A Study of Twelfth-Century Humanism* (Leiden, NL: Brill, 2004), 83–128, and on my "Reading Creation: Early Medieval Views of Genesis and Plato's *Timaeus*," in *The Creation of Heaven and Earth: Re-interpretations of Genesis 1 in the Context of Judaism, Ancient Philosophy, Christianity, and Modern Physics* ([Brill's] Themes in Biblical Narrative [8]), ed. G. H. van Kooten (Leiden: Brill, 2005), 225–43.

16. See Latour, *Politics of Nature*, 9–52.

17. Yet I do not think that simply because William is a premodern thinker it is therefore a confessional rather than a metaphysical position that drives him to see the world as such.

18. See Otten, *From Paradise to Paradigm*, 99n34, and William of Conches, *Philosophia* II.II §5, ed. G. Maurach (Pretoria: University of South Africa, 1980), 43.

19. On medieval humanism, see R. W. Southern, *Medieval Humanism and Other Studies* (Oxford: Blackwell, 1970), 29–60, and W. Otten, *From Paradise to Paradigm*, 9–44.

20. See note 19.

21. I find "surplus of power" as a description of what happens to the role of nature in the twelfth century more accurate than the concept of sacramentality used by Louis Dupré. See my discussion in *From Paradise to Paradigm*, 55–59 with reference to Dupré, *Passage to Modernity: An Essay in the Hermeneutics of Nature and Culture* (New Haven, CT: Yale University Press, 1993), 33–37.

22. See my "Reading Creation: Early Medieval Views of Genesis and Plato's *Timaeus*." See also W. Otten, "Nature, Body and Text in Early Medieval Theology: From Eriugena to Chartres," in *Divine Creation in Ancient, Medieval, and Early Modern Thought. Essays Presented to the Rev. Dr. Robert D. Crouse*, ed. M. Treschow, W. Otten, and W. Hannam (Leiden: Brill, 2007), 235–56.

23. See Otten, *From Paradise to Paradigm*, 116.

24. See W. Otten, "Nature, Body and Text in Early Medieval Theology: From Eriugena to Chartres," 252–55.

25. See *Glosae super Platonem* III, ed. Jeauneau, CCCM 203, 7–8.

26. The reason lies in the fact that recent studies of William emphasize his emancipation of nature as foreshadowing thirteenth-century natural phi-

losophy (*scientia naturalis*). See A. Speer, *Die entdeckte Natur Untersuchungen zu Begründungsversuchen einer 'Scientia naturalis' im 12. Jahrhundert* (Leiden: Brill, 1995), 130–221.

27. See William Paley, *Natural Theology or Evidence of the Existence and Attributes of the Deity, collected from the appearances of nature* (1802) (Oxford: Oxford University Press, 2008).

28. This is the thesis in Peter Harrison, *The Bible, Protestantism, and the Rise of Natural Science* (Cambridge: Cambridge University Press, 1998), which he has elaborated and extended in a different way, focused more on the Augustinian idea of original sin as promoting the trial-and-error method in science, in his *The Fall of Man and the Foundations of Science* (Cambridge: Cambridge University Press, 2007).

29. See P. Harrison, "Miracles, Early Modern Science, and Rational Religion," *Church History. Studies in Christianity and Culture* 75 (2006): 493–510, esp. 510: "The attempt to establish the religious utility of science had the unintended consequence of transforming religion itself, and was one factor in the creation of modern 'religion.'"

30. See Harrison, "Miracles, Early Modern Science, and Rational Religion," 510.

31. This development seems to continue in the movement of intelligent design, which is hence not so much a return to a longstanding Christian tradition as an extension of the Enlightenment defense of Christian creation à la Paley. See R. van Woudenberg, "Design in Nature: Some Current Issues," in *The Creation of Heaven and Earth*, 245–61.

32. See on this theme Hans Blumenberg, *The Legitimacy of the Modern Age*, trans. Robert Wallace (Cambridge, MA: MIT Press, 1983) and Louis Dupré, *Passage to Modernity*.

33. See Taylor, *A Secular Age*, 61–88 passim.

34. See on this latter theme, Susan E. Schreiner, *The Theater of His Glory. Nature and the Natural Order in the Thought of John Calvin* (Grand Rapids, MI: Baker Academic, 1995).

35. See Harrison, *The Bible, Protestantism, and the Rise of Natural Science*. See also the two conference volumes *The Book of Nature in Antiquity and the Middle Ages*, ed. K. van Berkel and A. J. Vanderjagt, *The Book of Nature in Early Modern and Modern History* (Leuven: Peeters, 2005–6) and *Nature and Scripture in the Abrahamic Religions*. 2 vols. in 4 parts, ed. J. M. van der Meer and S. Mandelbrote, (Leiden: Brill, 2008).

36. See especially my *From Paradise to Paradigm*, chap. 2 (Nature and Scripture), 51–55.

37. See Jean Scot, *Homélie sur le prologue de Jean*, ed. E. Jeauneau, SC 151 (Paris: Cerf, 1969), 270–73 and 327–28. As Jeauneau makes clear, in this

Eriugena is probably influenced by Maximus. See on this also (but without the Maximian reference) H. de Lubac, *Medieval Exegesis. The Four Senses of Scripture*, vol. 1, trans. Mark Sebanc (Grand Rapids, MI: Eerdmans, 1998), 40–41.

38. In what follows I have drawn on my article "The Parallelism of Nature and Scripture: Reflections on Eriugena's Incarnational Exegesis," in *Iohannes Scottus Eriugena: The Bible and Hermeneutics*, ed. G. van Riel, C. Steel, and J. McEvoy (Leuven: Leuven University Press, 1996), 81–102.

39. See the various contributions in *Eriugena, Berkeley, and the Idealist Tradition*, ed. S. Gersh and D. Moran (Notre Dame, IN: University of Notre Dame Press, 2006). On p. 147, Moran concludes his article on Eriugena's intellectualist immaterialism ["*Spiritualis Incrassatio*. Eriugena's Intellectualist Immaterialism: Is it an Idealism?," 123–50] with the following statement: "While 'idealism' may be too limited a term to encapsulate the full richness and complexity of his system, nevertheless, I want to conclude by affirming that Eriugena's philosophy of infinite nature is at least an idealism."

40. See Moran "*Spiritualis Incrassatio*. Eriugena's Intellectualist Immaterialism: Is it an Idealism?," 123–50.

41. See Eriugena, *Periphyseon* III.723C-724A, ed. Jeauneau, CCCM 163, 149 [trans. I. P. Sheldon-Williams and J. O'Meara, *Eriugena: Periphyseon (The Division of Nature)* (Montreal: Bellarmin, 1987), 357], where Eriugena compares *creatura* and *scriptura* as the two vestments of Christ at the time of his Transfiguration. See Maïeul Cappuyns, *Jean Scot Érigène. Sa vie, son oeuvre, sa pensée* (1933; reprinted *Bruxelles: Culture et Civilisation*, 1969), 276–80, and Henri de Lubac, *Medieval Exegesis. The Four Senses of Scripture*, vol. 1, 76–78. See also Donald F. Duclow, "Nature as Speech and Book in John Scotus Eriugena," *Mediaevalia* 3 (1977): 131–40.

42. See Richard Kearney, *Debates in Continental Philosophy. Conversations with Contemporary Thinkers* (New York: Fordham University Press, 2004), 15–32 ("Jean-Luc Marion, The Hermeneutics of Revelation"), at 24–25.

43. It is obviously a problematic feature of Eriugena's vision, related to his allegorical approach of language and especially scriptural language, that only the Gentiles will enjoy the special return.

44. See Eriugena, *Periphyseon* V.1005B, 203 [trans. *Eriugena, Periphyseon*, 694]

45. This is not unlike how Eriugena sees language also as a kind of clothing or robing of the divine, whose nudity remains outside our reach.

46. For earlier, and to some extent comparable analyses of Eriugena and Emerson, see my articles "Eriugena, Emerson, and the Poetics of Universal Nature," in *Metaphysical Patterns in Platonism. Ancient, Medieval, Renaissance,*

and Modern Times, ed. John F. Finamore and Robert M. Berchman (New Orleans: University Press of the South, 2007), 147–63, and "Nature as Religious Force in Eriugena and Emerson" in *Religion. Beyond a Concept,* ed. Hent de Vries (New York: Fordham University Press, 2007), 354–67.

47. See Hans W. Frei, *The Eclipse of Biblical Narrative. A Study in Eighteenth and Nineteenth-Century Hermeneutics* (New Haven, CT: Yale University Press, 1974).

48. See note 29.

49. With reference to Taylor, see note 11.

50. See Otten, *From Paradise to Paradigm,* 62–65.

51. See on this W. Otten, "In the Shadow of the Divine: Negative Theology and Negative Anthropology in Augustine, Pseudo-Dionysius and Eriugena," *The Heythrop Journal: A Quarterly Review of Philosophy and Theology 40* (1999): 438–55, at 451–52.

52. This observation should not blind us to the fact that there are many scriptural resonances in Emerson's texts, as is pointed out in the context of a discussion of the opening of his essay on nature by E. Cadava, *Emerson and the Climates of History* (Stanford, CA: Stanford University Press, 1997), 91–148. Cadava also comments how Emerson's *Nature* has the form of a Puritan jeremiad, or rather, is itself a kind of jeremiad against the jeremiad, 97–106.

53. By this I obviously refer to theology's combined roots in scripture and nature along the lines of my earlier discussion.

54. See Emerson, *Divinity School Address,* in: *The Complete Works of Ralph Waldo Emerson,* ed. Edward Waldo Emerson (Boston: Houghton Mifflin, 1903–4), vol. 1, 119–51, at 151.

55. Laura Dassow Walls (*Emerson's Life in Science: The Culture of Truth* [Ithaca, NY: Cornell University Press, 2003], 50) speaks in this respect about Emerson's intent to merge science and poetry, elevating the status of both to a new, prophetic power. Emerson goes back in this respect to Coleridge, who sees prophetic power as the essential privilege of science: see 6–7.

56. I am mindful here that Cavell sees Emerson's thought as a philosophy of moods, see "Thinking of Emerson," in Cavell, *Senses of Walden* [note 57], 127–28, and "An Emerson Mood," *Senses of Walden,* 141–60.

57. See Stanley Cavell, *The Senses of Walden. An Expanded Edition* (Chicago: University of Chicago Press, 1981), xiii. See also his *Emerson's Transcendental Etudes* (Stanford: Stanford University Press, 2005).

58. In this context it is important to note that Emerson found himself at a point in time where science was still a branch of natural philosophy, on the brink but not quite professionalized, see Walls, *Emerson's Life in Science,* 55–67.

59. See Cavell, *Senses of Walden*, 129–30.

60. I am referring to Kermode's brilliant analysis of the end of the Gospel of Mark here to underline how we should take the notion of ending, however abrupt or mysterious, seriously. In this respect I want to take issue with the argument in S. Mulhall, *Philosophical Myths of the Fall* (Princeton: Princeton University Press, 2005). Rather than thinking through the notion of ending to the very end, so to speak, Mulhall discusses the thought of Wittgenstein, Nietzsche and Heidegger as reaching the limits of secularity, as if their thought is somehow inherently conditioned to fold back into the Christian tradition of redemption.

61. See Cavell, *Senses of Walden*, 133.

62. Ibid., 133.

63. See Emerson, *Divinity School Address*, in *Collected Works*, vol.1, 126–27.

64. For Emerson metamorphosis applies both to nature (cf. *Method of Nature*, CW 1, 203; note 78*) and to man (cf. *American Scholar*, CW 1, 83; note 76).

65. It is important to note Cavell's connection here between the writing on the lintels, notably of "Whim," and the idea of constancy as opposed to randomness. For once crossing the threshold of "Whim" one is no longer the victim of arbitrariness, but rather embraces fate as one's own, "a matter of my life and death." See also Walls, *Emerson's Life in Science*, 146–47.

66. See Cavell, *Senses of Walden*, 137–38.

67. See Emerson, *Experience*, in *Collected Works*, vol. 3, 43–86, at 85: "Why not realize this world? But far be from me the despair which prejudges the law by a paltry empiricism;—since there never was a right endeavor but it succeeded." This essay with its warning against this paltry empiricism was written just after the death of his son Waldo in 1842, and is insightful not just in questioning experience but in associating it with despair. However, for a more critical look at overly emotional readings of this essay see Julie Ellison, "Tears for Emerson. *Essays, Second Series*," in *The Cambridge Companion to Ralph Waldo Emerson*, ed. J. Porte and S. Morris (Cambridge: Cambridge University Press, 1999), 140–61.

68. See Robert D. Richardson Jr., "Emerson and Nature," in *The Cambridge Companion to Ralph Waldo Emerson*, 97. See also his *Emerson. The Mind on Fire* (Berkeley: University of California Press, 1995). On nature, see further William Rossi, "Emerson, Nature, and Natural Science," in *A Historical Guide to Ralph Waldo Emerson*, ed. Joel Myerson (New York: Oxford University Press, 2000), 101–50.

69. On the impact of Thomas Paine's deism in *The Age of Reason* (1794) on Emerson, see E. Cadava, *Emerson and the Climates of History*, 119–23.

70. In fact, as Cadava makes clear, nature is in Emerson always only another name for reading and writing, see *Emerson and the Climates of History*, 94–95.

71. Cf. Pierre Hadot, *The Veil of Isis: An Essay on the History of the Idea of Nature* (Cambridge, MA: Harvard University Press, 2006).

72. Cadava points out that Emerson alludes here to 1 Cor. 13 (seeing God face to face) but reverses temporal order by seeing this not as a move in the future but one located in the past: see *Emerson and the Climates of History*, 117. While there is no space to discuss this further, Emerson's move here echoes Eriugena's reading of the fall of man in paradise as a matter of eschatology rather than protology: see W. Otten, "The Dialectic of the Return in Eriugena's *Periphyseon*," *Harvard Theological Review* 84 (1991): 399–421, esp. 409–17. In both cases it appears that temporality greatly matters in what is otherwise seen as a semipantheistic natural construct.

73. See Emerson, *Nature*, in *Complete Works*, vol. 1, 1–77, at 10: "Standing on the bare ground—my head bathed by the blithe air and uplifted into infinite space—all mean egotism vanishes. I become a transparent eyeball; I am nothing; I see all; the currents of Universal Being circulate through me; I am part or parcel of God."

74. The word "also" plays a crucial role here, see Richardson, "Emerson and Nature," 99. But Cadava makes clear that the dynamics of this text are more complex than a straightforward conflict between past and present, as there is an ongoing threat of the sepulchers of history within the American tradition itself, as exemplified in Daniel Webster's 1825 speech at the ceremonies for the Bunker Hill monument, as there too freedom is endangered by dependence. See Cadava, *Emerson and the Climates of History*, 97–123.

75. See R. W. Emerson, *Nature*, in *Complete Works*, vol. 1, 3. See also Richardson, "Emerson and Nature," 99.

76. See Richardson, "Emerson and Nature," 104. See also Richardson, *Emerson. The Mind on Fire*, 349–54.

77. As Emerson says in *The American Scholar* in: *Collected Works*, vol. 1, 70–115, at 86: "And science is nothing but the finding of analogy, identity, in the most remote parts."

78. See Emerson, *The Method of Nature*, in *Collected Works*, vol. 1, 189–224, at 213–14.

5. THE CARE OF THE PAST: THE PLACE OF PASTNESS IN TRANSGENERATIONAL PROJECTS
Charles Hallisey

1. "Men make their own history, but they do not make it just as they please; they do not make it under circumstances chosen by themselves, but

under circumstances directly encountered, given and transmitted from the past": from *The 18th Brummaire of Louis Bonaparte.*

2. Cavell identifies a key passage about nextness in Thoreau in *The Senses of Walden:* "For the most part we allow only outlying and transient circumstances to make our occasions. They are, in fact, the cause of our distraction. Nearest to all things is that power which fashions their being. *Next* to us is not the workman whom we have hired, with whom we love so well to talk, but the workman whose work we are." Stanley Cavell, *The Senses of Walden* (Chicago: University of Chicago Press, 1981), 105.

3. See, for a modern Islamic elaboration of this Qur'anic theme, Fazlur Rahman, *Major Themes in the Qur'an* (Chicago: Bibliotheca Islamica, 1980), 18, 37–64.

4. See, for example, Barack Obama's speech, "A More Perfect Union," delivered in Philadelphia, March 18, 2008.

5. South Bend, IN: University of Notre Dame Press, 1982.

6. New Haven, CT: Yale University Press, 1992.

7. New York: Norton, 2010.

8. The term "onwardness" is also Stanley Cavell's; see *Senses of Walden,* 135–6: There is a

> theme of [Emerson's] thinking that further stands it with the latter Heidegger's, the thing Emerson calls "onward thinking," the thing Heidegger means in taking thinking as a matter of getting ourselves "on the way." . . . In "Circles," Emerson invites us to think about the fact, or what the fact symbolizes, that every action admits of being outdone, that around every circle another circle can take its place. I should like to extend the invitation to think about how he pictures us as moving from one circle to another, something he sometimes thinks of as expanding, sometimes as rising. What is the motive, the means of motion of this [constantly onward] movement? How do we go on? (In Wittgenstein's *Philosophical Investigations,* knowing how to go on as well as knowing when to stop is exactly the measure of our knowing, or learning, in certain of its main regions or modes—for example, in the knowledge we have of our words. Onward thinking, on the way, knowing how to go on, are of course inflections or images of the religious idea of The Way, inflections which specifically deny that there is a place at which our ways end . . . .)

9. Jacob Carbine, *Sons of the Buddha: Continuities and Ruptures in a Burmese Monastic Tradition* (Berlin: Walter de Gruyter, 2010), 2. Carbine goes on:

> For example, one can be "inside the Sasana," a term often reserved "for those Buddhists with a heightened and special involvement with

the Sasana through ordination, the following of moral precepts, and meditation. This kind of identity apples especially to monks though lay practitioners of meditation and nuns have sometimes described themselves in this way. . . ."

"In contrast to supporting the Sasana "from being at the inside of it," one may support the Sasana "from being at the outside of it," as one who acquires the "heritage of the Sasana." To acquire this "heritage," one sponsors "the monastic ordination ceremony [and] provide[s] the eight monk requisites. [The phrase] implies that an individual is nearer to the [Sasana] than 'ordinary' laymen who have never sponsored an ordination." On occasion, the phrase may even be used to refer to those who have sponsored the construction of a religious building, such as an ordination hall. The epithet is traced back to the time of the Indian monarch Asoka (r. ca. 270–230 BCE). . . . Asoka, with all of his good works (e.g., the building of wells, reservoirs, pagodas, etc.), was only a "master of charity." To acquire the "heritage of the Sasana," he needed to sponsor an ordination. (2–3)

10. Guillaume Rosenberg, *Renunciation and Power: the Quest for Sainthood in Contemporary Burma* (New Haven, CT: Yale Southeast Asia Studies, 2010), 70.

11. Bernard Williams, *Ethics and the Limits of Philosophy* (Cambridge, MA: Harvard University Press, 1985), 129, 140.

12. See, from many examples, Allan Gibbard and Simon Blackburn, "Morality and Thick Concepts," *Aristotelian Society Supplementary Volume* 66 (1992): 267–99; Jonathan Dancy, "In Defence of Thick Concepts," *Midwest Studies in Philosophy* 20 (1995): 263–79; Michael Walzer, *Thick and Thin: Moral Argument at Home and Abroad* (South Bend, IN: University of Notre Dame Press, 2006); Matti Eklund, "What Are Thick Concepts?" *Canadian Journal of Philosophy* 41 (2011): 25–49.

13. Williams, *Ethics and the Limits of Philosophy*, 141.

14. *Majjhima Nikaya*, 1:265.

15. *The Fundamental Wisdom of the Middle Way: Nagarjuna's Mulamadhyamakakarika*. Translation and Commentary by Jay Garfield (New York: Oxford University Press, 1995), 50–51 [chapter XIX, verses 1–3, 5–6].

16. The aggregates are the constitutive elements that make up a person: body, predispositions, feelings, perceptions, and consciousness.

17. Bhadantācariya Buddhaghosa, *The Path of Purification (Visuddhimagga)*, trans. Bhikkhu Ñāṇamoli (Seattle: BPS Pariyatti Editions, 1999), 293.

18. Valuable surveys of the uses to which Theravada historical works have been put by scholars can be found in Stephen Berkwitz, *Buddhist History in the Vernacular: The Power of the Past in Late Medieval Sri Lanka* (Leiden: Brill,

2004) and Jonathan S. Walters, "Buddhist Histories: The Sri Lankan Pali Vamsas and Their Community" in *Querying the Medieval*, ed. Ronald B. Inden, Jonathan S. Walters, and Daud Ali (New York: Oxford University Press, 2000), 99–164.

19. See Charles Hallisey, "Auspicious Things" in *Buddhism in Practice*, ed. Donald Lopez (Princeton, NJ: Princeton University Press, 1995) 412–26.

20. *KhpA*, 90.

21. Max Weber, *From Max Weber: Essays in Sociology*, trans. Hans Gerth and C. Wright Mills (New York: Oxford University Press, 1946), 262–64.

22. *MhvT*, I.50–51, translation edited.

6. TREMBLING IN TIME: SILENCE AND MEANING BETWEEN BARTHES, CHATEAUBRIAND, AND RANCÉ
Mette Birkedal Bruun

1. François-René de Chateaubriand, *Vie de Rancé*, ed. Nicolas Perot (Paris: Librairie Générale Française, 2003), 143 on Poussin and *Le déluge*. Unless otherwise specified, translations are mine.

2. Roland Barthes, "Chateaubriand: *Vie de Rancé*," in *Le Degré zéro de l'écriture suivis de Nouveaux essais critiques* (Paris: Éditions du Seuil, 1972); first pub. (*Le Dégré*) 1953; first ed.: "La voyageuse de nuit," *La Vie de Rancé par Chateaubriand* (Paris: Union générale d'éditions, 1965), 9–21, 106–20, at 109; "Chateaubriand, *Life of Rancé*," trans. Richard Howard, *Roland Barthes: New Critical Essays* (Berkeley: University of California Press, 1990; first pub. New York: Hill and Wang, 1980), 41–54, at 44.

3. "Histoire ou Littérature?," *Sur Racine* (Paris: Éditions du Seuil, 1972; first publ. Club Français du Livre, 1960), 147–67, at 148–49.

4. "Qu'est-ce que l'écriture?," in *Le Degré zéro de l'écriture suivi de Nouveaux Essais critiques* (Paris: Éditions du Seuil, 1972; first pub. [*Le Dégré*] 1953), 11–17, at 15.

5. Ibid., 54–75, at 54.

6. Ibid., Introduction, 7–10.

7. "Littérature et méta-langage," in *Essais critiques* (Paris: Éditions du Seuil, 1964), 106–7.

8. Ibid.; "Écrivains et écrivants," 147–54, at 148–49.

9. "Écrivains et écrivants," 151–52, at 151; "Authors and Writers," trans. Richard Howard, *Roland Barthes Critical Essays* (Evanston, IL: Northwestern University Press, 1972), 143–50, at 147.

10. Concerning Rancé and his reform, see Alban J. Krailsheimer, *Armand-Jean de Rancé: Abbot of La Trappe* (Oxford: Clarendon Press, 1974); Chrysogonus Waddell, "The Cistercian Dimension of the Reform of La Trappe," in *Cistercians in the Late Middle Ages*, ed. E. Rozanne Elder (Kalamazoo, MI:

Cistercian Publications, 1981), 102–61; David Bell, *Understanding Rancé: The Spirituality of the Abbot of La Trappe in Context* (Kalamazoo, MI: Cistercian Publications, 2005).

11. Krailsheimer, *Armand-Jean de Rancé*, 7–10; Bell, *Understanding Rancé*, 169–96. For contemporary descriptions see for example Tallemant des Réaux, *Historiettes*, 2 vols., ed. Antoine Adam (Paris: Éditions Gallimard, 1970), vol. 2, 222; Louis de Rouvroy, duc de Saint-Simon, *Mémoires*, 8 vols., ed. Yves Coirault (Paris: Éditions Gallimard, 1983–88), vol 1: 1691–1701 (1983), 521–22; *Mémoires pour servir à l'histoire de France, vol. X: Mme de Motteville—Le Père Berthod*, ed. Joseph Fr. Michaud and Jean J. F. Poujoulat (Paris: Imprimerie de Firmin Didot Frères, 1838), 56–59.

12. Letter to Nicolas Pavillon, bishop of Alet, 30 May 1663, in *Abbé de Rancé: Correspondance*, 4 vols., ed. Alban John Krailsheimer (Cîteaux: Commentarii Cistercienses; Paris: Éditions du Cerf, 1993), vol. 1, 210. Rancé's enthusiasm for Duperron comes across in a letter to Robert Arnauld d'Andilly of 24 October 1658, in *Abbé de Rancé: Correspondance*, vol. 1, 109. See further Krailsheimer's note 110.

13. The Maurist Antoine-Joseph Mège wrote *Commentaire sur la Règle de saint Benoist, où les sentimens et les maximes de ce saint sont expliqués par la doctrine des Conciles, des SS. Pères [. . .]* (Paris: Veuve E. Martin, 1687); and Rancé, *La Régle de Saint Benoist: Nouvellement traduite, et expliquée selon son veritable esprit, par l'Auteur des Devoirs de la Vie Monastique*, 2 vols. (Paris: François Muguet and George & Louïs Josse, 1688).

14. "Avertissement," *La Régle de Saint Benoist*, vol. 1, unpaginated.

15. Ibid., chap. 6, vol. 1, 366.

16. Nicholas D. Paige, *Being Interior: Autobiography and the Contradictions of Modernity in Seventeenth-Century France* (Philadelphia: University of Pennsylvania Press, 2001).

17. *Éclaircissemens de quelques difficultez que l'on a formées sur les livre de sainteté et des devoirs de la vie monastique* (Paris: François Muguet, 1685), 367–79.

18. Saint-Simon, *Mémoires*, vol. 1, 521–52; Letter to Rancé of 29 March 1699; Saint-Simon, *Mémoires*, vol. 1, 1596–97.

19. *Les Véritables motifs de la Conversion de l'abbé de la Trappe avec quelques reflexions sur sa vie & fur ses écrits* (Cologne: Pierre Marteau, 1685), 27–28.

20. Chateaubriand, *Vie de Rancé*, 46.

21. Chateaubriand, *Génie du christianisme*, part 4, book 3, chap. 4; *Essai sur les révolutions/Génie du christianisme*, ed. Maurice Regard (Paris: Gallimard, 1978), 964–65; Louis Du Bois, *Histoire civile, religieuse, et littéraire de l'abbaye de la Trappe* (Paris: Raynal, Libraire, 1824), 259; Chateaubriand, *Vie de Rancé*, 162–63.

22. Emmanuelle Tabet, *Chateaubriand et le xviiᵉ siècle: Mémoire et création littéraire* (Paris: Honoré Champion Éditeur, 2002), 11–14.

23. Chateaubriand, *Génie du christianisme* I.I.I, 468; Tabet, *Chateaubriand et le xviiᵉ siècle*, 40.

24. Guillaume Peyroche d'Arnaud, "Enraciner la *Vie de Rancé*," in *Chateaubriand: Le tremblement du temps*, ed. Jean-Claude Berchet (Toulouse: Presses Universitaires du Mirail, 1994), 331–53.

25. Chateaubriand, *Vie de Rancé*, 121.

26. Tabet, *Chateaubriand et le xviiᵉ siècle*, 32.

27. D'Arnaud, "Enraciner la *Vie de Rancé*," 335–36.

28. Chateaubriand, *Vie de Rancé*, 87–88; see also the editor's note 2, 88–89.

29. Ibid., 92.

30. Ibid., 95.

31. For a list of literary works which attest to this interest, see Nicolas Perot, "Préface," in *Chateaubriand: Vie de Rancé*, 7–35, at 9.

32. Bell, *Understanding Rancé*, 15–17 and 339–40; Krailsheimer, *Armand-Jean de Rancé*, 342.

33. Herman Melville, *Confidence-Man* (New York: Random House, 2003; first pub. 1857), 142. It is possible that Chateaubriand was his source; Merton M. Sealts Jr., *Melville's Reading: A Check-list of Books Owned and Borrowed* (Madison: University of Wisconsin Press, 1966), entry 136, 49.

34. *Die Welt als Wille und Vorstellung*, Arthur Schopenhauer: *Sämtliche Werke*, ed. Wolfgang Frhr. von Löhneysen (Darmstadt: Wissenschaftliche Buchgesellschaft, 2004; first pub. 1968), vol. 1, book 4, 536; ibid., book 4, chap. 48, 788, 809.

35. Friedrich Nietzsche, "Unzeitgemässe Betrachtungen III: Schopenhauer als Erzieher," *Kritische Studienausgabe I: Die Geburt der Tragödie/Unzeitgemässe Betrachtungen*, ed. Giorgio Colli and Mazzino Montinari (Berlin: Walter de Gruyter, 1999; first pub. 1967–77 and 1988), 358.

36. Barthes, "Chateaubriand: *Vie de Rancé*," 106; trans. Howard, "Chateaubriand: *Life of Rancé*," 41.

37. Ibid., 106, 108; Howard, 43.

38. Barthes, "Le discours de l'histoire," in *Le Bruissement de la langue* (Paris: Éditions du Seuil, 1984), 163–66 ; see also Stephen Bann's introduction to his translation of the essay, "Introduction: Barthes' discourse," *Comparative Criticism* 3 (1981): 3–6, which positions the text within Barthes's oeuvre.

39. Barthes, "Chateaubriand: *Vie de Rancé*," 118, 111 (Barthes's italics); Howard, 53, 46.

40. Barthes, "La mort de l'auteur," in *Le Bruissement de la langue* (Paris: Éditions du Seuil, 1984), 61–67, at 64; "The Death of the Author," trans. Richard Howard, *The Rustle of Language* (New York: Hill and Wang, 1986), 51–52.

41. Barthes, "Chateaubriand: *Vie de Rancé*," 113–15; Howard, 50.

42. Ibid., 117.

43. Ibid., 111–15, at 112; Howard, 46.

44. Ibid., 106.

45. Ibid., 215, 215n2.

46. Ibid., 207.

47. Chateaubriand, *Génie du christianisme*, part 2, book 3, chap. 8, 710; *Vie de Rancé*, 91–2.

48. Ibid., 208–9.

49. Ibid., 111, 122.

50. Ibid., 98–99.

51. Ibid., 120; see also R. D. Middleton, "The Abbé de Cordemoy and the Graeco-Gothic Ideal: a prelude to Romantic Classicism I," *Journal of the Warburg and Courtauld Institutes* 25 (1962): 278–329.

52. Chateaubriand, *Génie du christianisme*, part 3, book 1, chap. 8, 801.

53. Chateaubriand, *Vie de Rancé*, 152; André Félibien des Avaux, "*Description de L'Abbaye de La Trappe a Madame la Duchesse de Liancour*," in *Reglemens de l'Abbaye de Nôtre-Dame de La Trappe* (Paris: Florentin Delaulne, 1718), 3–4.

54. Chateaubriand, *Vie de Rancé*, 104.

55. Ibid., 127.

56. Ibid., 210.

57. For references, see my "The wilderness as *lieu de mémoire*: Literary deserts of Cîteaux and La Trappe," in *Negotiating Heritage: Memories of the Middle Ages*, ed. M. B. Bruun and S. Glaser (Turnhout: Brepols, 2008), 21–42.

58. Letter of 31 December 1696, in *Abbé de Rancé: Correspondance*, vol. 4, 396.

59. Armand-Jean de Rancé, *De la sainteté et des devoirs monastiques*, 2 vols. (Paris: François Muguet, 1683), chap. 17, question 1, vol. 2, 162.

60. Rancé, *De la sainteté*, chap. 17, question 1–2, vol. 2, 162–67, at 167.

61. Gilles Ménage, *Ménagiana ou Les bons mots et remarques critiques*, 2 vols. (Paris: Chez la Veuve Delaulne, 1729), vol. 1, 34; another reference that has not slipped Chateaubriand who mentions it on 208.

62. "*Description de l'Abbaye de La Trappe*," 72; see also Bell, *Understanding Rancé*, 31–32.

63. Pierre le Nain, *La vie du reverend pere Dom Armand Jean le Boutillier de Rancé*, 3 vols. ([s.l.], 1715), vol. 3, 235–36, at 236 ; see also my *"Un autre Saint Bernard:* Representing Bernard of Clairvaux in the age of Louis XIV," in *Resonances: Historical Essays on Continuity and Change*, ed. N. H. Petersen, E. Østrem, and A. Bücker (Turnhout: Brepols, 2011), 173–98.

64. Rancé, *Éclaircissemens*, 35–47; Rancé, "Avertissement," *La Régle de Saint Benoist*, vol. 1.

65. Rancé, *La Régle de Saint Benoist*, chap. 6, vol. 1, 353.

66. Chateaubriand, *Vie de Rancé*, 209; see also *Génie du christianisme*, part 3, book 2, chap. 5, 822–24. Barthes is in agreement and identifies 1660 as the point around which clarity became a linguistic asset; "Triomphe et rupture de l'écriture bourgeoise," in *Le Degré zéro de l'écriture*, 41–48, at 43.

67. Chateaubriand, *Vie de Rancé*, 149.

68. Ibid., 208.

69. Ibid., 165–68.

70. Ibid., 109, 116.

71. Ibid., 118–19.

72. Ibid., 119–20; Howard, 54.

7. THE LITERARY COMFORT OF ETERNITY: CALVIN AND THOREAU
Ernst van den Hemel

1. Henry D. Thoreau, *Walden*, ed. James Lyndon Shanley (Princeton, NJ: Princeton University Press, 2004), 97.

2. Perhaps the most well-known modern exponent of this standpoint is R. T. Kendall, *Calvin and English Calvinism to 1649* (Oxford: Oxford University Press, 1979), discussed below. Also, for an early and controversial formulation of the problem see Basil Hall's "Calvin against the Calvinists" (in *John Calvin*, ed. G. E. Duffield [Grand Rapids, MI: Eerdmans, 1966], 19–37). For another canonical formulation of the standpoint that Calvin was corrupted by his followers see Brian G. Armstrong, *Calvinism and the Amyraut Heresy: Protestant Scholasticism and Humanism in Seventeenth-Century France* (Milwaukee: University of Wisconsin Press, 1969). Also, see Rolston Homes, *John Calvin versus the Westminster Confession* (Richmond, VA: John Knox Press, 1972), for an argumentation that explicitly defines Calvin as alien to the Westminster theology. As a result of the work of these authors, the standpoint that later Reformed writers turned Calvin's theology into a cold system is frequently found as a brief comment in books on Calvin. See for instance, Alistair E. McGrath in his *A Life of John Calvin: A Study in the Shaping of Western Culture* (Oxford: Blackwell, 1990): "Later Reformed writers are better described as philosophical rather than biblical theologians" (212).

3. Of the scholars that advanced this point most recently see first and foremost Richard A. Muller's *Post-Reformation Reformed Dogmatics: The Rise and Development of Reformed Orthodoxy, ca. 1520 to ca. 1725*, 2nd ed. (Grand Rapids: Baker Academics, 2003), further exponents of this view are Paul Helm, especially *Calvin and the Calvinists* (Edinburgh: Banner of Truth Trust, 1982), written as a reaction to Kendall's book on the matter. Also, see Paul Helm, *Calvin at the Center* (Oxford: Oxford University Press, 2010).

4. John Calvin, *Institutes of the Christian Religion*, trans. Henry Beveridge (Grand Rapids, MI: Eerdmans, 1957), III:ii, 7; 475.

5. *Institutes*, III:ii, 4; Beveridge, 472.

6. Ibid., III:ii, 16; Beveridge, 484.

7. Ibid., III:ii, 1; Beveridge, 470.

8. "The thing requisite is an explicit recognition of the divine goodness": Ibid., III:ii, 2; Beveridge, 471.

9. Ibid., II:ii, 16; Beveridge, 237.

10. Ibid.

11. Ibid., III:xiii, 4; Beveridge, 71.

12. Ibid., III:ii, 17; Beveridge, 484.

13. Ibid., III:ii,1; Beveridge, 478.

14. Ibid.

15. "For there is nowhere such a fear of God as can give full security, and the saints are always conscious that any integrity which they may possess is mingled with many remains of the flesh": Ibid., III:xiv, 19; Beveridge, 87.

16. Ibid., III:xxiv; Beveridge, 243.

17. Ibid., III:xxiv, 4; Beveridge, 244.

18. It is important to note here that Kendall seems to reiterate Brian G. Armstrong's characterization of Reformed orthodoxy, where syllogistic reasoning became the center, as opposed to a theology of revelation. See Armstrong, *Calvin and the Amyraut Heresy*, 32. It is a claim that has been fervently criticized by Richard A. Muller in *After Calvin. Studies in the Development of a Theological Tradition* (Oxford: Oxford University Press, 2003), and throughout his entire oeuvre.

19. Robert Tillman Kendall, *Calvin and English Calvinism to 1649*, 212.

20. Ibid., 210.

21. Ibid.

22. Ibid., 212.

23. Ibid., 28.

24. Ibid., 208.

25. Ibid., 56. See *Westminster Confession of Faith*, chapters 13, 14.

26. Ibid., 208.

27. Paul Helm, *Calvin and the Calvinists*, 9.

28. Ibid., 76.

29. Ibid.

30. Ibid., 77.

31. Ibid., 28.

32. Ibid.

33. Ibid.

34. Ibid.

35. Ibid., 57.

36. In the 1997 reprint of Kendall's *Calvin and English Calvinism*, a new preface was added in which Kendall replied to, amongst others, Helm's criticism. Due to space limitations I will not go into this part of the debate.

37. In fact, one can read Paul Helm's book as an attempt to prove precisely that later Reformed writers' language is in fact open, and not a philosophical-juridical closed-circuit. The only point is that this does not mean that Calvin used the *same* openness.

38. Hawthorne's *Scarlet Letter* versus Hawthorne's and the Transcendentalists' position on Puritanism and religion would be a suitable object to analyze here.

39. *Institutes*, III:ii, 11; Beveridge, 478.

40. Stanley Cavell, *The Senses of Walden* (Chicago: University of Chicago Press, 1992), 3.

41. Ibid.

42. *Senses of Walden*, 71.

43. *Walden*, 327.

44. Ibid., 328.

45. Ibid., 330.

46. Ibid.

47. *Senses of Walden*, 101.

8. THE PAST AND HISTORY IN ORDINARY LANGUAGE PHILOSOPHY
Asja Szafraniec

1. Richard Fleming, "The Self of Philosophy: An Interview with Stanley Cavell" in Stanley Cavell, *Philosophical Passages: Wittgenstein, Emerson, Austin, Derrida* (Oxford: Blackwell, 1995). Fleming's stake here is specifically the history *of philosophy*, but as far as I can see, Cavell's treatment of this question is coextensive with his more general remarks on history. In what follows I will refer to citations about the history of philosophy and about history *tout court* interchangeably.

2. "A Quarrel with God: Cavell on Wittgenstein and Hegel."

3. Stanley Cavell, *The Claim of Reason: Wittgenstein, Skepticism, Morality and Tragedy* (Oxford: Oxford University Press, 1979), 370.

4. The fact is that the "ordinary" stance toward time was misunderstood: ordinary language philosophy was attacked—by Bertrand Russell, among others—precisely on the grounds of its failure to account for an accurate representation of time events. We cannot, according to its detractors, rely on a language that continuously falsifies reality: a language that permits us to say that we see the sun, while what we see is in fact the state of the sun eight minutes ago. By extension, we must regard every statement about seeing something at this very moment as flawed. No philosophy can accept being founded on such a shaky foundation. Bertrand Russell, *Human Knowledge: Its Scope and Limits* (London: Allen and Unwin, 1948), 204. See also Bertrand Russell, "The Cult of Common Usage," *British Journal for the Philosophy of Science*, 3 (1952–53): 305. I am not going to discuss what was wrong with this view, since it has been done convincingly elsewhere. It can be found in Richard G. Henson, "Ordinary Language, Common Sense, and the Time-Lag Argument" *Mind*, n.s. 76, no. 301 (Jan. 1967): 21–33.

5. Stanley Cavell, *Philosophical Passages*, 61. Emphasis mine.

6. It needs emphasizing that Wittgenstein and Nietzsche are not brought together here for the major stakes they have in common: Nietzsche is deeply historical, just as Wittgenstein can hardly be called a-theological. What they share is rather the *reason* for their being willing to risk being understood as a-historical (Wittgenstein) and a-theological (Nietzsche): what Cavell calls their "desire for awakening." I discuss the form this awakening takes in the last section of this article.

7. Given in 1980. The sources referring to the address do not provide any information about the place, etc.

8. "An event is something to which some fairly definite public attaches some fairly definite importance." "The Ordinary as the Uneventful" in Stanley Cavell and Stephen Mulhall, *The Cavell Reader* (Cambridge, MA: Blackwell, 1996), 256.

9. Stanley Cavell, *Contesting Tears: The Hollywood Melodrama of the Unknown Woman* (Chicago: University of Chicago Press, 1996), 64.

10. Stanley Cavell, *The World Viewed: Reflections on the Ontology of Film* (Cambridge, MA: Harvard University Press, 1979), 210.

11. The notion of "playing off history" Cavell criticizes in Derrida (even if he grants that Derrida might deny that it is one continuity of history that is at stake) evokes a distant echo of Wittgenstein's explanation of why we tend to think that knowing how to go on must be a state of mind: We mix up a gramophone record with a tune. The implication is that the past is not avail-

able to us as a gramophone record but merely as a tune, and as such it can
only be heard in the present.

12. Stanley Cavell, *Must We Mean What We Say? A Book of Essays* (Cambridge: Cambridge University Press, 2002), 115–62.

13. Cavell, *Must We Mean What We Say?*, 334.

14. Cited in Stanley Cavell, *Philosophical Passages*, 92.

15. Quoted in Stanley Cavell, *Disowning Knowledge in Seven Plays of Shakespeare* (Cambridge: Cambridge University Press, 2003), 226.

16. Cavell, *Philosophical Passages*, 92.

17. Cavell, *Must We Mean What We Say?*, 337.

18. Ibid.

19. Stanley Cavell, *The World Viewed*, 121.

20. Stanley Cavell, *Must We Mean What We Say?*, 337; Stanley Cavell and Stephen Mulhall, *Cavell Reader*, 153; Stanley Cavell, *Disowning Knowledge in Seven Plays of Shakespeare*, 108.

21. Martin Heidegger, *Being and Time*, trans. John Macquarrie and Edward Robinson (San Francisco: Harper and Row, 1962), 211. *Sein und Zeit* (Tubingen: Max Niemeyer Verlag, 1993), 167.

22. Stanley Cavell, *Must We Mean What We Say?*, 337; Stanley Cavell, *Disowning Knowledge*, 108.

23. Ludwig Wittgenstein, *Tractatus Logico-Philosophicus* (London: Routledge, 2005), 87 (paragraph 6.4311).

24. *Contending with Stanley Cavell*, ed. Russell B. Goodman (Oxford: Oxford University Press, 2005), 107. Goodman points out that this attitude to the future is a significant difference between Cavell and the American pragmatists.

25. Stanley Cavell, *Contesting Tears*, 64.

26. Cavell, *Must We Mean What We Say?*, 334.

27. Ludwig Wittgenstein, *Philosophical Investigations*, trans. G. E. M. Anscombe, 3rd ed. (Oxford: Blackwell, 1967), II, 190.

28. While in Cavell the problem field of theatricality provides the key to the understanding of the role of the past, this foundational status of one with respect to the other is by no means clear; in Wittgenstein reflection on temporality seems to precede his reflection on other minds. Cf. Ludwig Wittgenstein, *Preliminary Studies for the "Philosophical Investigations" Generally Known as The Blue and Brown Books* (New York: Harper and Row, 1960), 26–27; Ludwig Wittgenstein, *Philosophical Investigations*, 36.

29. Ludwig Wittgenstein, *Philosophical Investigations*, 36 (para. 90).

30. Stanley Cavell, *This New Yet Unapproachable America: Lectures after Emerson after Wittgenstein* (Albuquerque, NM: Living Batch Press, 1989), 86.

31. This is what Cavell describes in the experiment of testing the humanity of the other: There is no end to this test. Also: "Even though there is no limit to the depth to which the publicness of our language reaches, there is no end to privacy either."

32. Ludwig Wittgenstein, *Philosophical Investigations*, 36.

33. Stanley Cavell, *The Claim of Reason*, 354–55. Emphasis mine.

34. Ludwig Wittgenstein, *Philosophical Investigations*, 36. (Augustine's investigation of time is here given as an example of a grammatical investigation.)

35. Ibid. (paras. 89–90).

36. Obviously, this solipsism must be taken with a grain of salt: "Wittgenstein is not maintaining that only the present moment of time is truly real, only that all comparisons between language and reality are transacted in the present." Jaakko Hintikka in *Time and History: Proceedings of the 28. International Ludwig Wittgenstein Symposium*, ed. Friedrich Stadler and Michael Stölzner (Heusenstamm: Ontos Verlag, 2006), 540.

37. Ludwig Wittgenstein, *Philosophical Investigations*, 3 (para. 353).

38. Ludwig Wittgenstein, *Philosophical Remarks* (Oxford: Blackwell, 1975), 81. Cf. German original, Ludwig Wittgenstein, *Philosophische Bemerkungen* (Frankfurt am Main: Suhrkamp, 1964), part V, 48. "*Sätze werden nur von der Gegenwart verifiziert. Sie müssen also so gemacht sein, dass sie von ihr verifiziert werden können. Dann haben sie also in irgendeiner Weise die Kommensurabilität mit der Gegenwart.*" There are some sentences however, that do not (cannot) have this commensurability: "*Die Kommensurabilität mit der Gegenwart . . . nicht haben (können), trotz ihrer raum-zeitlichen Natur, sondern diese muss sich zu jener verhalten wie die Körperlichkeit eines Maßstabes zu seiner Ausgedehntheit.*" The final judgment appears to be nevertheless "Isn't all that I mean: between the proposition and its verification there is no go-between negotiating this verification?" (56). For the discussion of the distinction between extension and materiality in this section I have relied on Gabriele M. Mras, "Das Jetzt bei Wittgenstein—Über Gegenwart und Wandel" in *Time and History*, 569–85.

39. "*Wie offenbart sich die Zeitlichkeit der Tatsachen, wie drückt sie sich aus, als dadurch, daß gewisse [Ausdrücke| Wendungen] in unsern Sätzen vorkommen müssen. D.h.: Wie drückt sich die Zeitlichkeit der Tatsachen aus, als grammatisch?*" Ludwig Wittgenstein, "Big Typescript," TS-212, 381 (1931).

40. Ludwig Wittgenstein, *Philosophical Remarks*, 85. (*Philosophische Bemerkungen*, 54).

41. Ludwig Wittgenstein, *The Blue and Brown Books*, 157.

42. Ludwig Wittgenstein, *Philosophical Investigations*, 47 (para. 90).

43. "Its [the clock's] knowledge is really its conscience." Stanley Cavell, *The Claim of Reason*, 343.

44. Ibid.

45. Stanley Cavell, *The Senses of Walden* (Chicago: University of Chicago Press, 1972), 10.

46. Ibid., 42.

47. Henry David Thoreau, *Walden and Civil Disobedience* (New York: Barnes and Noble Classics, 2003), 255–56.

48. Stanley Cavell, *The Senses of Walden*, 10.

49. Thoreau, *Walden*, 80 (chap. 2).

50. Cavell, *The Senses of Walden*, 11, Thoreau, *Walden*, 80.

51. Cavell, *Senses of Walden*, 44.

52. Ibid., 10.

9. FROM PAST TO PRESENT AND FROM LISTENING TO HEARING: FINAL INDEFINABLE MOMENTS IN BACH'S AND STRAVINSKY'S MUSIC
Rokus de Groot

1. John Eijlers (1943–2004) organized concerts of Indian classical music in Amsterdam and other Dutch cities from the 1970s through the 1990s, first in the Mozes en Aäron Church, later in the Theatre of the Royal Tropical Institute. During this period the Dutch public became amply acquainted with the great Indian masters of music.

2. Program booklet *Muziek uit India*, season 1998–99, Royal Tropical Institute, Amsterdam.

3. Sign in musical notation requiring the temporal suspension of counting time.

4. Trans. Derek Yeld, CD box J. S. Bach, *Les plus belles cantates*, Harmonia Mundi, HMX 2908091.95 (1999).

5. Since in musical composition and performance, counting is an essential tool, Arabic numerals instead of words will be used in the musical analysis, even for lower numbers.

The number 12 plays a crucial role in the examples from Stravinsky's work discussed below, *Les Noces* and *Requiem Canticles*. It may be taken as symbolic for the fulfillment of time.

6. Interestingly, Bach starts with a note of ambiguity: He does not open the piece with flute I on the beat, but after 1 unit (one-sixteenth) of rest. It leaves the listener in uncertainty for some time as to which meter is used, and to where the first beat of that meter is to be found. In this way the entrance of oboe I may be heard as "too early," even though it arrives on the beat. The composer thus creates an initial indefinable moment.

7. Trans. D. Yeld, J. S. Bach, *Les plus belles cantates.*

8. R. Craft, *Stravinsky: Chronicle of a Friendship, 1948–1971* (New York: Knopf, 1972; revised and expanded edition, Nashville: Vanderbilt University Press, 1994), 329.

9. J. N. Straus, *Stravinsky's Late Music* (Cambridge: Cambridge University Press, 2001), 139. The rhetorical topic of the coda is discussed in its own right in chapter 5.

10. *Stravinsky's Late Music*, 235.

11. L. Andriessen and E. Schönberger, *Het Apollinisch Uurwerk: Over Stravinsky* (Amsterdam: De Bezige Bij, 1983), 18; trans. J. Hamburg, *The Apollonian Clockwork: On Stravinsky* (Oxford: Oxford University Press, 1989).

12. See also the qualifications by Taruskin in n. 18.

13. Starting from rehearsal number 133.

14. Andriessen and Schönberger comment likewise. They call bridal and death bells the same, and therefore they regard the silence after *Svadebka* identical to the silence after *Requiem Canticles* (*Het Apollinisch Uurwerk*, 265).

15. In terms of Adorno, an impersonal, primitive, pre-individual, anti-humanist, collective-oriented, ritualistic, mechanical voice is taking over at this point at the expense of a humanistic, individual-oriented one. He was very critical about this tendency in Stravinsky's work. See Theodor W. Adorno, *Philosophy of Modern Music*, trans. A. G. Mitchell and W. V. Blomster (New York: Seabury Press, 1973), 145–47, 154–55, 157–60; "Stravinsky: A Dialectical Portrait" (1962), *Quasi una Fantasia: Essays on Modern Music*, trans. R. Livingstone (London: Verso, 1998), 145–75. See also the discussion in P. C. van den Toorn, "Stravinsky, 'Les Noces (Svadebka),' and the Prohibition against Expressive Timing," *The Journal of Musicology* 20, no. 2 (2003): 285–304.

16. Van der Toorn points in the same direction, countering Adorno's negative qualifications: "As internalized meters are brought to the surface of consciousness in the most disruptive cases of displacement, a heightened sense of attention, engagement and suspense may ensue." ("Stravinsky, 'Les Noces [Svadebka],'" 299.)

17. R. Craft, "Stravinsky: Letters to Pierre Boulez," *The Musical Times* 123, no. 1672 (June 1982): 396–402; see 401, n. 16.

18. The ending of *Les Noces* has widely elicited comments, which, in all their variety of perspectives, point to an experience of "inifinity" or "nonending." R. Taruskin: "Finally, after the choral climax has died away, theme A [the bridegroom's music] forms the melodic substance of what might be called the precoital coda, the groom's address to the bride, in which he speaks in distinctly self-centered terms of wedded bliss (adverting to his wife as 'my nocturnal amusement'), while bells—also to the modified tune of the bridal

plach [lament]—ring out eternity," *Stravinsky and the Russian Traditions* (Oxford: Oxford University Press, 1996), 1354.

Andriessen and Schönberger hear a contraction of time in *Svadebka* into one endless moment of synchronous events, which finally, when the voices become silent for the first and last time, freeze in bell-like chords. They note that there is no conclusion—there is silence. However, it is not possible to say where this silence enters. Does the sonorous ebbing away of the chords continue endlessly but inaudibly? They add that bells may confuse people, referring to a Russian saying: "At hearing the bell he did not know any more where he was," *Het Apollinisch Uurwerk*, 260.

19. *Chronicle of a Friendship*, 377.

20. Ibid., 415.

21. See also the analysis in *Het Apollinisch Uurwerk*, part 1, ch. 2.

22. *Stravinsky's Late Music*, 246.

23. Ibid., 248.

24. Ibid., 244.

25. Ibid., 243–48.

26. Matthew 11:15, 13:9:43; Mark 4:9:23, 7:16; Luke 8:8, 14:35.

27. See Van den Toorn, "Stravinsky, 'Les Noces (Svadebka),'" 299–300; Adorno, *Philosophy of Modern Music*, 155.

10. LATE STYLE MESSIAEN
Sander van Maas

1. Michel Foucault, *The Hermeneutics of the Subject: Lectures at the Collège de France, 1981–82*, trans. Graham Burchell (New York: Palgrave, 2001), 285.

2. See Burcht Pranger's work on the still life, "Henry James and Augustine on the Still Life," *Modern Language Notes* 119 (2004): 979–93.

3. See my *The Reinvention of Religious Music: Olivier Messiaen's Breakthrough Toward the Beyond* (New York: Fordham University Press, 2009).

4. Theodor W. Adorno, *Beethoven: The Philosophy of Music* (Stanford, CA: Stanford University Press, 1998), 123.

5. See Joseph N. Straus, "Disability and 'Late Style' in Music," in *The Journal of Musicology*, 25, no. 1 (Winter 2008): 3–45.

6. Adorno, *Beethoven*, 124.

7. Ibid.

8. Ibid., 125.

9. Ibid.

10. Edward Said, *On Late Style: Music and Literature against the Grain* (London: Bloomsbury, 2007), 13.

11. Arnold Whittall, *Musical Composition in the Twentieth Century* (Oxford: Oxford University Press, 1999), 262.

12. See van Maas, *The Reinvention of Religious Music*, 144–45.

13. Luke Berryman, "Messiaen as Explorer in *Livre du Saint Sacrement*," in *Messiaen the Theologian*, ed. Andrew Shenton (Aldershot: Ashgate, 2010).

14. Peter Hill and Nigel Simeone, *Messiaen* (New Haven, CT: Yale, 2005), 353.

15. Hill and Simeone, *Messiaen*, 370.

16. Ibid., 377.

17. Christopher Dingle, "Charm and Simplicity: Messiaen's Final Works," *Tempo*, n.s., no. 192 (April, 1995): 7.

18. Van Maas, *The Reinvention of Religious Music*, 126–57.

19. Said, *On Late Style*, 13.

20. These negative tendencies are balanced by the grand affirmative gestures of his nature music (landscapes, birdsong); that is, by everything in his music that exudes assuredness (as Messiaen once said, *"Ma musique n'est pas gentille, elle est* sûre"), and by the equally affirmative use of continuous lyricism. Messiaen, in *Olivier Messiaen: The Music of Faith* (1986), documentary directed by Alan Benson (Princeton: Films for the Humanities & Sciences, 2004).

21. Adorno, *Beethoven*, 152.

22. Perhaps this draws *Éclairs* close to the refracted world of late Beethoven (Adorno, *Beethoven*, 136). See also James Herbert's remarks on Messiaen and intimacy in "The Eucharist In and beyond Messiaen's *Book of the Holy Sacrament*," *The Journal of Religion* 88 (2008): 331–64.

23. See tables 1 and 2 in Straus, "Disability and 'Late Style' in Music," 8–12.

24. Adorno, *Beethoven*, 136.

25. See Said, *On Late Style*, 25–47. In Said's view Strauss's late work starts with the opera *Capriccio* (1940–41).

26. As the Mozart entry in the *Grove Music Online* (www.oxfordmusic online.com) has it, "On the whole the late works [1789–91, SvM] can be characterized as noticeably more austere and refined than the earlier works, more motivic and contrapuntal, more economical in the use of material and texturally less rich. There are fewer new themes in development sections or in exposition codas, and second-group material is frequently derived from primary ones by some form of extension or contrapuntal treatment" (accessed October 18, 2012).

27. G. W. F. Hegel, *Introductory Lectures on Aesthetics*, trans. Bernard Bosanquet (London: Penguin, 1993), 32. Incidentally this musical logic has recently been taken up by the media and now informs many television programs and features about one's "true" (biological, emotional, etc.) age as opposed to one's chronological age.

28. Jean-Luc Nancy, "The Deconstruction of Christianity," in *Dis-Enclosure: The Deconstruction of Christianity* (New York: Fordham University Press, 2008), 150.

29. The reference to Freud in this context is less than surprising if Messiaen's engagement with psychoanalytical and surrealist themes is taken into consideration. As I have argued elsewhere, in his work the birds carry meanings well beyond Messiaen's naturalistic and religious frames of reference. Also, their vital importance in his musical aesthetics calls for an account in terms of the libidinality. See my "Messiaen and Psychoanalysis" (forthcoming).

30. See Rokus de Groot's article in the present volume.

31. Jean-Luc Nancy, *Listening* (New York: Fordham University Press, 2007), 69, n. 6.

32. *Olivier Messiaen: Les couleurs du temps. Trente ans d'entretiens avec Claude Samuel.* Radio France, 2CD, 2000.

33. Foucault, lecture of 17 February 1982, Second Hour, in *The Hermeneutics of the Subject.*

34. Foucault, *The Hermeneutics of the Subject*, 283–84.

35. See my "Messiaen's Saintly Naïveté" in Shenton, *Messiaen the Theologian*, 41–62.

36. The most illuminated music of *Eclairs*' final movement, "Christ, lumière du Paradis," calls forth the demon of noontide that tends to appear when the sun reaches its apex. Following a similar logic the libidinality of the birdsong evokes the death drive. Messiaen's insistence on either one side of the equation announces the appearance of its reverse. On libidinality in Messiaen, see my *The Reinvention of Religious Music*, 138 and "Messiaen and Psychoanalysis" (forthcoming).

11. OF SHAKESPEARE AND PASTNESS
Brian Cummings

1. Ben Jonson, "To the memory of my beloved, the AUTHOR, Mr. WILLIAM SHAKESPEARE; And what he hath left us," *Mr. William Shakespeares Comedies, Histories, & Tragedies, Published according to the true originall copies* (London: Isaac Jaggard and Edward Blount, 1623), fol. A4r–v.

2. Horace, *Carminum*, 3.30.1–5; *Horatius. In quo quidem, praeter M. Antonii Mureti scholia, Io. Michaelis Bruti animadversiones habentur, quibus obscuriores plerique loci illustrantur* (Venice: Aldus Manutius, 1564), sig. h1r–v.

3. *Horace Odes III*, ed. and trans. David West (Oxford: Oxford University Press, 2002), 259.

4. *Shakespeare's Sonnets*, ed. Katherine Duncan-Jones, Arden Shakespeare, 3rd Series (London: Arden Shakespeare, 1997), 221.

5. Jacques Derrida, *De la grammatologie* (Paris: Minuit, 1967), 95.

6. Jacques Derrida, *Of Grammatology*, trans. Gayatri Chakravorty Spivak, corrected ed. (Baltimore: Johns Hopkins University Press, 1997), 65.

7. The origin of this proverbial classical phrase is traditionally ascribed to a speech to the Roman Senate by Caius Titus; see *Dialogue militaire entre anciens et modernes*, ed. J. P Bois, Université de Nantes Centre de recherches sur l'histoire du monde atlantique (Rennes: Presses universitaires de Rennes, 2004). The phrase was used by Lacan in his "Seminar on 'The Purloined Letter,'" in *The Purloined Poe: Lacan, Derrida, and Psychoanalytic Reading*, trans. Jeffrey Mehlman (Baltimore: Johns Hopkins University Press, 1997), 41. Derrida comments in reply in *The Post Card: From Socrates to Freud and Beyond*, trans. Alan Bass (Chicago: University of Chicago Press, 1987), 424.

8. Aeschylus, *Agamemnon*, 1–2; *Aeschyli septem quae supersunt tragoedias*, ed. Denys Page, Scriptorum classicorum bibliotheca oxoniensis (Oxford: Clarendon Press, 1972), 139.

9. Harold Bloom, *Shakespeare and the Invention of the Human* (London: Fourth Estate, 1999), 17.

10. See Harold Bloom, *The Western Canon: The Books and School of the Ages* (London: Warner Books, 1994), 519; and *Invention of the Human*, 726.

11. On the emergence of Shakespeare as an "author" in the eighteenth century, see Margreta de Grazia, *Shakespeare Verbatim: The Reproduction of Authenticity and the 1790 Apparatus* (Oxford: Clarendon Press, 1991), esp. chaps. 2–4; and Jonathan Bate, *Shakespearean Constitutions: Politics, Theatre, Criticism, 1730–1830* (Oxford: Clarendon Press, 1989).

12. Harold Bloom, *Hamlet: Poem Unlimited* (London: Riverhead Books, 2003), 137.

13. Bloom, *The Western Canon*, 65.

14. Bloom, *Hamlet: Poem Unlimited*, 3. The phrase is of course Northrop Frye's, from *The Secular Scripture: A Study of the Structure of Romance* (Cambridge, MA: Harvard University Press, 1976).

15. Act 5, scene 3, line 17.

16. Helen Cooper, *The English Romance in Time: Transforming Motifs from Geoffrey of Monmouth to the Death of Shakespeare* (Oxford: Oxford University Press, 2004), 405–7.

17. Geoffrey of Monmouth, *Historia Regum Britanniae*, 2.11; *The History of the Kings of Britain*, trans. Lewis Thorpe (Harmondsworth: Penguin, 1966), 81.

18. *History of the Kings of Britain*, 80.

19. *The True Chronicle History of King Leir, and His Three Daughters, Gonorill, Ragan, and Cordella* (London: Simon Stafford, 1605), sig. B3v–C1r.

20. *The True Chronicle History of King Leir*, sig. H4v.

21. *King Lear*, act 4, scene 1; text cited from the First Folio (see above, n. 1, *Mr. William Shakespeares Comedies, Histories, & Tragedies*), lines F2222–23. Further references in the text, using F line numbers.

22. On the "Aeschylean" dimension of *King* Lear, see A. C. Bradley, *Shakespearean Tragedy* (London: Macmillan, 1904), 226–30.

23. Harold Bloom, *Shakespeare and the Invention of the Human*, xx.

24. Oxford, Corpus Christi College MS 309; text reproduced in full in E. K. Chambers, *William Shakespeare: A Study of Facts and Problems*, 2 vols. (Oxford: Clarendon Press, 1930), 2:257.

25. The fullest examination of this evidence appears in E. A. J. Honigmann, *Shakespeare: The "Lost years"* (Manchester: Manchester University Press, 1985).

26. Patrick Collinson, "William Shakespeare's Religious Inheritance and Environment," in *Elizabethan Essays* (London: Hambledon Press, 1994), 252.

27. Chambers, *William Shakespeare*, 1:15.

28. Thomas Fuller, *The history of the worthies of England who for parts and learning have been eminent in the several counties: Together with an historical narrative of the native commodities and rarities in each county* (London: J.G.W.L. and W.G. for Thomas Williams, 1662), 126.

29. *The history of the worthies of England*, 116. I am grateful to Freya Sierhuis for commentary on this passage.

30. *Aubrey's Brief Lives, Edited from the Original Manuscripts*, ed. Oliver Lawson Dick (London: Secker and Warburg, 1949), lxii–iii.

31. *Aubrey's Brief Lives*, 275.

32. Stephen Greenblatt, *Hamlet in Purgatory* (Princeton, NJ: Princeton University Press, 2001), 240.

33. *King Lear*, act 3, scene 2; text cited from the First Folio (see above, n. 1, *Mr. William Shakespeares Comedies, Histories, & Tragedies*), lines 1702–07. Further references in the text, using F line numbers.

34. *William Camden*, Britain, or, a Chorographicall Description of the most flourishing Kingdomes, England, Scotland, and Ireland, *trans. Philemon Holland (London, 1610)*.(London: Georgii Bishop and Ioannis Norton, 1610).

35. Sir Thomas Browne, *Hydriotaphia, urn-burial, or, A discours of the sepulchral urns lately found in Norfolk together with the Garden of Cyrus, or, The quincuncial lozenge, or network of plantations of the ancients, artificially, naturally, mystically considered* (London: Henry Brome, 1669), sig. A2r.

36. Margaret Aston, "English Ruins and English History: The Dissolution and the Sense of the Past," *Lollards and Reformers: Images and Literacy in Late Medieval Religion* (London: Hambledon Press, 1984), 313–37.

12. THE ANGER OF ANGELS: FROM RUBENS TO VIRGINIA WOOLF
Peter Cramer

1. K. T. Parker, *Catalogue of the Collection of Drawings in the Ashmolean Museum, Vol. I, Netherlandish, German and French Schools* (Oxford: Clarendon Press, 1938), 86, no. 201 (WA1951.19). Parker attributes the drawing to Rubens.

2. Heinrich Wölfflin, *Kunstgeschichtliche Grundbegriffe*, 11th ed. (Basel: Benno Schwabe, 1948), 146–47.

3. Leon Battista Alberti, *On Painting*, trans. Cecil Grayson with an introduction by Martin Kemp (London: Penguin, 2004), book 3 for *istoria*: The whole of book 3 might be read as a struggle between method (above all, the geometry of perspective) and working from nature.

4. Svetlana Alpers, *The Making of Rubens* (New Haven, CT: Yale University Press, 1995), 101–57.

5. Avigdor Arikha, "On Drawing from Observation," in *On Depiction: Selected Writings on Art 1965–94* (London: Bellew Publishing, 1995), 112.

6. Stanley Cavell, quoted by Michael Fried, *The Moment of Caravaggio*, The A. W. Mellon Lectures in the Fine Arts, Bollingen Series XXXV: 51 (Princeton, NJ: Princeton University Press, 2010), 104. Remarks in square brackets are Fried's.

7. Baudelaire, "Le Peintre de la vie moderne," *Œuvres complètes*, ed. Claude Pichois (Paris: Gallimard, 1976), vol. 2, 692.

8. *To the Lighthouse*, ed. Stella McNichol, with an introduction and notes by Hermione Lee (London: Penguin, 1992), 137. I have used this Penguin edition throughout.

9. Hermione Lee, *Virginia Woolf* (London: Chatto and Windus, 1996), 735–36, quoting the 22 June 1940 entry in *The Diary of Virginia Woolf*, 5 vols., ed. Anne Olivier Bell and Andrew McNeillie (London: Hogarth Press, 1977–84), vol. 5, 298; and VW, "The Man at the Gate," *Collected Essays*, ed. Leonard Woolf (London: Chatto and Windus, 1966–67), vol. 3, 217–26.

10. Virginia Woolf, "The Man at the Gate," *Collected Essays*, vol. 3, quoted in Hermione Lee, *Virginia Woolf*, 736.

11. Shakespeare, Sonnet 98, in *To the Lighthouse*, 132.

12. Ibid., 134.

13. Ibid., 133.

14. Ibid., 131.

15. Ibid., 194.

16. Edgar Wind, "Pan and Proteus," in *Pagan Mysteries in the Renaissance* (Oxford: Oxford University Press, 1980), 197. He comments: "The fable

[of the Judgment of Paris] teaches, according to Bruno, that when divine perfections become finite, they disclose through their discord an overruling harmony, of which each is only a partial expression. Their finite collisions carry the overtone of their coincidence in the infinite; and thus one dominant consonance emerges from a variety of discords."

17. Rainer Maria Rilke, *Gedichte, Erster Teil* (Frankfurt am Main: Insel Verlag, 1987), 264.

18. *To the Lighthouse*, 134.

19. Ibid., 148.

20. Hermione Lee, *Virginia Woolf*, 736.

21. *Diary*, vol. 5, 316–17, quoted by Hermione Lee, *Virginia Woolf*, 741.

22. George Steiner, "Absolute Tragedy," in *No Passion Spent* (London: Faber and Faber, 1996), 130.

23. Erich Auerbach, *Mimesis: The Representation of Reality in Western Literature*, trans. Willard R. Trask (Princeton, NJ: Princeton University Press, 1968), 525–57.

24. *To the Lighthouse*, 129.

25. Ibid., 131.

26. Ibid., 144–45. A few pages earlier (141): "Only once a board sprang on the landing; once in the middle of the night with a roar, with a rupture, as after centuries of quiescence, a rock rends itself from the mountain and hurtles crashing into the valley, one fold of the shawl loosened and swung to and fro." See note 39 for Empson's handling of this passage.

27. Ibid., 145.

28. Ibid., 88.

29. *Cahiers* i: *Oeuvres complètes*, ed. André A. Devaux and Florence de Lussy, vol. 6 (Paris: Gallimard, 1994), 290.

30. *To the Lighthouse*, 140.

31. Ibid., 146.

32. Ibid., 145.

33. *Mimesis*, 549–50.

34. *L'archéologie du savoir* (Paris: Gallimard, 1969), 33–36.

35. "The Rise of Antiquarian Research," in *The Classical Foundations of Modern Historiography* (Berkeley: University of California Press, 1990), 54–79.

36. *Les armées révolutionnaires. Instrument de la Terreur dans les départements. Avril 1793–Floréal An II* (Paris: Mouton et Co., 1961–63).

37. Dionysus the Areopagite, *Celestial Hierarchy*, ed. G. Heil, trans. M. de Gandillac, introduced by R. Roques: Denys l'Aréopagite, *La Hiérarchie céleste*, SC 58 bis, 2nd edition, 81. (I have translated from the French.)

38. Michel de Certeau, *La Fable mystique: XVIe-XVIIe siècle* (Paris: Gallimard, 1982), 198.

39. Ibid., 200–204. Empson takes Virginia Woolf to task for the plunge into plotlessness of the later novels and turns his complaints (woven in with admiration) partly on the shawl that roars. *To the Lighthouse*, 141: "Only once a board sprang on the landing; once in the middle of the night with a roar, with a rupture, as after centuries of quiescence, a rock rends itself from the mountain and hurtles crashing into the valley, one fold of the shawl loosened and swung to and fro." The force of this, he observes, comes from what has been said before: Cam is frightened by the skull of a boar hanging on the wall of the nursery, and can't go to sleep, so Mrs. Ramsay winds her shawl round the horned head. "'Now it was lovely,' she said to Cam, 'it was like a bird's nest; it was like a beautiful mountain such as she had seen abroad, with valleys and flowers and bells ringing and birds singing and little goats and antelopes . . . '" (124). The irony of Mrs. Ramsay's associations is admirable, says Empson. The familiar shawl, which she had gathered round her shoulders against the cooling evening, is an inhuman (if beautiful) landscape. The sudden anticipation, which calms the child but in the same breath drops away into uninhabited waste, brings home the bleakness of Mrs. Ramsay's death. Yet Empson cannot help feeling that the whole of part 2 ("Time Passes") is wanting. The uncovering of motivation by the study of moods as they soak up their surroundings—the complicity of character and the detail of surroundings—is let down in these pages by the absence of figures in whom the surroundings cohere; by the absence of the human. And the coherence of character in a setting, the portrait in a landscape, is broken, for Empson, by the lack of thread between the intense patches of color. Yet he hovers unsure. V. W. is like nature, working from preconsciousness. One can say of her what can be said of Shakespeare, that "any of his stones may have been made bread, and repay turning." But her brilliance is "wilful and jumping." One can never be sure of a form. The hesitation is expressed finely at the end of his short essay: her work is "very lifelike, in short; and I do not know how far it may be due to just this quality; to the fact that so many of her images, glittering and searching as they are, spreading out their wealth of feeling, as if spilt, in the mind, give out just that sense of waste that is given by life itself." Or of interrupted joys, one might add. (William Empson, "Virginia Woolf," in *Argufying: Essays on Literature and Culture*, ed. John Haffenden [London: Chatto and Windus, 1987], 443–49).

40. Henry James, in his preface to *The Awkward Age* (Harmondsworth: Penguin, 1966), 21, delights in the unity of his novel as he rereads it; but what he finds is a unity not simply of the relation of parts (as in a play), but one

which arises out of the identity of form with substance, and where substance necessarily runs the risk of the loose end: "'Exhibition' may mean in a story twenty different ways, fifty excursions, alternatives, excrescences, and the novel, as largely practised in English, is the perfect paradise of the loose end. The play consents to the logic of but one way, mathematically right, and with the loose end as gross an impertinence on its surface, and as grave a dishonour, as the dangle of a snippet of silk or wool on the right side of a tapestry." Nanda, the unmarriageable antiheroine of *The Awkward Age*, is a sort of glorious and touching loose end. The colliding idioms of this novel of dialogue are so many others.

41. *La Fable mystique*, 205.

42. *To the Lighthouse*, 169–70.

43. Ibid., 194. And *La Prisonnière*, the sixth volume (1923) of Proust's *A la recherche du temps perdu*, is a great study of desire and grief in balance, and then of the almost morbid plenitude to be found in their balancing. The aftermath of love, the grief of possession, has a perfection all its own.

44. "To Spain," in *Moments of Being* (London: Hogarth, 1947), 173–74.

45. *Tristram Shandy*; but also see the astonishing attention to dashes and indentions, etc. in Joakim Garff, *Søren Kierkegaard: A Biography* (Princeton, NJ: Princeton University Press, 2007), 258–61.

46. *To the Lighthouse*, 226.

METTE BIRKEDAL BRUUN is Professor of Church History at the University of Copenhagen. She is the author of *Parables: Bernard of Clairvaux's Mapping of Spiritual Topography* (Brill 2007) and the co-editor of *Negotiating Heritage: Memories of the Middle Ages* (with Stephanie Glaser; Brepols 2008) and *Commonplace Culture in Western Europe in the Early Modern Period I: Reformation, Counter Reformation and Revolt* (Brepols 2011) and *Negotiating Heritage: Memories of the Middle Ages* (with Stephanie Glaser; Brepols 2008).

PETER CRAMER published a study on the shifting perception and effect of baptism in the early Middle Ages (*Baptism and Change*, Cambridge 1993) and is at present interested in aspects of Europe from the twelfth to the fifteenth centuries, and also in the relation between history and fiction in various periods. He teaches History, History of Art, and Literature at Winchester College in the UK.

BRIAN CUMMINGS is Anniversary Professor of English at the University of York and Leverhulme Trust Major Research Fellow. He is the author of *The Literary Culture of the Reformation: Grammar and Grace* (Oxford 2002). From 2009 to 2012 he was a research professor as the recipient of the Leverhulme Trust Major Research Fellowship, working on his project "The Confessions of Shakespeare." In 2011 he published his edition of *The Book of Common Prayer: The Texts of 1549, 1559, and 1662* (Oxford).

ROKUS DE GROOT held a personal chair for "Music in the Netherlands since 1600" at the University of Utrecht (1994–2000). From 2000 until his retirement in 2012 he was Professor of Musicology at the University of Amsterdam. He has published extensively on the aesthetics and techniques of contemporary music composition, on the re-use in contemporary music of past religious concepts, and on Edward Saïd's concept of polyphony and counterpoint. He is also a composer, working with musicians from different cultural backgrounds on projects of mutual learning (*Songs of*

Songs: The Life of Mirabai, Dehli 2005; *Layla and Majnun*, Amsterdam 2006; *ShivaShakti*, Chennai 2009).

CHARLES HALLISEY is Yehan Numata Senior Lecturer at Harvard Divinity School. He joined the faculty of Harvard Divinity in 2007 after teaching at the University of Wisconsin in the Department of Languages and Cultures of Asia and the Religious Studies Program. His research centers on Theravada Buddhism in Sri Lanka and Southeast Asia, Pali language and literature, Buddhist ethics, and literature in Buddhist cultures.

BABETTE HELLEMANS earned her PhD at the École des Hautes Études en Sciences Sociales and Utrecht University. She is currently Assistant Professor in History at the University of Groningen, The Netherlands. Hellemans has published on historiographical and intellectual themes such as the anthropology of eschatology in Western medieval culture, including modern theories of temporality, semantics, and images. She is the author of *La Bible Moralisée: une oeuvre à part entière. Temporalité, sémiotique et création au XIIIᵉ siècle* (Brepols 2010). At present she is completing a monograph, *Peter Abelard (1079–1142) and the Varieties of the Self: An Intellectual Biography*.

ERNST VAN DEN HEMEL completed a research MA in Cultural Analysis at the University of Amsterdam in 2006. In his dissertation, *Tracing Circles: Literary Dimensions in the Work of John Calvin* (2011), he combined an emphasis on literature and philosophy to analyze the poetic structure of John Calvin's *Institutes of the Christian Religion*. He is the author of *Calvinisme en Poltitiek: Tussen Verzet en Berusting* [*Calvinism and Politics: Between Resistance and Resignation*] (Boom 2009). Van den Hemel teaches at the Amsterdam University College.

SANDER VAN MAAS is Buma Professor of Dutch Contemporary Music at Utrecht University and Assistant Professor of Contemporary Music at the University of Amsterdam. His research focuses on the philosophy and criticism of twentieth- and twenty-first-century music. His publications include *The Reinvention of Religious Music: Olivier Messiaen's Breakthrough Toward the Beyond* (Fordham 2009) and forthcoming volumes on *Liminal Auralities* and *Contemporary Music and Spirituality*. In 2010–11 van Maas held visiting positions at Boston and Harvard universities.

WILLEMIEN OTTEN was Professor of the History of Christianity at Utrecht University from 1997. Since 2007 she has been Professor of the Theology and the History of Christianity at the University of Chicago. She has published on Western medieval and early Christian theology, including the continuity of (Neo) Platonic themes. Among her books are *The Anthropology of Johannes Scottus Eriugena* (Brill 1991) and *From Paradise to Paradigm: A Study of Twelfth-Century Humanism* (Brill 2004). With Karla Pollmann she is the co-editor of *The Oxford Guide to the Historical Reception of Augustine* (forthcoming 2013). Her current project involves a comparison between Johannes Scottus Eriugena and Ralph Waldo Emerson on the role of nature and the self.

BURCHT PRANGER is Professor Emeritus in the History of Christianity at the University of Amsterdam. He has published extensively on medieval monasticism, in particular Anselm of Canterbury and Bernard of Clairvaux. Among his books are *Bernard of Clairvaux and the Shape of Monastic Thought* (Brill 1994) and *The Artificiality of Christianity: Essays on the Poetics of Monasticism* (Stanford 2003). In 2010 he published his *Eternity's Ennui: Temporality, Perseverance and Voice in Augustine and Western Literature* (Brill).

ASJA SZAFRANIEC teaches at the University of Amsterdam. She is the author of *Beckett, Derrida, and the Event of Literature* (Stanford 2007) and of articles on the relation between continental and ordinary language philosophy, on the question of the specificity of the nature of philosophical discourse, and on the relation between philosophy and various forms of literary experiment. Her current research on the work of Stanley Cavell focuses on contemporary philosophy's response to the questions of skepticism, faith, and religion.

JAMES WETZEL is Professor of Philosophy at Villanova University and the first permanent holder of the Augustinian endowed chair in Augustine's thought. He writes extensively on sages and saints, and Augustine especially. He is the author of *Augustine and the Limits of Virtue* (Cambridge 1992) and *Augustine: A Guide for the Perplexed* (Continuum 2010) and the editor of *Augustine's City of God: A Critical Guide* (Cambridge 2012).